THE EARLIEST
Complete English Prose Psalter.

BERLIN:　　　ASHER & CO., 5, UNTER DEN LINDEN.
NEW YORK:　　C. SCRIBNER, & CO.; LEYPOLDT & HOLT.
PHILADELPHIA: J. B. LIPPINCOTT & CO.

THE EARLIEST
Complete English Prose Psalter

TOGETHER WITH

Eleven Canticles

AND A

Translation of the Athanasian Creed

EDITED FROM THE ONLY TWO MSS. IN THE LIBRARIES OF THE
BRITISH MUSEUM AND OF TRINITY COLLEGE, DUBLIN,

WITH

Preface, Introduction, Notes, and Glossary

BY

KARL D. BÜLBRING M.A. Ph.D.

EDITOR OF DANIEL DEFOE'S "COMPLEAT ENGLISH GENTLEMAN."

PART I

PREFACE AND TEXT.

LONDON

PUBLISHT FOR THE EARLY ENGLISH TEXT SOCIETY
BY KEGAN PAUL, TRENCH, TRÜBNER & CO., LTD.

1891.

Unaltered reprint 1998

ISBN 0 85991 853 X

Distributed for the Early English Text Society by
Boydell & Brewer Ltd, PO Box 9, Woodbridge, Suffolk IP12 3DF
and Boydell & Brewer Inc, PO Box 41026, Rochester, NY 14604-4126

PREFACE.

OF all the books of the Bible none has been Englished so often as the Psalter. Numerous versions in Prose as well as Verse were written before Wyclif's, some of which I notice below. The reasons for the Psalms getting this preference over the other parts of Scripture are, no doubt, to be found in their poetical language,—which recommended them to the contemplative mind of the monks,—in their fitness for prayers and singing, and in the fact that they could be detached from the rest of the Bible without any inconvenience. In most MSS. we find them connected with several other biblical prayers and songs, like the Song of Moses, of Hannah, of the Three Men in the Fiery Furnace, and others, and this distinctly indicates their destination.

The oldest English Psalter is Anglo-Saxon; only the first 50 Psalms are in Prose, and are ascribed to King Alfred. There are several Old English interlinear versions, glossing the Latin word by word; and during the Middle-English period the Psalter was repeatedly translated into English Verse.

Most of these older versions have been printed; but the Earliest Complete English Prose Psalter,[1] which at the same time is also the earliest version in English prose of any entire book of Scripture, is now published for the first time.

It is preserved in two MSS.: one is the well-known Additional MS. 17,376 of the British Museum, which also contains William

[1] Richard Rolle of Hampole's Commentary on the *Psalter*, which was edited by the Rev. H. R. Bramley in 1884, dates from about the same time as the text now printed, and contains also a literal English prose translation of the whole Psalter following the Latin and preceding the commentary on it verse by verse. This seems to forbid my styling the present Psalter the **Earliest** Complete English Prose Psalter. But I think I have done right, considering that the comments form by far the larger portion and more important part of Hampole's work; the oldest MS. known of the *Commentary* is, moreover, considerably later than the MS. from which the present edition is derived.

of Shoreham's Religious Poems. It forms a small thick octavo volume, and contains 220 leaves of vellum. Both pieces are written by the same scribe, but there are a few corrections made by different hands, which, so far as the Psalter is concerned, will be found pointed out in the foot-notes. The date of the MS., according to Sir Frederic Madden, is the earlier half of the fourteenth century. At the end of the Psalter, on the back of leaf 149, a hand of the sixteenth century has written the following notices; they are very indistinct, and have caused great trouble to me and Mr. Bickley, of the British Museum, who has very kindly helped me to decipher them :—

Anno domini M° CC° xxiiij° in festo beati bartholomei fratris minores primo venerunt in angliam.

Ville anglie torrentes (?) scaccario regis anglie preter villas aliorum dominorum anglie sunt .xxv. M^a & octoginta.

Item feoda militum anglie sexaginta M^a CC^a & xv de quibus religiosi occupant .xxviijj^a M^a & xv.

Item comitatus anglie .xxv^{a}vi cum dimidio.

Item ecclesie perochiales .xlv. M^a & quatuor.

Anno domini M° CC° vi° incepit ordo minorum & predicatorum.

Anno domini .M° CC° xxviiij fuit regula beati francisci confirmata.

In eodem anno in exaltacione sancte crucis intrauerunt fratres angliam.

Anno domini M° CC° xxvi° obijt beatus franciscus.

Item anno domini M° CC° xx8° leuatur a cimiterio.

Anno domini M° CC° 31° beatus antonius migrauit ad dominum.

A fly-leaf prefixed to the MS. contains the following notice of the history of the MS., written by Sir Frederic Madden :—

"This MS., in 1828, belonged to Thomas Rodd, of whom it was purchased by the late Alexander Henderson, Esq., of Edinburgh, who caused the printed specimens of the Psalter to be set up,[1] with the intention of printing the whole, and he proposed to myself to be the Editor. For the purpose of transcription, Mr. Henderson took off the old binding, and divided the MS. into two portions, in which state it appeared in the Sale Catalogue of his library, sold in London, at Sotheby's rooms, in June, 1846,

[1] They are bound up with the MS. at the end, and contain the first three Psalms printed in two columns on two leaves with the Latin text on the left and the English on the right hand. On a preceding leaf is another note, which runs thus :

"Ediny., Aug. 4, 1832.

This first and last portion of a MS was given me for the purpose of the printed specimen of the first three pages and a half, and for copying the last half page.

JAMES KILGOUR."

Lots 3329 and 3332. Lot 3329, containing the Psalter, was purchased by Tho. Rodd for the Museum for £18; but Lot 3332, on being called for, was found to have been stolen from the Auction-room. It was, however, put up,[1] and purchased by Rodd for the Museum, for £5 12s. 6d. In March, 1849, this missing portion of the MS. again made its appearance in private hands, and was eventually made over to Messrs. Sotheby & Co., by whom it was delivered to the Keeper of the MSS. in the Museum, in May, 1849. The two parts have been now re-united together in one volume. F. M., 8 June, 1849."

Mr. Thomas Wright, the editor of William of Shoreham's *Religious Poems*, which, as has just been noted, are found together with the Psalter in the London MS., thought that the MS. was written by the poet himself. But this is quite impossible, as has already been shown by Professor Konrath.[2] William of Shoreham spoke his Kentish dialect,[3] but in the MS. his poems contain numerous forms of other dialects, and—which is more important— they are full of corruptions, the readings of many passages being nothing but bare nonsense. Thomas Wright's edition does not contain any corrections, but R. Morris, Maetzner, Wülker and Konrath have since given a large number of emendations. The Psalter is in a like bad state, as a glance at the numerous footnotes to the text printed below will show at once.

The second MS. is preserved in the library of Trinity College, Dublin. Formerly it had the mark H. 32, and is now numbered A. 4. 4. It was also written in the fourteenth century, and a note at the end of the Psalter, in the hand of the original scribe,[4] gives the name of John Hyde[5] as the owner of the book.

The Psalter fills the first 55 leaves of the MS., and is followed

---

[1] On Sir F. Madden's insistance. He knew (thro' the Percy Society) that Thomas Wright was editing Shoreham's Poems, and must have stolen the MS. from Sotheby's shelves. Sir F. Madden told me this.—F. J. FURNIVALL.

[2] M. Konrath, *Beiträge zur Erklärung und Textkritik des William von Schorham*, Berlin, 1878, p. 3.

[3] Cp. Danker, *Laut- und Flexionslehre der mittel-kentischen Denkmäler*, Dissert. Strassburg, 1879.

[4] "Explicit Psalterium translatum in Anglicum ; Johanni Hyde constat."

[5] In Baliol College, Oxford, is a MS. (numbered 354) which contains legends, songs, etc , and was written by a certain John Hyde. But this must be a different person; for the handwriting is at least a hundred years later, as I have ascertained myself. Cp. also *Anglia*, vol. xii. p. 16.

next by Wyclif's *Commentary on the Apocalypse* written in the same hand, which begins with this rubric:—

Hic incipit prologus libri decretis celestib*us* qui dicit*ur* apocalipsis in anglicis.

(*Beginning.*) Saynte poule þe apostel sayþ þat aⱡⱡ þo þat wyⱡⱡ pr*i*uylych leue*n* on Ih*e*su cryste schal sofre p*er*secucyons *and* angwysches, bot o*u*r swete lorde Ih*e*su cryste wyll noȝt þat his chosen faile in tribulacious. (14 *leaves.*)

The third piece is a *Tale of Charite*, written by the same scribe. Begins: *Many man spekeþ of charite þat wote neue*r *what it is.* (In Prose.)

Next, an *Exposition of the Decalogue.* (Prose, 7 pages.) Then, a *Description of Jerusalem*, in Latin prose; one page and a half. Besides these, the MS. contains Richard Rolle's poem, *The Pricke of Conscience*; but this work is written by a different scribe. Eight leaves, containing the lines 4071–5525 of the poem, are inserted in a wrong place of the MS., in the middle of Wyclif's Commentary on the Apocalypse.[1]

Josiah Forshall and Frederic Madden, who, in the Preface to their large quarto edition of the Wycliffite Bible,[2] have given an historical survey of the English translation of Scripture, also treat of the two MSS. which have just been described.

From the facts that in the older one the Psalter is found together with William of Shoreham's Poems, and that the MS. belongs to the time when William lived, they infer that the Psalter also is his work. But this supposition is contradicted by other and weightier facts. A comparison of the dialectical forms and the modes of spelling in the two works at once shows that they cannot have had their origin in the same part of England, and that they were written together from different MSS. The Psalter does not contain any traces of the Kentish dialect worth mentioning, or perhaps none whatever; its language

---

[1] I have discussed the relation of this version of the *Pricke of Conscience* to those of other MSS. in a paper "On twenty-five MSS. of Richard Rolle's *Pr. of C.*," read before, and shortly to be published in the Transactions of, the Philological Society.

[2] The Holy Bible, in the Earliest English Versions made by John Wycliffe and his Followers, edited by the Rev. Josiah Forshall and Sir Frederic Madden, Oxford, 1850.

is almost pure West Midland, which differs very distinctly from the Southern forms of the Poems. Only by chance were the two works put together, possibly on account of the similarity of their contents, the scribe's intention being to make a collection of religious songs.

It is not improbable even that it was the very writer of our MS. who collected them. Judging from the mechanical manner in which he did his copying, he must have been a very ignorant man, who understood neither much Latin nor English, though we cannot blame him for excessive carelessness. In a certain way he has bestowed much attention on his original, and has apparently done his best to make an exact copy, writing letter by letter, so far as he could decipher the original before him, which very likely was difficult to read. He has very often produced most ridiculous results. In such cases he does not seem to have used his brains at all, but to have purposely abstained from making emendations. The blunders in the Latin text of the Psalter are legion. For instance, he writes *adorabum* instead of *adorabo*, *sabitis* instead of *salutis*, *uniuersente* instead of *universe uie*, *into* instead of *intimo*, etc.

The English translation also exhibits a great number of corrupted forms which have no sense at all; for instance, *arengþe* for *strengþe*, *hi mi* for *huni*, *gogged* for *goddes*, *shi iuges* for *shininges*, *len* for *ben*, *den* for *hem*, *kycked* for *wycked*, *Vn* for *þou*, *herne de fulnes* for *her nedefulnes*, *mid fouleing* for *mi defouleing*, etc.

Now if we keep in mind that the copier introduced very little of his own, and realize how widely the Psalter on the one hand and the Poems on the other differ both in dialectical forms and peculiarities of spelling—two facts which I propose to discuss at length in the Second Part of this edition—it will appear very likely that the two works had not before been transcribed by another and the same copier; or they would have more resemblance in their language and spelling.

At all events, there remains no reason to attribute the Psalter to William of Shoreham.

In a similar way, the Psalter of the Dublin MS. had been ascribed to John Hyde, whose name stands at the end of it;[1] but as Forshall and Madden have already suggested, it is only a revision of the text in the London MS. and not an independent translation, and John Hyde was only the owner of the MS.

The Dublin MS. is very carefully and distinctly written, and there are only very few mistakes in it. It is of invaluable help in mending the numerous senseless readings of the London copy.

Both MSS. contain the Latin text as well as the English translation, which follow each other verse by verse. To the Psalter are added eleven Canticles, and the Athanasian Creed.

The Latin text is that of the Vulgate, of course with the readings of the time, which sometimes differ from the modern editions. All deviations will be given in the *Notes*.

Another difference exists in the division of some of the Psalms. Thus, counting the Psalms as they stand in the two MSS., their number would exceed 150. But in order to avoid the difficulty which the numbering according to the MSS. would cause to anybody desirous of comparing this Psalter with other versions, I have not adhered to those deviations; all peculiarities of the two MSS. are, however, pointed out in foot-notes. Following the example which Forshall and Madden have set in their edition of the Wycliffite Bible, I have adopted the numbering of the Psalms used in the ordinary editions of the Vulgate version. But as this deviates to a great extent from that employed in the Authorized English Bible, I have added the English numbering within marks of parenthesis, wherever there is a difference. I have borrowed this expedient from Professor Skeat's reprint of *The Books of Job, Psalms, Proverbs*, etc., *according to the Wycliffite Version*.[2] His brief explanation of the double numbering is as follows:—

The difficulty begins after verse 21 of Psalm ix., where the Vulgate

---

[1] Cp. the summary of the contents prefixed to the MS. and written by a hand of the seventeenth century; also Le Long, *Bibliotheca Sacra*, vol. i. p. 425.

[2] Oxford, 1881.

version has the remark "Psalmus x. secundum Hebræos," with a fresh numbering of the remaining verses in the Psalm. The English version makes Psalm x. begin here. But the Vulgate version heads our Psalm xi. with the title: "In finem, Psalmus David x." This throws the whole numbering out for a long way, down to the end of Psalm cxlvi. Psalm cxlvii. has its verses numbered from 12 to 20, and agrees with the latter part of Psalm cxlvii. in the English version. The last three Psalms are the same in both versions. Psalms cxiii., cxiv., cxv. in the Vulgate are strangely divided. The first is Psalms cxiv. and cxv. of the English version; the other two make up Psalm cxvi.

The only difference from his numbering (which I have left unaltered) is the position of Psalms 136 and 137, which are transposed in both MSS.

In neither MS. have the numbers themselves been added throughout. In the London MS. they are written in the margin by a later hand, but very carelessly; several numbers are skipped, and in other places Psalms are not counted. The last number in the London MS. is 97, put at the beginning of Psalm 99. The numbers in the Dublin MS. are added by the rubricator, and the last numbered Psalm is the forty-first, bearing the incorrect number 39.

As to the numbering of the verses, I have not thought it advisable to change anything, as in many cases the peculiar way in which the text is divided has resulted in quite a different meaning. Besides, this discrepancy in the numbering is usually but slight, and will cause no serious difficulty.

What makes this Psalter especially curious is the fact that the Latin text is largely explained and interpreted by Latin glosses, and that in the translation—which, apart from this, is generally faithful and literal,—the words of the gloss are substituted for those of the text.

In the Dublin MS. most of the Latin glosses of the first few Psalms are omitted; but their English translation is always retained.

In both MSS. all the Latin glosses are written after the word explained, and in the London copy they are, as a rule, underlined with red paint. They will be printed in the *Notes*, which will form part of the second volume of this work.

PREFACE.

At present I will give only a few instances, in order to show the character of the glosses and the mode in which they are Englished. The last clause of the Latin of Psalm 1, 1 reads thus in L (the London MS.) :—*et in cathedra .i. iudicio pestilencie .i. falsitatis non sedit*; in D (the Dublin MS.) the glosses are omitted. The English rendering in L is :—*ne sat nauȝt in fals iugement*, the translator rejecting *cathedra pestilencie*, and adopting the gloss *iudicio falsitatis*. In the revised text of D, both the glossed words and the glosses are translated :—*& haþ not syt in þe chayer of pestilence, þat is to seyne, of vengeaunce, or of fals iuggement*. It is no literal translation, though; for the words *of vengeaunce* have no equivalent in the Latin text, but are an addition made by the reviser. Moreover, the end of the verse should be *in* instead of '*of* fals iuggement.'

This is, however, not the usual way of translating in D, which (as a rule) Englishes only the glosses.

I add also the other glosses of the first and second Psalms, distinguishing them from the surrounding text by the use of italics :—1, 4, quecumque *justus* faciet ; 1, 5, Non sic *sunt* impij. 2, 1, Quare fremuerunt *.i. dubitaverunt de lege* gentes *sine lege* ; 2, 2, aduersus Christum *.i. sacerdotem crismate unctum* eius ; 2, 3, Dirumpamus, *pater dixit filio et spiritui sancto*, vincula *.i. incredulitatem* eorum; et proiciamus a nobis iugum *.i.*[1] *pondus peccati* eorum ; 2, 5, in furore suo *.i. vindicta* conturbabit eos ; 2, 6, ab eo patre super Sion [*.i.*] *celum* ; 2, 7, Dominus *pater* dixit . . . genuit te *cum me* ; 2, 8 in virga ferrea *.i. asperitate* ; 2, 13, Cum exarserit *.i. sit commotus* . . . . , beati *sunt* omnes.

Compare also Psalm 137, 1 :—Super flumina *.i. insultus* Babilonis *.i. diaboli*, illic sedimus et flevimus : cum [2] recordaremur Sion *.i. celi*. (2) In salicibus [3] *.i. transitorijs* in medio eius suspendimus organa *.i. gaudia* nostra. (3) Quia illic interrogaverunt nos, qui *.i. diaboli* captivos duxerunt nos, verba cantionum.

Such passages are significant of the way in which the scholastic theologians of the Middle Ages used to explain the Bible. The

---

[1] MS. *et*. [2] MS. dum. [3] MS. psallicibus.

most curious interpretation occurs in the first verse of Psalm 78, which, with its additions, reads thus :—

De terra Vs, Deus, venerunt gentes *sine lege* in hereditatem tuam *.i. Judee*,[1] polluerunt templum sanctum tuum: posuerunt Jerusalem in *quarundam gencium vocatarum* pomorum custodiam.—The English translation shows that the last word but one was thought to mean *a maner of folk¹ þat was cleped Pomos.*

I have taken considerable trouble to find out something about the origin of these glosses, but all my endeavours have hitherto been in vain. There are numerous glossed Latin Psalters of various ages in the British Museum; but of all of them, (so far as I have been able to ascertain,) our glosses are independent. Such MSS. are Royal 2. B. v; 3. B. ix; 4. B. iv; 4. D. x; 1. E. iii; 2. E. ii; 2. E. v; 4. E. vi; Harl. 628; 3654; 4804; Addit. 9350; 10924; 16903; 18043.

As to the mode of my reproducing the text of the MSS., only a few more remarks are necessary.

In the London MS., all the Psalms begin with a large capital letter in blue and red on a fresh line. The first letter of all Latin verses is written with blue paint, and the English translation is always prefixed by a red ¶.

Punctuation occurs only in the English text, on the first pages of the MS. The only sign used is a thin downward stroke, which is found after the following words:

1, 1 wicked | sinȝeres | —1, 2 was | lord | lawe | —1, 3 tre | — 1, 6 iugement | —2, 2 vpstonden | lord | —2, 3 gost | mysbeleue | —2, 4 hem | —2, 5 wraþe | —2, 7 to me | —2, 8 men | habbinge | —2, 11 doute | —2, 12 noȝt | noȝt | —2, 13 ire | hij | — 3, 1 trublen me | —3, 2 soule | —3, 3 Keper | glorie | —3, 4 uoyce | —3, 5 aros | —3, 6 folk | me | god | —3, 8 lord | lord | —4, 1 me | —4, 3 sones | —4, 4 wele | name |

Capitals are not used in the MS., except for all first letters of the Latin as well as the English verses; only once (in Ps. 50, 7) *ffor* is spelt with two f's.

I have first printed the text of L, the London MS. The nearest

---

[1] *tuam .i.* is omitted in the British Museum MS.

foot-notes underneath point out the numerous blunders, etc., of that MS. At the bottom of the page follow the various readings of D, the Dublin copy, with only a few foot-notes belonging to this text. Usually differences of spelling and dialect are not given, so that the alterations of the reviser will be more readily perceived. The dialectical forms of D, of which I have made a full list, will be discussed at length in the *Introduction*.

I have preferred not to try and correct all the errors of L, but have restricted myself to mending the grossest and most ridiculous blunders and such as were quite senseless; full attention will be given to the subject in the *Notes*, where many puzzling questions remain to be settled.

I had intended to publish the *Introduction*, *Notes*, and *Glossary* with the text; but other work has prevented me from completing my task in time. The type of the text was set more than eighteen months ago, and its sheets have been ready for issue a long time. So, in order not to cause more inconvenience and loss to the printers,—to whom I am indebted for their patience as well as for the great care with which they have treated my puzzling copy,— I have determined to divide the work into two parts, and I trust that the second volume will be completed within the course of next year.

I return my sincerest thanks to Professor Konrath, of Greifswald, who presented me with his very careful copy of the first thirty-seven Psalms in the London MS., when I asked him whether he intended to edit the Psalter. I myself completed the copy, and also collated the Dublin MS. I take this opportunity of expressing my great obligations to the Rev. T. K. Abbot, the courteous Librarian of Trinity College, Dublin, who very readily placed the Dublin MS. at my disposal when I had only a few days in Dublin. My grateful acknowledgments are again due to him, as well as to Mr. Thomas French, his Sub-Librarian, who I am sorry to say has since left this life, for ascertaining the manuscript readings of a great number of passages about which I was doubtful. To Mr. A. K. Donald I am indebted for once reading the proof-sheets with the London text. I also tender my best thanks to Professor Logeman, of Ghent, for his kind communications regarding a number of Latin Psalters, with Latin glosses. And last, not least, I sincerely thank Dr. Furnivall for always very obligingly complying with my wishes and proposals regarding my editorial work, and for his kind and friendly advice in many cases.

KARL D. BÜLBRING.

HEIDELBERG,
    October 31*st*, 1890.

ERRATA IN THE TEXT.

Ps. 6, 2 L.	*instead of*	have	*read*	haue.
9, 27 D.	,,	have	,,	haue.
14, 6 L.	,,	that	,,	þat.
14, 7 L.	,,	shall	,,	shal.
27, 4 D.	,,	*ieuls*	,,	*iuels*.
33, 9 D.	,,	no	,,	no nede.
60, 4 D.	,,	scha	,,	2. *shal*] scha.
67, 15 L.	,,	souless hul	,,	soules shul.
78, 13 L.	,,	seven	,,	seuen.
82, 11 L.	,,	scu*n*ari	,,	san*ct*uari.
88, 25 L.	,,	Gode	,,	gode.
90, 10 D.	,,	cam	,,	com.
93, 23 L.	,,	departem	,,	departen.
97, 4 L.	,,	merey	,,	mercy.
101, 26 D.	,,	26—*Ne*	,,	25.—*Ne.* 26.
108, 18 L.	,,	cloyþng	,,	cloþyng.
117, 23 D.	,,	: þou	,,	].
134, 11 L.	,,	Kyng	,,	kyng.
187, 24 L.	,,	cleþed	,,	cleped.

Early English Psalter.

[BRITISH MUSEUM, ADDITIONAL MS. 17376.]

[1] PSALM 1.

1. Blesced be þe man, þat ȝede nouȝt in þe counseil of wicked, ne stode nouȝt in þe waie of sinȝeres, ne sat nauȝt in fals [2] iugement.

2. Ac hijs wylle was in þe wylle of oure Lord, and he schal þenche in hijs lawe boþe daye and nyȝt.

3. And he schal be as þe tre, þat hijs sett by þe ernynges of waters; þat schal ȝeue his frut in hijs tyme.

4. And hijs lef [3] schal nouȝt fallwen; [4] and alle þynges þat þe ryȝtful doþ schal multiplien.

5. Nouȝt so ben þe wicked, nouȝt so; as a poudre, þat þe wynde casteþ fram þe face of þerþe.

6. For-þi ne schal nouȝt þe wicked arise in iugement, ne þe sinners in þe conseyl of þe ryȝtful.

---

[1] fol. 1.   [2] *fals* written on erasure in a later hand.   [3] By a later hand an *a* is added over the *e*.   [4] The *w* is added above the line by a different hand.

[TRINITY COLLEGE, DUBLIN, MS. A. 4. 4.]†

*1. 1. ȝede n.] haþ noght go: wicked ... nouȝt] wykkyd men & haþ not stond: sinȝeres ...] synful men, & haþ not syt in þe chayer of pestilence, þat is to seyne, of vengeaunce, or of fals iuggement.

2. But in þe law of *our* Lorde the wyl of hym schal be, & in hys law he schal haue mynde day & nyght.

3. a trow: be-syde þe *cours*: ȝuld.

4. *fallwen*] fade or falow: þe r. doþ] he schal do: *mult.*] welfare or multyplie.

5. þe wykkyd men schal noþer be so no so, but as pouder.

6. þer-fore þe wykkyd schal noȝt aryse, no þe synners in þe counseyl of ryȝtful men.

---

* fol. 1.   † The signs + and − will be used to indicate additions and omissions; words preceding them are given in the spelling of D. The numerous repetitions in L, which are notified under the text, do not, of course, occur in D.

7. For oure Lord knew þe waie of þe ryȝtful, and þe waye of synners schal perissen.

PSALM 2.

1. Whi douteþ hij hem [1] of þe lawe, þe folk wyþ-outen lawe, & folk þoȝt idel þynges?

2. Þe kynges of erþe vpstonden, and þe princes acorden in on oȝains our Lord and oȝain hys preste anoint wyþ creme.

3. Þe fader seiþ to þe sone and to þe holi gost, Breke we here mysbyleue, and cast we oway fram vs þe charge of here synnes.[2]

4. He þat woneþ in heuen schal scornen[3] hem, and oure Lord schal vnder-nymen[4] hem.

5. Þan schal God speken to hem in hys wraþe, and schal trublen hem in hijs wreche.

6. Ich for-soþe am stablyst kyng of þat fader up heuen, hys holy hyl, precheand hys comaundementȝ.

7. Þe Lord, oure fader, seide to me, Þou ert my sone; ich biȝat þe today wyþ me.

8. Aske of me, and ich schal ȝeue[5] to þe men þyn eritage, and þin habbinge þe terme of þerþe.[6]

9. Þou schalt gouernen hem in sharpnes; and þou schalt breken hem as an erþen pott.

10. & ȝe kynges, vnderstondeþ nov; beþ lered, ȝe þat iugen þerþe.

11. Serueþ our Lord in doute, and gladeþ to hym wyþ quakeing.

12. Take disciplin, þat our Lord wraþ noȝt, and þat ȝe peris noȝt out of þe ryȝt waie.

---

[1] fol. 1b.   [2] y corrected from u.   [3] MS. tornen.   [4] Between vnder and nymen, ne is dotted out.   [5] ȝ on erasure in a different handwriting.   [6] fol. 2.

---

7. knowþ: of ryȝtfull men: synful men.

2. 1. Why doutyd or gruchyd þe folk withowten law of þe law & thogth ydel thyngeȝ.

2. of þe erþe stod up: acordyd: aȝen: aȝen.

3. sayde: mysb.] bondes of her m.

4. scorne.

5. trublen] schende.

6. For-soþ ich am ordeynde a kyng: up] of: þe hesteȝ of hym.

7. Our Lorde fader.

*8. habb.] possessions: termes.

9. sharpn.] a ȝurde of yse or in scherpenes: a pott of erþe.

12. Takeþ lore: wr. n.] be noȝt wraþt: þe] þis.

* fol. 1b.

13. Whan he be styred in hys short ire, blisced ben hij, þat afien in hym.

PSALM 3.

1. Lord, why ben hij multiplied þat trubles me? mani arisen aʒeins[1] me.
2. Many siggen[2] to my soule, þer nys non helþe to hym in hys God.
3. Þou, Lord, for-soþe ys my keper, my glorie, and heʒand min heued.
4. Ich cried to my Lord wyþ my uoyce, & he herd me fram hys holy heuen.
5. Ich slepe and slomered and a-ros; for our Lord toke me.
[3] 6. Ich ne schal nouʒt doute þousaundes of folk' þat bysetten me; aryse þou, Lord, þat art my God, ande make me sauf.
7. For þou smete[4] alle þat were oʒains me wyþ-outen enchesoun; and þou defouledest þe wickednes of sinʒeres.
8. Helþe ys of oure Lord, and þy blisseing,[5] Lord, hys on þy folk'.

PSALM 4.

1. As ich cleped, God of my ryʒt herd me; þou, Lord, forbare me in my tribulacioun.
2. Haue mercy on me, Lord, and here my prayere.
3. Ha ʒe mennes sones, why ben ʒe heuy of herte? wherto loue ʒe ydelnes and secheþ lesyng'?
4. Wyte ʒe wele, þat our Lord haþ made wonderfulliche hys holy name; my Lord schal here me, whan ich haue cried to hym.
5. Wraþþes ʒou, & wil ʒe nouʒt synʒen;[6] þat ʒe[7] saie in ʒour hertes and beþ prikked in ʒour[8] chouches.

---

[1] aʒe on erasure. [2] s on erasure of v, by a later hand. [3] fol. 2b. [4] Corrected from smote by erasing a little off the right part of the o. [5] MS. vlisseing. [6] ʒ on erasure in a later hand. [7] ʒ corrected from h, which is erased, by a later hand. [8] MS. our.

---

13. is mouyd : trysteþ.   8. blyssyng.

3. 2. sayþ.
3. ert: keper & my ioie & enhying.
4. hyl or heuen.
6. —ne : drede : þ. b.] bysegyng.
7. smote : cause : to-brast þe teþe or þe wykkydnes of synners.

4. 1. When : God] to my Godd : ryʒt+he.
3. —Ha : men : segeþ.
4. & wyt : haue c.] schal cry.
5. Wr. ʒ.] Beþ wroþ : ʒe s.] saþ :
* our] ʒour : couches.

* fol. 2.

6. Sacrifieþ sacrifice of ryʒt, and hopeþ in our Lord; mani siggen[1] Who schal shew vs gode þynges?

[2]7. Lord, þe lyʒt of þy face hys merked vp vs; þou ʒaf liʒtnes[3] in my hert.

8. Of þe frute of hys whete and of hys win and of hys oile ben þe gode multiplied.

9. In pees schal ich slepe, and in þat ich resten.

10. For þou, Lord, haþ on-liche[4] stablist me in hope.

PSALM 5.

1. Lord, take myn wordes wyþ þyne eren; vnderstonde my crye.

2. Vnderston (!) þe voice of myn praier, þou my king and my God.

3. For y schal praie to þe, Lord, and tou schalt erlich here mye uoice.

4. Erlich shal ich stonde to þe and sen; for þou nert nouʒt God willand wyckednes.

5. Þe wycked shal nouʒt wonen bisid þe, ne þe vnryʒtful schal nouʒt dwellen a-forn þyn eʒen.

6. Þou hatest alle þat wirchen wickednes, and þou shalt lesin alle þat speken lesyng.

7. Our Lord shal haue in abhominacioun[5] þe man þat sinʒeþ and þe treccherous; ich am, Lord, in þe miclenes[6] of þy mercy.

8. Y shal entren in-to þyn houus; y shal praie to þyn holy temple in þy doute.

9. Lade me, Lord, in þy ryʒtfulnes for myn enemys; adresce my way in þy siʒt.

---

[1] MS. *singgen.* seems to be erased. [2] fol. 3. [3] ʒ corrected from a *t*. [4] Between *on* and *liche, e* seems to be erased. [5] fol. 3b. [6] MS. *cl* (which is expuncted) *vnclennes.*

---

6. Sacrifyþ+þe: seyn: *schal sh.*] haþ schewyd to.
7. *vp*] on: hast ʒyue.
8. —1. *and*: *þe gode*] þey.
9. *ich rest.*] same schal y rest.
10. hast: sett.

5. 1. eres+&.
2. Take hede to þe voce (!).

4. ert.
5. *ne þe v.*] no vnriʒtful men: to-for.
6. —*and*: lese.
7. A man of synnes & a tricherus man our Lord schal haue in abhominacion: mychelnes.
8. entry: drede.
9. & dresse.

EARLY ENGLISH PSALTER. PSALM 6.   5

10. For soþenes nys nouȝt in her mouþe; her hert ys ydel.

11. Her þrote ys a graue open; hij diden trecherouslich wyþ her tonges; God, iuge þou hem.

12. Fallen hij fram her þouȝtes; and put hem ouȝt fro þe, Lord, efter þe mechelnes of her iuels; for hij wraþed þe.

13. & gladen all þat hopen in þe; hij schul ioyen wyþ-outen ende, and þou shalt wonen wyþ hem.

14. & alle þat louen þy name shalt (!) gladen in þe; for þou shalt blisse þe ryȝtful.

15. Lord, þou hast crouned us as wyþ þe shelde[1] of þy gode wylle.

PSALM 6.

1. Lord, ne repruce me nouȝt in þy vengeaunce; ne reproue me nouȝt in þyn yre.[2]

2. Lord, haue mercy on me, for ich am sik; hele me, Lorde, for alle myn bones ben trubled.

3. & my soule ys mychel trubled, & þou, Lord, sum dele.

4. Be þou, Lord, turned, and defende[3] my soule; make me saufe for þy mercy.

5. For þer nys non in dampnacioun, þat hys þenchand on þe; and who schal shryue to þe in helle?

6. Ich trauayled in my sorowynges; ich shal wasshe my bed [by][4] uch nyȝt; ich shal dewey[5] my[6] couertour wyþ min teres.

7. Myn eȝen (!) hys trubled wyþ wraþe; ich wex olde amonge al myn enemys.

8. Departeþ fro me, ȝe alle þat wyrchen wickednesse[7]; for our Lord herd þe voice of my wepe.[8]

---

[1] shelþe MS., þ being written on an erasure by a different hand.   [2] fol. 4.
[3] MS. defended, the last d being expuncted.   [4] After bed two letters are erased, and after this erasure the space of four letters is left empty.   [5] The y of dewey is added over the line.   [6] y corrected out of i.   [7] MS. wickenednesse.   [8] MS. wepeg¹, of which g¹ is written on an erasure by a later hand.

---

10. For þer is no soþnes : mouþe +&.
11. an open byryel+& : gylefullych : deme.
12. wykkydnees (!).
13. glade be all þo þat.
14. schal be gladyd : ryȝtful+man.*
15. schelde.

6. 1.—ne : reproue : ne] no.
2. sturbuld.
3. sturbuld.
4. defend : soule+and.
5. nys] is : —schryue.
6. haue tr. : sorow : bed by ech : watery.
7. ye is sturbuld.
8. wykkydnes : wepe (distinct).

* fol. 2b.

9. Our Lord herd my praier, our Lord toke myn oreisoun.

10. Wax alle myn enemys asshamed, and ben hij greteliche trubled; ben hij conuerted, & shame hij ful swyftlich.[1]

PSALM 7.

1. Lord, my God, ich hoped in þe; make me saufe of alle þat pursuen me, & deliuer me fram alle yuel;

2. þat þe enemi ne rauis nouȝt my soule as a lion, þer-whyles þat þer nys non to raunsoun it, [ne to] makᵗ it sauf.

3. Lord, my God, ȝyf ich did þys þyngᵗ, ȝyf wycked[nesse][2] hys in myne hondes,

4. Ȝyf ich ȝelde euel to hem þat ȝelden iuel to me, y schal falle by desert idel fram myne enemys.

5. Pursue þe enemy my soule, and take it, and de-foule my lyf in erþe, and lade mi glorie in-to poudre.

6. Aryse, Lord, in þyn yre, & be þou hered in þe cuntres of myn enemys.

7. Lord, my God, aryse in þe comaundement þat tou sent,[3] &[4] synagoge of folke shal encumpas þe.

8. & for þat ich þinge cum up oȝain on heȝe; our Lord iugeþ þe folk.

9. Juge me, Lord, efter my ryȝtfulnesse, and after myne innoce[nce] be þou vp[5] me.

10. þe wickednesse of synȝeres shal be wasted; and þou shal drescen þe riȝtful, God, sechaund[6] hertes and reiners.[7]

---

[1] fol. 4b.   [2] *nesse* is added in margin by another scribe.   [3] MS. *lent*.   [4] MS. *in*.
[5] fol. 5.   [6] *a* corrected from *e*.   [7] MS. *and ry reiners*. *Reiners* is probably only a blunder instead of *reines*.

---

9. praier+&.
10. sturbuld: schamyd ful hastylych.

7. 1. My Lord God ych trust: all purseuyng.
   2.—*ne*: to-whyls þer is: raunson + yt no to: saue.
   3. My Lord Godd: wykkydnes.
   4. do: doþ: fall wylfullych fram myn ydel enemys.

5. ioye.
6. enhyed.
7. Aryse my Lord God: þi commaunment (!): þou sent & þe s.: besett.
*8. —*ich*: go aȝeyne on hye+ þer: demeþ.
9. Deme: ryȝtwysnes: —*innoce*.
10. destrued: riȝtful + man: —*God*: schechyng (!): & reynes.

* fol. 3.

11. Min helpe ys ryʒtful of our Lord, þe which makeþ sauf þe ryʒt-ful of hereť.[1]

12. God ys iuge stalworþe, ryʒtful, and suffrand, and ne wraþes hym nouʒt ich daie.

13. Bot ʒyf ʒe be styred fram iuel, he shal shew[2] hys vengeaunce; he made hys manaces, and he dyted hem.

14. And in þat dyʒted he pynes of deþe, and made hys woundes to þe brynnand in pynes.

15. Lo, þe sinner doþ vnryʒt-fulnesse; he conceiued sorow, and childed wickednesse.

16. He opened helle & dalf it, and fel in þe diche þat he made.

17. Hys sorowe shal be turned oʒains hys heued, and hys wickenesse(!) shal fallen doun oʒayn þe haterel of hys heued.

18. Ich shal shryue to our Lord after hys ryʒtful[3]nesse, and synge to þe name of þe heʒest Lord.

PSALM 8.

1. Ha þou, Lord, our Lord, ful wonderful hys þy name in al þerþe.

2. For þy mychelnes ys heʒed up þe heuens.

3. Þou madest heryynge of þe mouþe of childer and of þe sukand, for þyne enemys; þat þou destruye þe enemy and þe wrecher of Adam sinne.

4. For ich schal sene[4] þyn heuens, þe werkes of þyn fyngers, þe mone and þe sterres, þat þou[5] settest.

5. What þynge ys man, þat þou ert þenchand on hym? oþer mannes sone, þat-ou visites hym?

---

[1] hereť· MS. (t¹ on erasure and by a later hand). [2] MS. sw (expunged) shew.
[3] fol. 5 b. [4] MS. se new, the w being added by a later hand. [5] þ is corrected from t.

---

11. þe which] þat: safe —þe: ryʒtful+men: hert.
12. is a domes-man ryʒtful, strong, & sofferyng, no is he noʒt wraþed be all dayes.
13. turnyd: braundesch or schew his swerd or vengaunce, his bow or his manece he bent or made & haþ engrayde hym.
14. he dygth: paynes: byrnyng: paynes.

15. childed] brogth forþ.
16. def(!) it vp and+he.
17. wykkydnes.
18. to þi n.

8. 1.—Ha.
2. vp þe] aboue.
3. of sowkyng: Adames.
4. se—new.
5. theching(!).

EARLY ENGLISH PSALTER. PSALM 9.

6. Þou madest hym a lyttel lasse þan þyne au*n*gels; þou corouned hym wyþ glorie and hon*ur*, and stablist hym vp þe werkes of þyn hondes.

7. Þou laidest alle þynges vnder hys fet, alle shepe and nete and also þe bestes of þe felde;

8. Þe briddes of heue*n*, and þe fisshes of þe see, þat gon by þe bystees of þe se.

9. Ha Lord, our Lord, ful wonderful ys þy name in alle erþe.

[1] PSALM 9.

1. Ich shal shryue to þe, Lord, in alle myn hert; ich shal tellen al þyn wonders.

2. Y shal ioien and gladen in þe, y shal syngen heȝestlich to þyne name.

3. I[*n*] turnand oȝainward myn enemy, þe wicked shul ben vnstabled & p*e*rissen fram þy face.

4. For þou madest my iugement and myn e*n*chesun; þou, þat iuges riȝtfulnes, sittest vp þe trone.

5. Þou blamed þe folk', and þe wicked p*e*rissed; þou dedest owai her name wyþ-outen ende and in heue*n*.

6. Þe ve*n*gcau*n*ce of myn enemys defailed in-to þende, and þou destruedest her heritage.

7. Her mund[2] p*e*rissed wyþ noyse, and our Lord dwelleþ wyþ-outen ende.

8. He made redi his trone in iugement, and shal iuge þe folk' in riȝtfulnes.[3]

9. And our Lord hys made refut to þe pou*er*, helper in nedfulnes in tribulaciou*n*.

---

[1] fol. 6.   [2] Altered to *mende* by a later hand.   [3] MS. *riȝtiles*.

---

6. —*a* : þan þyne] fram : crouned : —*wyþ* : ioie : settest : þe] þine.
7. castest aH+aH(!) : fete—*alle*.
*8. goþe þe paþes.
9. vt supra.

9. 1. Lord y schaH schr. to þe.
2. gladen & ioye : hylych.
3. In t*u*rnyng : wykkyd+men : be seke or dye & schal p*e*rysche.

4. dome : cause : demest : þi.
5. blamyd—þe : wykkyd+ma*n*.
6. vengances : failed : her cytes or her herytages.
7. þe mynde of he*m*.
8. dome, & he schal deme þe worlde in eue*n*nes, and he schal deme folk in riȝtfulnes.
9. pouer+and.

* fol. 3*b*.

10. And hopen hij[1] in þe, þat knowen þy name; þou, Lord, for-sake nouȝt þe sechand þe.

11. Singeþ to our Lord, þat woneþ in heuen; sheweþ[2] his studyynges amonge men.

12. For he schand[3] þouȝt[4] [on her] synne; he ne forȝate nouȝt þe crye of þe pouer in gost.

13. Haue mercy on me, Lord;[5] se mi[6] lowenes of myn enemys.

14. Þou þat heȝest me, Lord, of ingoynge of deþ, þat ich swewe al þyn heryynges of þe goynges of þe soules of heuen.

15. Y shal gladen in þyn helþe; þe folke ben ficched in deþ of synne þat hij diden.

16. In þe gnares þat þe folk' hid, is her fote[7] taken.

17. Our Lord shal be knowen doand iugementȝ; þe sinȝer hys[8] taken in þe workes of his hondes.

18. Ben þe synners turned in-to helle, alle þe folkes þat for-ȝeten God.

19. For forȝetyng' of pouer in gost ne shal nouȝt be in ende; þe suffraun[9]ce of þe pouer ne shal nouȝt perisse in ende.

20. Arise up, Lord; be nouȝt[10] man conforted; be þe[11] folkes iuged in þy syȝt.

21. Sett, Lord, up hem þe berer of lawe; witen þe folkes þat hii ben men.[12]—(PSALM 10).

23. Þer-whiles þat þe wicked proudeþ, þe pouer in gost ys bre[n]t; hij ben taken in þe[13] counseil in wich hij þenchen.

---

[1] fol. 6b. [2] MS. sw (expunged) sheweþ. [3] Instead of sechand'. [4] MS. nouȝt.
[5] d on erasure. [6] semi MS. [7] MS. forte. [8] hys on erasure. [9] fol. 7.
[10] MS. nauȝt (expuncted) nouȝt. [11] MS. boþe. [12] Verse 22 is omitted in this text.
[13] in þe, on erasure.

---

10. name + for: forsakeþ noȝt men scheyng (!) þe.

11. heuen+and.

12. sechyng† recoredid (!) her synn & he for-ȝat.

13. Lorde before haue: me+&: on.

14. enhiest me fram þe gates or þe entre of deþ or of hell þat y may schew: h. in þe gates.

15. gl.] ioie: stykkyd or sett in +þe.

16. grynnes: hid ... forte] made or hydd is her fote.

17. makeyng dome.

18. Synners be þey turnyd; hell & all folk.

*19. of+þe: —in gost ne: in+þe: ende+&: pacience:—ne: in +þe.

20. Lord+&: be þe folk denyd (!).

21. of þe lawe & know þe folk.

22. Wharto Lord went þou afer? þou despyest in nedes in tribulacione.

23. To-whyls—þat: brent and hey (!) beþ take in her counseiles þat þey thenche in.

† Before sechyng, schyng with e added over the y is struck out.   * fol. 4.

24. For þe synȝer is[1] heried in þe desires of hys soule, and he blisced of þe wicked.

25. Þe synner greued our Lord; he schal nouȝt seche efter þe mechelhede of hys ire.

26. God nys nauȝt in his syȝt; hys waies ben filed in alle time.

27. Þyn iugement ben don oway fram þe face of þe synȝer; þe ryȝtful shal lord-shipen of alle hys enemys.

28. For þe wicked seid in hys hert, Y ne schal nouȝt ben styred fram kynde to kynde wyþ-outen iuel.

29. Of wich þe mouþe [2] ys ful of waryingʻ[3] and of bitternesse and of trecherie, trauail and sorow is vnder his tunge.

30. He sitteþ in waieteynges wyþ þe riche in[4] priuetes, þat he slo þe[5] nouȝt a-noiand.

31. Hys eȝen loken oȝain þe pouer in gost; he waiteþ in priuite as lioun in hys denne.

32. He waiteþ þat he rauis þe pouer; forto rauis þe pouer in gost, þerwhiles þat he drawe him to him.

33. Þe wicked lowed in hijs wickednes[6] þe riȝtful, he enclined hym to synne, and he shal fallen, whan þat he haþ lordshipped of þe pouer in gost.

34. For þe wicked seid in his hert, God haþ forȝeten synnes; he turneþ his face fram euel, þat he ne se nouȝt at ende.

35. Arise, Lord, and be þin[7] honde an-heȝed,[8] þat þou ne forȝete[9] þe pouer in gost.

---

[1] MS. synȝeris.   [2] fol. 7b.   [3] i added over the line.   [4] MS. and.   [5] MS. sloþe.   [6] -js wi- on erasure.   [7] MS. beþ in.   [8] MS. and heȝed.   [9] te added over line in a different hand.

---

24. praysid: hert: he (!) wykkyd is blyssyd.
25. Lorde+and: mychelnes.
26. is: syȝt+&: defoilyd.
27. domes: synner+&: schal haye lordship.
28. kyn to kyn.
29. Whas mouþe: cursyng: bitterness and gyle.
30. waytynges: ryche men in preuytes þat he slee þe vngylty.
31. aȝens: p.+man: goste+&. as+a.
32. pouer+and: p. —in gost: towhylles.
33. w.+man: made lowe: w.+or falshode: r.+man &: when he schal have lordschip.
34. synnes+&: fram þe wykkyd: —ne: into þe ende.
35. enhied: —ne: forȝete+noȝt.

EARLY ENGLISH PSALTER. PSALM 10 (11).

36. For what þynge stired þe wicked God? for he seid in his hert, He ne shal nouȝt sechen.

37. Seþ þou, sinner? for[1] þou seþ trauail and sorowe, þat þou heue[2] hem into þyn hondes.

38. Ha God, þe pouer in gost ys bilaft to þe; þou shal [3] be helpere to þe faderles.

39. Defoule þe miȝt of þe synȝer and of þe wicked; hys sinne[4] shal be souȝt, and ne shal nouȝt be founden in þe riȝtful.

40. Our Lord shal regnen wyþ-outen ende in þe worled of worldes; ha ȝe men wyþ-outen lawe, ȝe shulle perissen fram hys erþe.

41. Our Lord herd þe desire of þe [pouer] in gost; Lord, þin ere herd[5] þe red[i]nes of her hertes.

42. To iuge þe moderles and þe meke, þat man sett nouȝt to herien hem vp þerþe.

PSALM 10 (11).

1. Ich affie me in our Lord; hou saie ȝe wicked to mi soule, Wende þou in-to heuen as a sparwe?

2. For whi se! þe synȝers made her þretynges; hij diȝted her malices in hardnesse, þat hij herten in derknesse þe riȝtful of hert.

3. For hij destruiden þat tou made; what þyng of iuel did þe riȝtful?

4. Our Lord hys[6] in hys holi temple; our Lord his in heuen, þer his sete ys.

5. Hys eȝen loken to þe pouer in gost; his [7] eȝeliddes asken þe childer of me[n].

6. Our Lord askeþ þe riȝtful and þe wicked; and he þat loueþ wickednesse, hateþ hys soule.

---

[1] *for for* MS.   [2] Read *ȝeue*.   [3] fol. 8.   [4] A later hand has added an *s*.
[5] MS. *ereberd*.   [6] Before *hys*, *in* is struck out by the corrector.   [7] fol. 8b.

---

36. greuyd þe wykkyd+man: —ne.
37. Sest tow sinner for þat þou hast sorow & trauayle: take.
38. —Ha: Godd+to: 1. *to þe*] &: f.+chylde.
*39. Defoile: synn: *ne*] it.
40. — ha: lawe—ȝe: perisch.
41. of pouer men: goste+&: eres herd þe redynes.

42. Forto deme to þe m.: put noȝt ouer to make hym grete or hie vp þe erþe.

10. 1. *aff. me*] tryst: w.+men: pass.
2. For lo how þe s.: *hij*] &: ordeynd: males: *herten*] myȝt greue.
5. g.+&: sonnes of men.
6. wykkyd—*and*.

* fol. 4b.

7. It shal rayne up þe synȝers droppes of fur and of brunstone; and þe gost of tempestes ys partener[1] of her wyckednesse.

8. For our Lord ys riȝtful, ande he loueþ riȝtfulnes; hys semblaun saiȝ euennis.[2]

PSALM 11 (12).

1. Ha Lord, make me sauf, for þe holi failed in parfit holynes; for soþnes ben litteled fram mennes sones.

2. Ichon han i-spoken[3] idel þynges to her neȝeburs, trecherous lippes ben[4] in her hert, and hij spaken trecherie in hert.

3. Our Lord desp[ar]ple alle trecherous tunges & þe tunge miches (!) spekand.

4. Hij þat saiden, We shal praysen our tonges, our lippes ben fram us; who is[5] our Lord?

5. For þe chaitifte of nedeful and þe waimentyng' of pouer y shal aryse nov, saiþ our Lord.

6. Y shal sett þe gode in helþe; y shal make hem faiþliche[6] þer ynne.

[7]7. Þe wordes of our Lord ben chast wordes, siluer ytried wyþ fur þryes, eft purged seuen siþes.

8. Þou, Lord, shal kepen us and loke vs wyþ-outen ende fram þat biȝetyug'.

9. Þe wicked ȝeden abouten, þou multiplidest mennes sones efter þyn eȝenes.

PSALM 12 (13).

1. Ha Sir, hou longe forȝetestou[8] me on ende? hou longe turnestou þy face fram me?

---

[1] *parceuer* MS.   [2] MS. *enemis.*   [3] MS. *ham spoken.*   [4] MS. *hem.*
[5] *who is* on erasure.   [6] *faiþlicle* MS.   [7] fol. 9.   [8] MS. *-toū.*

---

7. He: dr.] grynnes: & brunstone: spirites: is partiner.
8. louyd: face segh euennes.
11. 1.—*Ha*: Godd: h.+man: made liteH: men.
2. haþ: neȝpurs & gileful: *hem*] beþ: hertes: gyle.
3. disparple: muchel.
4. Hei (!).

5. wrechidnes: waylyng.
6. h.+&: —*hem*: fayþlych.
7. chaste (—*wordes*) as siluer examynd in þe fure prouyd thryse & purgyd seuen syþe.
8. schalt ȝeme vs & schalt kepe vs: þis kynred.
*9. hynes.
12. 1. *Ha S.*] Lord: into þe e.

* fol. 5.

2. Hou longe shal ich sett cou*n*seil in my soule, sorow in my hert bi day?

3. Hou long¹ shal myn enemy ben heȝed up me? Lord, my Gode, loke, and here¹ me.

4. Liȝt myn eȝen, þat y slepe no time in deþ; þat myn enemy ne say nauȝt, Ich was more worþy oȝains hym.

5. Hij þat trublen me shal joie*n*, ȝif ich haue ben stired; and y hoped in þy mercy.

6. Min hert shal ioie*n* in þyn helþe; ich shal singe to our Lord, þat ȝaf to me godes, and y² shal synge to þe ³name of our Lord alderȝeste (!).

PSALM 13 (14).

1. Þe vnwyse seid in⁴ his hert, It nys God.

2. Hij ben corru*m*ped and made loþeliche in her studies; þer nys non þat doþ gode, þer nys non vnto on.

3. Our Lord loked fram heue*n* vp mennes sones, þat he se, ȝyf þer be ani vnderstand[and]⁵ oþer sechand⁶ God.

4. Alle boweden, to-gider hij ben vnp*r*ofitable; þer nys [non þat doþ gode, þer nys] non vn-to on.

5. Her gorge is an open biriel, hij deden trecherou*u*sliche wiþ her tunges; veni*m* of aspides, .i. nedders, is vnder her lippes.⁷

6. Of whiche þe mouþe ys ful of waryynge⁸ and bitternysse, her fete ben swift to shade blode.

7. Defoule and vnhappe ys in her waies; and hij ne knewen nouȝt þe waie of pees; þe drede of God nys nouȝt to-fore her eȝen.

---

¹ MS. *heȝe*. ² MS. *h* (struck out) *y*. ³ fol. 9*b*. ⁴ MS. *and*. ⁵ MS. *end* added in margin in a different handwriting. ⁶ Another hand has added an *e* to *sechand*. ⁷ In margin *notabile* by a later hand. ⁸ MS. *þaryynge*.

---

2. conseyles: soule+and.
3. enhied: here.
4. y ne sl. noȝt i*n* any tyme :—*ne*.
5. sturbeleþ: y schal be : *and y h.*] ych for-soþe hope.
6. alderhiest.

13. 1. v.+ma*n*: *and*] in : þer is no Godd.
2. abho*m*inabil: is: is noȝt to one.

3. *be*] is : vnde*r*stondyng or.
4. declinyd to-geder & þei beþ + aH : þer is none þat doþ gode þer is noȝt to one.
5. throte is +as: gilefullych :— *aspides .i.*
6. þe mouþ of wham : c*ur*syng & +of : b.+&.
7. Defulyng : —*ne* : is.

8. Alle þat wirichen wickednesse, ne shal hij nouȝt knowen; wyche[1] de-uouren mi folk as mete of brede?

[2]9. Hij cleped nouȝt our Lord; hij trembleden þer for doute, þer no doute nas.

10. For our Lord his in riȝtful biȝetyng'; þou, Lord, confoundest þe counseil of þe mesais; for our Lord hys hys hope.

11. Who shal ȝyf fram þe heuen helþe to Israel? whan our Lord haþ turned oway þe chaytifnesse of hijs folk', þe kynreden of Iakob shal gladen, and þe folk' of Israel shal ioyen.

PSALM 14 (15).

1. Lord, who shal wonen[3] in þy tabernacle, oþer who shal resten in þyn holy hill?

2. He þat entreþ wyþouten wemm[4] and wyrcheþ ryȝtfulnesse;

3. He þat speke soþnes in hys hert, and ne dide no trecherie in hys tunge;

4. Ne did non yuel to his neȝbur,[5] ne toke no reprusynge oȝayn hys neȝburs.[6]

5. Þe wicked hys brouȝt to nouȝt in hys siȝt, and God glorifieþ þe dredand our Lord.

6. He þat swcreþ to hys neȝbur and decoiueþ [7]hym nouȝt and ȝaf nouȝt hys tresour to oker and ne tok ȝiftes up innocent:

7. He þat doþ þes þynges, ne shal nouȝt be stired wyþ-outen ende.

PSALM 15 (16).

1. Kepe me, Lord, for ich hoped in þe; ich seide to our Lord, þou art my[8] God, for þou ne hast no nede of myn godes.

---

[1] Corrected from weche. [2] fol. 10. [3] In margin notabile, by later hand.
[4] After wemm, two letters are erased. [5] After neȝbur an e seems to have been erased.
[6] In MS. with an o written over u by later hand. [7] fol. 10b. [8] MS. lord þou art my lord þou art mi.

8. wyrch: —ne: —hij: know no þes swalouþ.
9. d. were was no d.
10. generacioun: confoundid: m.] pouer man.
11. fram—þe: thraldome: kynred: gl.] ioie: ioyen] be glade.

14. 1. oþer] &.
*2. wemm] synn.

3. spekeþ soþfastnes: —ne: gyle.
4. Ne] & he þat: & did no reprofe aȝens.
5. þe dr.] men dredyng him.
6. dissaȝuyþ: & he þat ȝaf: mony to vsurye ne toke noȝt ȝ. vp on innocentes.
7. ne] he: mouyd.

15. 1. —ne.

* fol. 5b.

2. Unto halwen þat ben in his londe he made wonderful alle my willes in hem.

3. Her syknesses ben multiplied, and efterwardes hij hasteden to hym.

4. Ich ne shal nouȝt gader to-gideres, seid our Lord Dauid, her wicked felawe-shippes of synȝes;[1] ne ich ne shal nouȝt be þenchand on her names by my lippes.

5. Our Lord is part of myn heritage and of mye ioie; þou art þat shal restoren to me myn heritage.

6. Foundeinges fellen to me in godenesces; for min heritage his ful clere to me.[2]

7. Y shal bliscen our Lord, þat ȝaf me vnderstondyng, and vp þat unto nyȝt my kydnaies blamed me.

8. [3] Y puruaiede our Lord in my siȝt, for he is at my riȝt half, þat ich ne be nouȝt stired.

9. For þat[4] min hert ioide,[5] and my tunge shal gladen, and my flesshe shal al-so resten in hope.

10. For þou ne shal nouȝt [laten my soule in helle, and þou ne shal nouȝt] ȝyf þyn holy to se corupcioun.

11. þou madest knowen to me þe waies of lyf, þou shalt fulfillen me of ioie wyþ [þy] face; delitynges ben in þy riȝt honde vnto þe ende.

PSALM 16 (17).

1. Here, Lord, my riȝt; vnderstonde my praier.

2. Receiue my praier wyþ þy neren nouȝt in trecherous[6] lippes.

3. Forþ go þi iugement out of þy semblant; se þyn eȝen euennes.

---

[1] Over *e* and *s* a later hand has added an *n*. [2] After *me* a letter is erased.
[3] fol. 11. [4] *at* on erasure in a later hand. [5] MS. *seide*. [6] MS. *trecherour*.

2. To his holy men.

3. sekenes beþ: afterward: *hym*] me.

4. *Our* Lord sayd to Dauyd, Y schall noȝt g. to-geder her wykkyd felyschyppes: y — *ne*: be þe thencher of.

5. *party*: schalt restore myne h. to me.

6. Temptacions: *god.*] clerete of godenes.

7. ȝaf+to: ouer þat myne kydners blamyd me vnto n.

8. *at*] on: syde: —*ne*.

9. & þer-for myne h. was gladyd: ioie: also schal.

10. For þou schalt noȝt lete my soule in hell, ne þou schalt noȝt ȝif þine holy seruant forto see corrupcion.

11. m. þe ways of lyfe know to me: with+þine: delites: into.

16. 1. riȝt*fulnes+&.

2. Take: þine eres: gileful.

3. þi dome pas out of þi semblaunte+&.

* fol. 6.

4. Þou prouedest myn hert, and uisited it on niȝt; þou assaidest me þurȝ fur, and wickednesse nys nouȝt founden in me.

5. Þat my mouþe ne speke nouȝt werkes of men, ich kept hard waies for þe wordes of þy lippes.

6. Fulfyl my goynges in þy bestiȝes, þat m[i] traces ne be nouȝt stired.

[1]7. Ich cried, God, for þou herd me; bow þyn eren to me, and here myne wordes.

8. Make þy mercies wonderful, þou þat makest sauf þe hopand in þe.

9. Kepe me fram hem, þat oȝain-stonden þyn ryȝt-half, as þe appel of þyn eȝe.

10. Defend me vnder þe shadow of þy mercies fram þe face of wicked, þat tormented me.

11. Myn enemys ȝede aboute my soule wyþ synnes; hij shetten to-gideres her fattnes; her mouþe spekeþ pryde.

12. Þe kestand oway godnesse han nov gon abouȝt me, and han stablyst her eȝen to bowe into þerþe.

13. Hij token me as a lyon redy to his praie, and a welpe of a lyon wonand in hydels.

14. Aryse vp, Lord, and cum to-forne hym and put [hym] out; defende my soule fram þe wycked, defend þy makeyng' fram þe enemys of þyn honde.

15. De-part hem, Lord, fram fewe of þe erþe in her libbynges, and her wombe [2] [3]ys fild of þyn hydynges.

16. Hij ben fulfild of wickednesses hid, and hij departed to her lytel her iuel toknes.

17. And y shal apperen in ryȝt to þy siȝt [4]; y shal be fild, whan þy glorie haþ shewed.

---

[1] fol. 11b. [2] S. an (expuncted) wombe. [3] fol. 12. [4] MS. fiȝt.

---

4. in: examyndest: with: was.
5 —ne: for þe wordes of þi l. y kepid h. wayis.
6. Fulfil+þou: b.]paþes: my: —ne.
7. —God: ere.
8. 1. þe] men.
9. K. me as þe appiH of þin ye fram men aȝenstondyng þi riȝt honde.
11. to-geder: spak.

12. þai castyng away me or her godnes fram me haþ: sett: forto.
13. and+as: dwellyng.
14. put+hym: wykkyd+&.
15. leuyng: preuy þingis.
16. wykkydnes preuy: departid +or left: smale chyldern her releues or toknes of wykkydnes.
17. to] in: siȝt+&: ioie schal schew.

PSALM 17 (18).

1. Ha Lord, y shal loue þe, my strengþe, my fasteninge, my refut, and my deliuerer of iuel.

2. My God ys myn helper, and y shal hopen in hym;

3. My defendour and þe helpe of myn helþe and my taker.

4. Ich heriand shal clepe our Lord, and y shal be sauf fram myne enemis.

5. Sorowes of deþ ȝeden aboute me, þe welles of wickednes han trubled me.

6. Þe sorwes of helle encumpassed me, þe trappes of deþ han taken me.

7. Ich cleped our Lord in my tribulacioun, and ich cried to my God.

[1] 8. And he herd my uoice fram hys holy temple, and my crie entred in-to hys eren in-to hys syȝt.

9. Þe erþe hys styred, and hyȝt trembled; þe foundemenȝt[2] of þe mounteyns ben trubled, and hij ben styred, for he hys wraþed to hem.

10. Smeke mounted up yn hys wraþe, and fur brent of hys face; coles ben þer-of alyȝted.

11. He bowed þe heuens, and com adoune; and derknes ys vnder his[3] fete.

12. And he mounted vp cherubyn, & fleȝe; he fleȝe vp þe liȝtnesse of þe wyndes.

13. And he sett derknesses hys dwellyng, o-bouten hym hys tabernacle, as derk water in cloudes of þe aier.

14. Þe cloudes passeden in hys siȝt to-fore þe shininge, hail and coles of fur.[4]

---

[1] fol. 12b.   [2] Thus in MS., the ȝ being written over another t.   [3] MS. her.
[4] Verse 15 omitted, both Latin and English.

17. 1. —Ha: f.] stedfastnes.
*2. The English translation is omitted, as well as the Latin in the next verse.
3. helþe] help.
5. me+ &: reuers: han] &: sturbelyd me+me (!).
6. enc.] ȝede aboute: grynnes: han taken] ocupied.
7. —cleped: —ich.
8. eren into] eres in.
9. of — þe: trubled . . styred]

sturbled & mouyd: wroþ.
10. Sm. m.] þe s. went: & þe fure of his face b. & þe c. beþ aneled þer-of.
11. enclynyd—þe: his fote.
12. went vp aboue ch. & fleȝ & fleȝ aboue þe feders or þe swyftnes of þe w.
13. derknes.
14. schynig (!).
15. & our Lord thunderd in fram heuen, & ful hye he ȝafe his voice; haiel & coles of fure.

* fol. 6b.

16. And he sent hys manaces and wasted hem; he multiplied leuinges, and trubled hem.

17. & þe welles of waters appered, and þe foundement of [1] þe worled ben y-shewed,

18. For þy blamyng' & for þe inspiracioun of þe spiriȝt of þyne ire.

19. He sent fram heȝe, and toke me fram many tribulaciouns.

20. He defended me fram myn stronggest enemis and fram hem þat hated me; for hij ben conforted vp me.

21. Hyy com to-fore me in þe day of [my] tourmentyng', & our Lord ys made my defendour.

22. And he lad me in brede; he made me sauf, for he wold me.

23. And our Lord shal ȝyf to me efter my ryȝt; and he shal heue [2] to me efter þe clennesse of myn hondes.

24. For ich kept þe waies of our Lord, ne ich ne bare me nouȝt yuel oȝain my God.

25. For al hys iugementȝ ben in my siȝt, & ich ne putted nouȝt hys riȝt-wysnesse oway fram me.

26. And ich shal be unfiled wyþ hym, and ich shal kepe me fram my wickednesse.

[3] 27. And our Lord shal ȝeue to me efter my ryȝtfulnesse and efter þe clennesse of myn hondes in syȝt of hys eȝen.[4]

28. Þou shalt ben holy wyþ þe holy, and þou shalt be innocent wyþ þe innocent man.

29. And wyþ þe chosen þou shalt be chosen, and wyþ þe wycked þou shalt be wicked.

30. For þou shalt mak' sauf þe mild folk', and þou shalt lowen þe eȝen of þe prowde.

---

[1] fol. 13.   [2] Blunder for ȝeue.   [3] fol. 13b.   [4] Here the MS. makes a paragraph, and begins the next Latin verse with a large and ornamented letter. Accordingly a later hand has added the number 18 in the margin.

---

16. sparpild: liȝtynynges: sturbled.
17. foundementes.
18. Fram þe blame of þe Lord & fram þe i.
19. hye+a-boue.
21. of+my.
22. into brode+&: wolde me+.s. be safe.
*23. þe] my.
24. & y did noȝt yuyll.
25. domys: & & (!) y putt.
26. vnfulyd.
27. in+þe.
28. with holy men: holy with —þe.
30. þe m.] meke: þe p.] proud men.

* fol. 7.

31. For þou alyȝtest myn lanterne; ha þou, Lord my God, alyȝt my derk‍nesse.

32. For in þe shal ich be defended fram temptacioun, and y shal passen þe yuel in my God.

33. My God ys, and hys waie ys vn-filed; þe wordes of our Lord ben proued wyþ fur, and he hys defendour of alle þe trowand in hym.

34. For who ys God bot our Lord, oþer who is God [1] bot our God?

35. God þat girt me wyt uertu and sett my waye vnfiled;

36. Þat made my fete lyȝt as [2] of þe hertes, and stablissand me up heȝe þynges;

[3] 37. He þat techeþ myn hondes to fiȝt oȝayn þe fende; and þou sett myn arme stable as a bow of brasse.

38. And þou ȝaf to me defens of [4] myn helþe, and þy poste toke me.

39. And þy discipline amended me on ende, and þy discipline onlich shal teche me.

40. Þou madest large my goynges vnder me, and my traces ben nouȝt made syke.

41. Y shal pursue myn enemys, and y shal taken hem; and ich ne shal nouȝt turne oȝain, vn-to þat hij faile.

42. Y shal breken hem, and hij shul nouȝt mow stonde; hij shul fallen vnder my fete.

43. And þou girt me wyþ vertu vnto batail; þou put out þe vparisand oȝaines me.

44. & þou ȝaf [5] myn enemys riggen to me, [6] and þou desparplist þe hatand me.

45. Hij criden to our Lord; ac þer nas non þat made hem sauf, ne he ne herd hem nouȝt.

---

[1] MS. *wheisgod.*   [2] MS. *af.*   [3] fol. 14.   [4] MS. *of of.*
[5] MS. *h* (expuncted) ȝaf.   [6] MS. *men.*

---

31. *al.*] makest liȝt:—*ha þou*: my Lord Godd lyȝten.
32. *in*] þurȝþ: skape euyH by.
33. *þe tr.*] men trowyng.
34. or who.
35. gird.
36. as þe fete of h.: settyng.
37. stronge.
38. —*to*: power.
39. *on*] into þe: *onlich*] þat.

40. brode: waies: vnfast.
41. —*þat.*
42. —*nouȝt.*
*43. *vnto*] to: bataile + &: þe .... *me*] men rysyng aȝens me vnder me.
44. *men*] me: disparpeld: þe] men.
45. was: *ne he ne*] no he.

* fol. 7b.

46. Y shal littelel (!) hem[1] as poudre to-fore þe face of þe [2] wynde, and y shal don hem o-way as lome of þe stretes.

47. Þou shalt defende me of oȝain-syggeynges[3] of þe folkᵢ; þou shalt sett me oȝain þe heued of men wyþ-outen lawe.

48. Þe folkᵢ, þat ich ne knewe nouȝt, serued me, and bowed to me in herynge[4] of eren.

49. Straunge children leiȝed to me; straunge childer ben elded, and hij ben made lame fram þy waies.

50. Our Lord lyueþ; and blisced be my God, and þe God of myn helþe be heȝed.

51. Ha God, þat ȝeueþ to me uengeaunces and settest þe folkᵢ vnder me, be þou my delyuerer of myn enemys wraþful.

52. Þou, Lord, shal an-heȝe me fram þe arisand oȝains me, and þou shal defende me fram þe wycked man.

53. For-þy, Lord, y shal shryuen to þe in cuntreys, ande y shal synge psalme to þy name,

54. Heriand þe helþes of his kynge and doand mercy to hys Dauid anoit wyþ creme and hys sede vnto þe world.

[5] PSALM 18 (19).[6]

1. Þe heuens tellen þe glorie of God, and þe firmament telleþ þe werkes of his hondes.

2. Þe daye putteþ forþe þe worde to þe day, and þe nyȝt sheweþ conyngᵢ to þe nyȝt.

3. Hij ben nouȝt speches, ne wordes of wiche þe voices of hem ben nouȝt herd.

4. Þe soune[7] of hem ȝede out in-to alle erþe, and her wordes in-to þe contreis of þe world.

---

[1] MS. *ham*, the *a* being dotted out and an *e* written over it. [2] fol. 14*b*. [3] MS. *oȝain-syngeynges*. [4] MS. *heryynge*. [5] Fol. 15. [6] Ps. 19, MS. [7] MS. *seune*.

---

46. +And: littyl: cley.
47. fram aȝene-siggynges of f.+&.
48. —*ne*: and in heryng of ere þat bowyd to me.
49. were elde: *b.m.l.*] haltyd.
50. be made hie.
51. —*Ha*: *e.w.*] w.e.
52. +And: enhie: *þe a.*] men arisyng.
53. nacyons: sigge.
54. anoityd: &+to: into.

18. 1. *þe h.*] h.: ioie: scheweþ.
2. scheweþ word.
3. *Hij . . . wordes*] þe speches & þe wordes beþ noȝt.
4. soune: endes of all þe w.

5. He sett his tabernacle in þe sunne, and he as a spouse comand forþe of hys chaumbre.

6. He ioyed as a giaunt to erne his waye; his going-out is fram þe heȝest heuene,[1]

7. And hys oȝayn-ernyng' vnto hys heȝest; and þer nys non þat hideþ hym fram his hete.

8. Þe lawe of our Lord hys nouȝt filed, turnand soules fram yuel; þe witnessyng' of our Lord ys trew, ȝifand wisdom vn-to þe littel[2] of vnderstondynge.

9. Þe ryȝtfulnesses of our Lord [ben] makand ioy[3]ful ryȝtlich þe hertes, þe comaundementȝ of our Lord his clere, liȝtenand eȝen to heuens.

10. Þe holy doute of our Lord ys wyþ-outen ende, þe iugementȝ of our Lord ben soþe, made riȝtful in hym self,

11. Desiderable michel[4] more þan gold and precious stones, and swetter þan hony [&] honykombes.

12. For þy saruaunt kept him; mechel ȝeldyng' is it in keping' hem.

13. Who vnderstondeþ my trespasses? Lord, make me clene of my dedelich priueteȝ, and spele of þe oþer ueniales to þyn seruaunt.

14. Ȝif þat hij ne[5] haue nouȝt lord-shipped of me, þan shal ich be vnfiled, and y shal ben clensed of my grettest trespasse.

15. And þe wordes of my mouþe shul ben, þat hij plesen to þe, and þe þouȝt of myn hert alwaies in þy siȝt.

16. Lord, þou art myn helper and myn oȝainbyger.

PSALM 19 (20).

[6] 1. Ha þou my soule, her our Lord þe in þe day of þy tribulacioun; þe name of þe God Jacob defende þe fram iuel.

---

[1] MS. heuenē. [2] Second t over line. [3] fol. 15b. [4] MS. minchel. [5] MS. h (dotted out) ne. [6] Ps. 20, MS.

6. to his way to be ȝorne: —þe: heuen.
7. aȝen-goyng+is: is.
8. wytnes: vnto þe] to: cunnyng.
*9. Lord beþ gladyng riȝtfullych hertes þe heste: —clere: heuen.
10. drede: domes: soþe & iustified: hem self.
11. Des. m.] And þe domes of our Lord beþ desirabil: & muchel sw.: hony or h.

12. kepeþ hem & muchel reward is in hem to be kepid.
13. trespas: preuy .s. dedelich synnes & spare þi seruant fram oþer .s. venialles synnes.
14. — ne: lordeschipet: vnfulid: grete.
15. alw.] schal be euer more.

19. 1. O: Godd+of.

* fol. 8.   † i added over the line.

[1] 2. Sende he to þe helpe of þe holy gost, and defende he þe fram iuel.

3. Be he þenchand on al þy sacrifice, and be þyn offryng⸱ made gode.

4. ȝif he to þe eft*er* þyn hert, and conferme he alle þyn conseil.

5. Whe shul ioyen in þyn helþe, and we shul herien in þe name of our Lord.

6. Our Lord fulfille al þyn askynges; nou haue ich knowen þat our Lord made sauf hys preste anoint wyþ creme.

7. He shal here hym fram hys holy heue*n*; þe helþe of hys mercy ys in his miȝtes.

8. Hij in carres, and hij in horses, and we shul herien þe name of God, our Lord.

9. Hij ben bou*n*den and feld adou*n*, and we ros vp, and ben adresced.

10. Lord, make þou þe kyng⸱ sauf, and her us in þe daie þat we haue cleped þe.

[2] PSALM 20 (21).

1. Lord, þe kyng⸱ shal gladen in þy vertu, and he shal gre[3]teleche ioyen vp þyn helþe.

2. Þou ȝaf to hym þe desire of his hert, and þou deceiuedest[4] hym nouȝt in þe wille of his lippes.

3. For þat þou comest to-for hym in bliscin*g*es of swetnes; þou sett on his heued a croune of pr*e*cious stones.

4. He asked lif of þe, and þou ȝaf to hym len*g*þe of daies in þe world and in þe world of worldes.

5. Þe gloŕie of hym ys grete in þyne [helþe]; þou shalt sett vp him glorie and michel honou*r*.

6. For þou shalt ȝyf hym in bliscyng⸱ in þe world of worldes; þou shalt liȝten hym in ioye wyþ [þy] semblant.

---

[1] fol. 16. [2] Ps. 21, MS. [3] fol. 16*b*. [4] MS. *dece inuedest*.

---

2. to þe+þe: —*he*.
4. ȝif he+he.
6. ẏch haue.
8. þai + clepid: cartes: —*hij*: *herien*] clepe in.
9. *f.a.*] þai feḻḻ doune: *adr.*] arered vp.
10. —*þou*.

20. 1. *glad*e*n*] ioie.*
2. desayuedest
3. —*þat*: come: stone.
5. ioie: þine + helþe Lord: —*sett*: *vp*]on: ioie: grete.
6. blyssẏngys: of world: *liȝten*] glade: *semblant*] þi chere.

* fol. 8*b*.

7. For þe kyng hopeþ in our Lord, and þe mercy of þe heȝest shal nouȝt be stired.

8. Be þy merci founden to alle þyne enemys, þyne helpe finde al þo þat hated þe.

9. Þou shalt sett hem as ouen of fur in þe time of iugement; our Lord shal trublen hem, and þe fur of helle shal deuoure hem.

[1] 10. Þou shalt lese her frute of þerþe & her seide fro mennes sones.

11. For iuels boweden in þe; hij þouȝten conseils, which þat hij ne myȝt nouȝt stablice.

12. For þou shalt sett hem a-rigge, and þou shalt make rady her semblant in þy leuinges.

13. Be þou, Lord, an-heȝed in þy vertu; we shul syngen & psalmen þy vertuȝ.

[2] PSALM 21 (22).

1. Ha God, my God, loke in me; whi for-soke þou me? þe wordes of min trespases ben fer fram myn helþe.

2. Ha my God, y shal crien bi daie, and þou ne shalt nouȝt here; and by nyȝt, and nouȝt to unwitt to [3] me.

3. Þou forsoþe wonest in holy heuen, heryyng of þe folk' of Israel; our fadres hopeden in þe, and þou deliueredest hem of iuel.

4. Hij criden to þe, and hij ben made sauf; hij hopeden in þe, and hij ben nouȝt confounded.

5. And ich am worme and no man, reproceyng' of men and out-[4] castyng of folk'.

6. Al þat seȝen me scorned me, and spaken wyþ her lippes, and stired her heued,

7. Saiand, He hoped in þe Lord; defende he hym, make he hym sauf; for he wil hym.

---

[1] fol. 17.   [2] Ps. 22, MS.   [3] MS. te.   [4] fol. 17b.

---

7. mouyd.
8. m.] honde of mercy.
9. as+ane: dome: sturble.
10. sede: men.
11. euyl þingis declined: — which: —ne: stable.
12. put: a-bache: chere.
13. enhied: v.+&.

21. 1. Ha] þou: into.
2. —Ha: —ne: vnwysdome to.
3. For-soþe þou: Israel+þai hopid in þe.
5. am+a: reprouyng.
6. mouyd.
7. þai said: delyuer: m.he] & make.

8. For þou art[1] þat drawe me out of þe wombe; þou art myn hope fram þe tettes[2] of my[3] moder; in þe[4] am ich out-caste of þe wombe.

9. Þou art my God fram þe out-going· of my mod*er*; dep*ar*t þou nouȝt fro me.

10. For tribulacion is nere to me; for þer nys non þat helpeþ me.

11. Many temptaciou*n* ȝeden a-boute me; mani uices bisegeden me.

12. Hij maden her sautes vp me as a lyon rauissand and rumiand.

13. Ich am helded out as wat*er*, and alle myn bones ben desp*ar*plist.

14. Myn hert ys made as wex meltand a-middes of my wombe.

15. My uertu defailed as a shelle, [5] and my tunge drowe to myn chekes; and þou ladde me in-to passyng· of deþ.

16. For many fendes han en-cumpassed me, þe cou*n*seil of wicked vmseged me.

17. Hij doluen myn honden and myn fete, and tolden alle my bones.

18. Hij for-soþe seȝe iuel and lokeden, & dep[*ar*]teden to hem myn cloþynges, & up myn cloþynges hij casten lott.

19. And þou, Lord, make nouȝt þyn helþe fram me; loke to my defendyng·.

20. De-fende, God, my soule fram ve*n*geau*n*ce and myn on soule fram þe honde of þe fende.

21. Sauue me fram þe mouþe of helle and my mekenes fram iuels[6] of pr*i*de.

22. Y shal tollen þy name to my neȝburs, and y shal herien þe amiddes of myn hert.

---

[1] MS. þo uart.   [2] Or *tittes*? the letters are written too close together.   [3] MS. þy.
[4] MS. *mod*e*rin*þe.   [5] fol. 18.   [6] MS. *iueld*.

---

8. drowe: *of—þe: tetis: my: þurȝ þe y am cast oute of.
10. nyȝ: *for*] &: is.
11. te*m*ptacions: me+&.
12. *m. her s.*] opynd her mouþe: roreyng.
13. *h.*] sched: disparpyld.
14. —*of.*
15. dryde or failid: cleuyd: clekes(!): pouder or passyng.

16. *enc. me*] go aboute me &: w.+me*n*: by-segid.
17. deluyd: telde.
18. *Hij fors.*] & for-soþe þai: departyd: 1. *cloþynges*] cloþes.
19. *make n.*] schalt noȝt make: me+or þi help bot.
20. Godd defend: *on*] onelich.
21. *helle*] þe fende i*n* heɫɫ: fra*m* þe euyls.
22. teɫɫ: —*of.*

* fol. 9.

23. ȝe þat douten our Lord, herieþ ȝe hym; alle þe sede of Jakob, glorifieþ hym.

24. Ich man[1] of Israel [2]doute hym; for he for-soke nouȝt, ne despised nouȝt þe praier of þe pouer in gost.

25. Ne he ne turned nouȝt his face oway fram me; and he herd me, as [y] cried[3] to hym.

26. Myn heryynge his to þe in a grete chirche; y shal ȝelde my vowes in þe syȝt of þe doutand hym.

27. Þe pouer shul eten, and shul ben fild; and hij shul herien our Lord; hij þat sechen hym, þe hertes of hem shul liuen in þe world of worldes.

28. Alle þe cuntreis of þe erþe shul biþe[n]chen, and shul turne to our Lord.

29. And alle þe meinȝeis of folkes shul aouren in hys syȝt.

30. For þe kyngdom ys of our Lord, and he shal lord-shippe þe folkes.

31. Hij eten and aoured alle þe fatnes of[4] þerþe; alle þo þat fallen in-to þerþe shul fallen in hys syȝt.

32. And my soule shal leuen to hym, and my sede shal seruen hym.

33. Þe kynde þat hys to comen shal be shewed to our Lord, and þe heuens shul shewe hys riȝtfulnes to þe folk' þat shal ben borne, which our Lord made.

[5]PSALM 22 (23).[6]

1. Our Lord gouerneþ me, and noþyng' shal defailen to me; in þe stede of pasture he sett me þer.

2. He norissed me vp water of fyllyng'; he turned my soule fram þe fende.

3. He lad me vp þe bistiȝes of riȝtfulnes for his name.

---

[1] MS. am.   [2] fol. 18b.   [3] ascried.   [4] MS. of of.   [5] fol. 19.   [6] Ps. 23, MS.

23. ȝe hym] him & ȝe.
24. Ech man : ne] no : of pouer men—in gost.
25. Ne he ne] And he : —oway : & when y cride to hym, he herd me.
26. wonnes: of men drededyng (!).
*27. 1. &+þai : Lorde+& : sechen] sche (!) : her hertes.
28. be-þench : turne] be tourne (!)
29. meynȝe : anoure.

30. lordsh.] have lordschyp of.
31. honourid : fattesses (!).
33. which] þat.

22. 1. faile : he haþ sett me in þe st. of p. þer.
2. broȝt me forþe vp þe w. of fulfillyng+&.
3. paþes.

* fol. 9b.

4. For ȝif þat ich haue gon amiddes of þe shadowe of deþ, y shal nouȝt douten iuels; for þou art wyþ me.

5. Þy discipline and þyn amendyngᵗ conforted me.

6. Þou madest radi grace in my siȝt oȝayns hem þat trublen me.

7. Þou makest fatt myn heued wyþ mercy; and my drynkᵗ makand drunken ys ful clere.

8. And þy merci shal folwen me alle daies of mi lif;

9. And þat ich wonne in þe hous of our Lord in lengþe of daies.

[1] PSALM 23 (24).

1. Þe erþe is our Lordes and his plente, þe world and ichon þat woneþ þer-inne.

2. For he bigged it vp þe sees, and made it redi vp þe flodes.

[2] 3. Who shal climben in-to þe mountein of our Lord, oþer who shal stonde [3] in his holy stede?

4. Þe innocent in honde and of clene hert, þat ne toke nouȝt his soule in idelnesse and ne swore noȝt in gileri to his neȝbur.

5. He shal take bliscyngᵗ of our Lord, and mercy of God, his helpe.

6. Þis his þe biȝetyngᵗ of þe sechand hym, sechand þe face of God Jacob.

7. Openeþ ȝour ȝates, ȝe princes of helle, and beþ ȝe lifted, ȝe euerlastand ȝates; and þe kynge of glorie shal entre.

8. Which is he, þat kyngᵗ of glorie? Þe Lord stronge and miȝtful, þe Lorde myȝtful in batail.

---

[1] Ps. 24, MS. [2] fol. 19b. [3] *stonden* MS., with the final *n* dotted out.

---

4. F. ȝif y schal go amiddes—*of*: —*iuels*.
5. lore: am.+þes þinges.
6. sturbleþ.
7. madest: with+þi.
8. all+þe.
9. in þe lengeþ.

23. 1. & þe plentusnes þer-of.
2. sett.

3. cl.] go vp: m.] hill: or: place.
4. clene of hondes and clene of h.:—*ne*: *id.*] vayne: —*ne*: gile.
5. helpe.
*6 generacyon of men scheyng hym & of men scheyng: Godd+of.
7. heuyd vp.
8. Who is þis kyng of glorye? he is a str. L. & a myȝty, he is a myȝty Lord in batayle.

* fol. 10.

EARLY ENGLISH PSALTER. PSALM 24 (25). 27

9. Openeþ ȝour ȝates, ȝe pr*i*nces of heuene,[1] and beþ ȝe lifted, ȝe ȝates euerlastand ; and þe kynge of glorie shal entren.

10. Which is he, þat kynge of glorie ? Þe Lord of uertu, he his kynge of glorie.

[2] PSALM 24 (25).

1. Lord, ich lefted my soule to þe : þou art my God ; ich affied me in þe, ich ne shal nouȝt shame.

[3] 2. Ne ne schorne nouȝt myn enemis me; for alle þo þat susteine þe shal nouȝt be confou*n*ded.

3. Alle þat don iuels vp idelshipp*e*, be confou*n*ded.

4. Lord, shewe me þyn waies, and teche me þyne bisties.[4]

5. Dresce me, Lord, in þy soþenesse, and teche me; for þou art my God, my sauiour, and ich susteined in þe aldaie.

6. By-þenche þe, Lord, of þy pites and of þy mercius þat ben of þe world.

7. Þe trespases of my ȝengþe and my vncona[*n*]dnes ne þenche þou nouȝt.

8. Lord, for þy godnes þenche on me eft*er* þy mercy.

9. Our Lord is swete and riȝtful ; for-þy he shal ȝeue lawe to þe trespassand in þe waie.

10. He shal drescen þe mylde i*n* iugement, and he shal teche þe de-boner his waies.

11. Alle þe waies of our Lord ben mercy and soþenes vnto þe sechand his testame*n*tȝ and his wittenes.

12. Lord, for þy name be merciable to my synne ; for it is michel.

[5] 13. Who is þe man þat douteþ our Lord ? he stablist to hi*m* lawe in þe waie þat he ches.

---

[1] MS. *heuenē*. [2] Ps. 25, MS. [3] fol. 20. [4] Before *bisties* stands a þ, which is struck out. [5] fol. 20*b*.

---

9. heuen : arered vp — ȝe ȝat*es* e. : ioie ; entre+in.
10. Who is þis k. of ioie.

24. 1. lift+vp : Godd+& : —ne.
2. Ne scorne noȝt me my*n* e. : susteineþ.
3. euyl to ydelfullych.
4. schew+to : *b.*] paþes.

5. haue susteynd.
7. ȝouþe ; vnknowynges haue þou noȝt i*n* my*n*de.
9. þer-for : 1. þe] me*n*.
10. meke : dome : debono*ur*.
11. soþefastnes to me*n* scheyng his testame*n*t.
13. þe] þat : ordeyneþ law to hy*m* : haþ chosyn.

14. His soule shal dwellen in gode, and his sede shal enheryte þerþe.

15. Our Lord is fastenynge to þe dredand hym, and his testament þat it be shewed to hem.

16. Myn eȝen ben alway to our Lord; for he shal drawe out myn feet of þe gnare.

17. Loke to me, and haue pyte on me, for þat ich am on and pouer.

18. Þe tribulaciouns[1] of myn hert ben multiplied; deliuer me fram my nedefulnes.

19. Se, Lord, my lowenesse and mi trauail, and forheue[2] me alle my trespas.

20. Loke to my enemis; for hij ben multiplied, and hij hated me wyþ wycked hatyngˑ.

21. Kepe my soule, and defende me; y ne shal nouȝt be asshamed, for ich hoped in þe.

22. Þe nouȝt noiand[3] and þe ryȝtful drow to[4] me; for ich susteined þe.

23. Delyuer þou, God, þe folk of Israel of alle her tribulacions.

[5]PSALM 25 (26).[6]

1. Iuge me, Lord, for ich entred in myn innocens; and ich hoped in our Lord, nc shal nouȝt be made syke.

2. Prque me, Lord, and assaie me; kepe my kydnaies and myn hert.

3. For þy mercy ys to-fore myn eȝen, and ich plesed in þy soþenesse.

4. Y ne satt nouȝt wyþ þe conseil of ydelnes, and y ne shal nouȝt entren wyþ hem þat iuel beren hem.

5. Ich hated þe techyng of þe wicked, and y ne shal nouȝt sitte wiþ þe wicked.

6. Y shal wasshen myn honden omonges þe innocentȝ, and y shal gon aboute þin auter, Lord,

---

[1] The stroke is only over the last *u*.   [2] i.e. *forȝeue*.   [3] MS. *noinad*.
[4] MS. *drowte*.   [5] fol. 21.   [6] Ps. 26, MS.

---

14. godes.
15. fastnes to men dredyng & þat h. t. be schewyd to hem.
*16. grynne.
17. mercy: —þat.
19. for-ȝif.
21. —ne.
22. þe innocentes: to.

25. 1. Deme: ennocence: ne]
and y.
2. kydneres.
4. —ne: —ne: with men euyl beryng hem.
5. —ne.
6. among þine innocentes.

* fol. 10b.

7. Þat ich here¹ þe voice of þyn heryyng' and telle al þyne meruayles.
8. Lord, ich loued þe fairnes of þyn hous and þe stede of þe wonyng' of þy glorie.
9. Ne lese nouȝt, Lord, my soule wyþ þe wicked, and my lif wyþ þe filed wyþ dedelich synnes.
10. In whas hondes wickednesse ben, her ryȝtfulnes is fulfild of ȝiftes.
11. Ich am for-soþe entred in myn innocence; raunceoun me, Lord, and haue mercy on me.
12. My fote stode in stede dresced; Lord, ich shal blisse þe in chirches.

²PSALM 26 (27).

1. Our Lord, which ich shal douten, is my liȝtyng' and my helpe.
2. Our Lord is defendour of my lif; for what þyng shal ich drede?
3. To þat noiand³ comen neȝe vp me, þat hij etand my flesshes:
4. Myn enemys, þat trubleden me, ben made sike, and hij fellen.
5. Ȝif hij setten manaces oȝains me, myn hert ne shal nouȝt drede.
6. Ȝyf myn enemy arere bataile oȝains me, y· shal hopen in þat.
7. Ich asked þe lif þat euer shal last of our Lord; ich shal bisechen þat, þat ich mai wonne in þe hous of our Lord alle þe daies of my lif;
8. Þat ich se þe wille of our Lord and uisite his temple.
9. For he⁴ hid me in his myȝt, he defended me fram ⁵þe dedes of wicked in þe priuete of his tabernacle.
10. He heȝed me in stablenes, and nou he haþ en-heȝed myn heued vp alle myn enemis.

---

¹ MS. bere.   ² Ps. 27, MS.   ³ MS. noinand.   ⁴ Here þat is expuncted and struck out.   ⁵ fol. 22.

---

7. here: wonders.
8. habitacion of þi ioie.
9. —Ne: þe f.] men defulid.
10. riȝtf.] riȝthonde or her riȝt-wysnes: with.
11. For-soþe ych am: inn. + .s. clennes þou.
12. riȝtful.

26. 1. þat: helþe.

3. To-whyles noyng+men: ete.
*4. sturbeleþ.
5. manes+or strenkeþ: —ne.
6. þer-in.
7. þe lif . . Lord] one askyng of our lorde and: mai w.] dwell: Lord+in: —daies.
9. miȝt+&: wykkyd+men.
10. made me hyȝe in stabilnes: aboue.

* fol. 11.

11. Y ȝede a-bout, and sacrified in his tabernacle offerand berand voice; i¹ shal synge and saie salme to our Lord.

12. Here, Lord, mye voyce, wyþ which hij² cried to þe; haue pite on me, and her me.

13. Myn hert seid to þe, my face soȝt þe; Lord, y shal seche þy face.

14. Ne turne nouȝt fram me þy face, ne bowe nouȝt owaie in ire fram þy seruaunt.

15. Lord, be þou myn helper, and for-sake me nouȝt; ha God, myn helþe, ne despise me nouȝt.

16. For my fader and my moder han for-saken me, and our Lord haþ taken me.

17. Sett to me, Lord, lawe in þy waie, and dresce me in þy bistie for myn enemys.

18. Ne ȝyf me nouȝt, Lord, into þe soules of þe trubland me; for fals witnesses aros oȝains me, and her wickednesse ³ leiȝe to hem.

19. Ich hope to se þe godes of our Lord in þerþe of liuiand.

20. Abyde our Lord, and do manneleche; and þyn hert be conforted, and kepe wyþ þe our Lord.

⁴ PSALM 27 (28).

1. Lord, my God, y shal crye to þe; ne stylle nouȝt fro me, ne let nouȝt fro me; and y shal be liche to þe descendand in þe diche.

2. Here, Lord, þe uoyce of my praier, þer-whyles þat ich byseche to þe; þer-whyles þat ich an-heȝe myn honden to þyn holy temple.

3. Ne ȝyf me nouȝt to-gidres wyþ synȝers, and ne lese me noȝt wyþ hem þat wirchen wickednes;

---

¹ MS *in*.   ² i.e., *y* (ego).   ³ fol. 22*b*.   ⁴ Ps. 28, MS.

---

11. *offerand b. v. in*] y schal syngt þe sacrifice of voice beryng y.
12. *hij*] y : mercy.
14. —*Ne*: —*ne*: fram þi seruant in þi wraþ.
15. —*ha*: —*ne*.
17. Lord sett to me : paþe.
18. —*Ne*: þe *tr.*] men sturblyng: lyed.
19. of men lyfyng.

20. be þyn h.

27. 1. *Lord*] Lor: —*ne*: still+ þou: ne holde noȝt preuy fram: to men fallyng into.
2. to-whils y pray: & to-whils ych holde vp.
*3. —*Ne*: —*ne*: with men wyrchyng.

* fol. 11*b*.

† *but* y schal syng *is expuncted*.

4. Þat speken [pees] wyþ her neȝbur, iuels for-soþe in her hertes.

5. Ȝeue to hem efter her werkes and efter þe wickednesse of her fyndynges.

6. Ȝyf to hem efter her werkes of her hondes; ȝelde her rewarde to hem.

7. For hij ne vnder-stode nouȝt þe werkes of our Lord, and þou [1] shalt destrue hem in þe werkes of her hondes; & þou ne shalt enhabite hem in heuens.

8. Blisced be our Lord, for he herd þe voice of my praier.

9. My Lord his myn helper and my defendour, and myn hert hoped in hym, and ich am hulpen.

10. And my flesshe florissed oȝain, and y shal shryue to þe of my wylle.

11. Our Lord ys þe strengþe of his folk¹, and he his defendour of þe bliscynges [2] of his prest anoint wyþ creme.

12. Make, Lord, þy folk¹ sauf, and blisce þyn heritage, and gouerne hem, [& anheȝe hem] vnto wyþouten ende.

[3] PSALM 28 (29).

1. Ha ȝe Goddes sones, bringeþ to our Lord, bryngeþ to our Lord sacrifice of weþers.

2. Bryngeþ to our Lord glorie and honour; bringeþ to our Lord glorie to his name; aoureþ [4] our Lord in his holi temple, þat ys, mannes body.[5]

[6] 3. Þe voice of our Lord is vp waters; God of maieste, þou þunred; Lord vp many waters.

4. Þe voice of our Lord is in vertu, þe voice of our Lord his in heryng¹,

5. Þe voice of our Lord brekand cedros; and our Lord shal breke þe cedros of Liban.

---

[1] fol. 23. [2] *of his folk¹ and he his defendour of þe bliscynges* twice in MS.
[3] Ps. 29, MS. [4] An *n* is added over *ao* by another hand. [5] *þat ys mannes body* underlined with black and red ink in MS. [6] fol. 23b.

---

4. þai þat spekeþ+pees; *ieuls*] & euyl: for-soþe+beþ.
7. —*ne*: —*nouȝt*: —*ne*: schalt+noȝt.
9. helpyd.
11. strenþe(!): saluacion: anoyntyd.
12 hem+& enhye hem.
 † *s* added over the line.

28. 1. —*Ha*: sunnes of Godd.
2. ioie & wyrschypt† bryng: ioie: honoureþ.
3. þou þ. *Lord*] Lord thunderd‡: —*many*.
4. herying.
5. cedres: cedres of + þe:
 ‡ *e* added over the line.

6. And he shal littelen hem as folk of Liban, and loued as cautel of vnicorn*us*.

7. Þe voice of our Lord pr*ai*and makeþ flamne of fur; þe voice of our Lord smytand to-gidres desert, and our Lord shal stiren þe des*er*t of Cades for þe wickedness*e* of hem þat wone*n* þer-inne.

8. Þe voice of our Lord makand rady h*er*tes; and he shal shewe þe hidels, and alle folk*es* shal saie glorie to hym in his temple.

9. Our Lord makeþ þe flode to wone*n*, and our Lord shal siten kyng wyþ-outen ende.

10. Our Lord shal heue [1] v*er*tu to his folk', and our Lord shal blisc*en* his folk*es* in pes.

[2] PSALM 29 (30).

1. Y shal heʒe þe [3] Lord, for þou herdest me, and madest nouʒt myn [4] enemys on brede vp me.

2. Lord, my God, ich cr*i*ed to þe; and þou madest me hole.

3. Lord, þou lad my soule out of helle, and sauedest me fra*m* þe falland into synne.

4. Syngeþ to our Lord, ʒe his halwen, and shryueþ to þe mynde of his holinesse.

5. For ire ys in his dignacio*u*n (!), and lif in his wylle.

6. Wepynge shal dwellen at even, and ioie at morwen,

7. Ich for-soþe seid in my wexi*n*g, Y shal nouʒt be stired wit-outen ende.

8. Lor, in þy wylle þou ʒaf vertu to my fayrenesse.

9. Þou t*ur*nedest þy face fram [me], & ich am made trubled.

10. Lord, i shal cr*i*en to þe; and y shal pr*ai*e to my God.

11. What pr*o*fit is in my penau*n*ce, þ*er*-whiles þat ich descende [5] in-to synne?

---

[1] Read ʒeue. [2] Ps. 30, MS. [3] fol. 24. [4] MS. þyn. [5] MS. *descended*.

6. of+þe: as+þe: vnicorns.
7. famne (!)
8. folk: ioie.
9. dweH.
10. —2. *Lord*: *folk.

29. 1. my*n*: on brod.

2. My Lord Godd: heledest me.
3. þe] me*n*.
5. i*n*dignacyon.
6. atte m.
7. For-soþe y: ple*n*teousnes.
8. Lord.
9. fra*m*+me: *am*] was: heuy.
11. faH.

* fol. 12.

12. Ys to wyten ȝif¹ man shal shryue to þe, [oþer] tellen þy soþenes?

13. Our Lord herd me, & ²had pite of me; our Lord hys made myn helper.

14. Þou turnedest my waymentyng' in-to ioie; þou carf my sak', and compasedest me wyþ gladnes,

15. Þat mi glorie synge to þe, and y ne be nouȝt prikked; Lord, my God, y shal shryue to þe wyþ-outen ende.

³PSALM 30 (31).

1. Ich hoped in þe, Lord; y ne shal nouȝt be counfounded wyþ-outen ende for þy riȝtfulnes; deliure me fram iuel.

2. Bowe to me þyn ere, and heiȝe þe, þat þou deliure me of yuel.

3. Be to me in-to God defendour, & in-to þe hous of refut, þat þou mak' me sauf.

4. For þou art my strengþe and my refut; and for þy name þou shalt lade me and norisse me.

5. Þou shalt lade me out of þe gnare which þe fendes hidden to me; for þou art my defendour fram iuel.

6. Lord, [ich] ȝyf my gost in-to þyn hondes; þou, Lord of soþenes, bouȝtest me.

7. Þou hatedest hem þat kept uanites vp idelnes.

⁴8. Ich for-soþe hoped in our Lord; y shal gladen and ioien in þyn mercy.

9. For þou lokedest to my lowenes, and þou sauedest my soule fram nedfulnesses.

10. Ne þou ne shettest me nouȝt in þe hondes of þyn⁵ enemy; þou stablisced my fete in large stede.

11. Haue mercy on me, Lord; for ich am trubled; myn eȝe is trubled in ire, my soule [& my wombe].

---

¹ MS. ȝis.   ² fol. 24b.   ³ Ps. 31, MS.   ⁴ fol. 25.   ⁵ MS. of þyn twice.

12. Wheþer noȝt man schal schryue hym to þe, oþer tell þi soþnes?
13. mercy on.
14. ioie+to me: enclosed.
15. ioie: —ne: schryue+me.

30. 1. y .. be] þat y be noȝt: for] pro (!).

2. haste.
5. grynne þat þe deuyl hydd.
6. Lord+y: soþfastnes.
8. For-soþe ych.
*10. And þou closyd: settest.
11. sturbled: sturbled: soule +& my wombe.

* fol. 12b.

12. For-þy my lif fayled in sorowe, and my ȝeres in waymentynges.

13. My uertu is made sike in pouert, and my bones ben trubled.

14. Ich am made reproce up alle myn enemis, and greteliche to my neȝburs, and drede to hem þat knowwen me.

15. Hij þat seȝen me flowen out fram me, and ich am ȝeuen vnto forȝetyng' as deþ fram hert.

16. Ich am made as vessel loren;[1] for ich herd blamyng' of many dwelland abouten.

17. Þer-whiles þat hij comen to-gidres in þis oȝains me, hij conseiled hem to take my soule.

[2] 18. Ich hoped in þe, Lord; ich seid þou art my God; myn lottes ben in þyn hondes.

19. Defende me fram þe honde of myn enemis and fram hem þat pursuen me.

20. Alyȝt þy face up þy seruant, Lord; make me sauf in þy mercy, and ich be nouȝt confounded; for ich cleped þe.

21. Ben þe wicked made asshamed, and ben hij ladd in-to helle; and þe trecherous lippes ben made doumbe,

22. Which speken wickednes oȝayns þe ryȝtful in pride and in abusion.

23. Ha Lord, ful michel his þe multitude of þy swetnes, þatou hidest to þe doutand þe.

24. Þou madest ioie to hem þat hopen in þe, in þe siȝt of mennes sones.

25. Þou shal hiden hem in þe hydyng' of þy face fram þe trublyng of men.

26. Þou shal defende hem in þy tabernacle fram oȝainsiggeing of tunges.

27. Blisced be our Lord, for he made his mercy wonderful to me in heuen.

---

[1] MS. *lord.*   [2] fol. 25*b.*

---

12. —þy.
13. sturbled.
14. reproue: to my knouen men.
15. out] away: vnto] to.
16. as a vessel lore.
17. —me: —hem.
20. Lord aliȝt: Lord] &: be ych.

21. be þe trichourus lippis.
22. which] þai þat: pride +also.
23. —Ha: þe] þi: —þy: þe d.] men dredyng.
24. hopid: men.
25. sturblyng.
26. with-siggyng.
27. me] men.

28. Y seid *in* pas'syng' of my þou3t, Ich am owaie cast fram þe ly3t of þyn e3en.

29. For-þy þou herdest þe voice of my p*r*aier, þer-whyles þat ich cried to þe.

30. Loueþ our Lord, 3e alle his halwen; for our Lord shal sechen soþenes, and 3eue ve*n*geance plentiuouseliche² to hem þat don pr*i*de.

31. Doþ ma*n*neliche, and beþ 3our he*r*t co*n*forted, 3e alle þat hopen in our Lord.

³PSALM 31 (32).

1. Ben hij blysced⁴ of wich þe wickednesses ben for-3euen and of which þe synnes ben hed.

2. Blisced be þe man to whom our Lord aretted nou3t synne, ne gilery nys nou3t in his gost.

3. For ich held me stylle; my bones wexen olde, þer-whyles þat ich c*r*ied alday.

4. For þyn honde ys greued vp me day and ny3t; ich am t*ur*ned in my chaitifte,⁵ þer-whiles þat vices ben ficched in me.

5. Ich made myn trespas⁶ knowe*n* to þe, and ich ne hid nou3t myn vnry3tfulnesses.

6. Ich seid, Y shal shryue o3ayns me myn ⁷vnry3tfulnesse to our Lord; and þou for-3af þe ⁸ wickednesse of myn synne.

7. For-þy shal ich an halwe p*r*aie to þe in couenable tyme.

8. For-soþe hij ne shal nou3t come nere hym in þe gaderyng of mani synnes.

---

¹ fol. 26. ² Second *u* added over the line. ³ Ps. 32, MS. ⁴ *y* corrected from *e*. ⁵ MS. *chaitiste* (with a long *s*). ⁶ MS. *trappes*. ⁷ fol. 26*b*. ⁸ *o3ayns me myn vnry3tfulnesse to our lord and þou for-3af þe o3ains me myn vnri3tfulnesse to our lord and þou for-3af þe* MS.

---

28. passyng+oute: cast away.
29. þ*er*-fore: —*voice*.
*30. plentefullych.
31. he*r*tes: 3e] 3 (!).

31. 1. þai beþ blissyd þe wykkydnes of wha*m*: whas synnes beþ hydd or p*r*euye.

2. put no s. & gyle is: hert or goste.
4. myschefe: þorne or vices er prikkyd.
5. trespas: —*ne*: vnry3tfulnes.
7. ech halow schal: behoueable.
8. —*ne*: —*nou3t*: gederyng.

* fol. 13.

9. þou art my refuit[1] fram þe tribulacioun þat cumpassed me; my gladnesse de-liuere[2] me fram hem þat conpassen me wyþ iuel.

10. Y shal heue[3] to þe vnderstondyng, seid our Lord, and y shal en-fourme[4] þe, and y shal fasten vp þe myn eȝen in þat wai þatou[5] shalt gon.

11. Willeþ ȝe nouȝt, mennes sones, ben made as horses and mule, to which vnderstondyng nis nouȝt.

12. Constreingne her cheken in bernache[6] and bridel, Lord, þat ne neȝed nouȝt to þe.

13. Mani tourmentes ben of synȝers; and mercy shal cumpassen þe hopand in our Lord.

14. Gladeþ, ȝe ryȝtful in our Lord, and beþ ioyful and glorieþ, ȝe alle riȝtful of hert.

[7] PSALM 32 (33).

1. Gladeþ, ȝe ryȝtful in [8] our Lord; heryynge bicomeþ to þe ryȝtful.

2. Shriueþ to our Lord in uertuȝ, and doþ to hym þe techynges of þe .x. comaundementȝ.

3. *The translation is omitted.*

4. For þe worde of our Lord is ryȝt, and alle hys werkes ben in faiþe.

5. He loueþ mercy and iugementȝ; þerþe is ful of þe mercy of our Lord.

6. Þe heuens ben fastened þurwe þe worde of our Lord, and alle her uertue is of spiriȝt of ys mouþe.

7. Gaderand to-gidres as in a gourde þe waters of þe see, settand depe helles[9] in tresours of yuiles.[10]

---

[1] MS. *restut?* [2] MS. *de-liuere*r. [3] Read ȝeue. [4] *u* added over line. [5] MS. þa tou. [6] MS. *bernathe.* Or ought to be *bernacle?* [7] Ps. 33, MS. [8] fol. 27.
[9] MS. *belles.* [10] MS. *hilles.*

---

9. refute: —þe: enclosid: dediuer: encloseþ.

10. enfourme: festen myn eȝen vp þe: þat þou: go+in.

11. ȝe sonnes of men wiH ȝe noȝt be made as hors or mule in whych is none v.

12. chekes in barnakle: *lord*] þai: *ne n. n.*] cum noȝt neȝ.

13. enclosye man hopyng.

14. beþ .. ȝe] ioieþ & ioieþ.

32. 1. ȝe] ȝ (!): for riȝtful b. herying.

3. Do ȝe gode warkes, & serueþ to hym in all ȝour strengþ.

4. feye.

5. dome.

*7. hellis: *hilles*] yuyH.

* fol. 13b.

8. Drede al þerþe our Lord; and alle þat wonen in þe worled ben styred of hym.

9. For he seid, and hij ben made; he comaunded, and hij ben fourmed.

10. Our Lord wasteþ þe counseiles of men wyþ-outen lawe, and he reproceþ þe[1] counceils of princes.

11. Þe counseil of our Lord woneþ wyþ-outen ende; þe þouȝtes of his hert ben in kynde and kynde.

[2]12. Þe folkᶦ ben blisced of which our Lord is her God; þe folkᶦ þat he chees to hym in heritage ben blisced.

13. Our Lord loked[3] fram heuen; he seiȝe alle mennes sones.

14. He loked fram his tabernacle made redi vp alle þat wonen on erþe;

15. Which feined onliche her hertes & vnderstondeþ alle her werkes.

16. Þe kyngᶦ nys nouȝt saued þurȝ michel uertu, and þe geant ne shal nouȝt be saued in þe michelhede of his uertu.

17. Þe hors is deceiuable vnto helþe; and he ne shal nouȝt be saued in þe wexing of his uertu.

18. Se! þe heȝen of our Lord ben vp þe dredand hym, and in hem þat hopen in his mercy;

19. Þat he defende her soules fram deþ & noris hem in grete desire.

20. Our soule loueþ our Lord; for our Lord is our helper and our defendour.

21. For [in] þat our hert shal glade in hym; and we hoped in his holy name.

22. Be, Lord, þy merci made up us [4]as we hoped in þe.

[5] PSALM 33 (34).

1. Y shal bliscen our Lord in al time; be his heryyngᶦ euermore in my mouþe.

2. My soule shal be heried in our Lord; heren þe milde, and gladen hij.

---

[1] MS. *he.*   [2] fol. 27b.   [3] MS. *lokeþ.*   [4] fol. 28.   [5] Ps. 34, MS.

9. beþ m.: be fourmyd.
10. *Our .. princes*] & he reproueþ þe þouȝtes of folkes, & he reproueþ þe conseils of pr.
11. fram k. into k.
12. þat f. is: wham: ben] beþ.
13. loked: h. +&: men sonnes.

16. is: —*ne* : gretnes.
17. dis[. . . .]ble †: help: —*ne.*
18. þe] men.
21. For+in.
22. Lord þi mercye be.

33. 2. meke+men.

† Part of the word is stained and illegible.

3. Þe folk' herieþ our Lord wyþ me;[1] and heȝe we his name wyþ hym seluen.

4. Ich bi-souȝt our Lord; and he herd me, and defended me fram alle my tribulaciouns.

5. Comeþ to hym, & beþ aliȝted; and [ȝ]our faces ne shul nouȝt be confunded.

6. Þis pouer crie[d]; and our Lord herd hym, and deliuered hym of alle his tribulaciouns.

7. Þe aungel of our Lord goþ about þe dredand hym, and he shal defenden hem fram iuel.

8. Swelweþ and seþ, for our Lord is liþ; blisced bi þe man þat hopeþ in him.

9. Doute our Lord al is halwen; for misais nys nouȝt to hem þat douten hym.

10. Þe riche were nedeful, and hungred; and þe sechand our Lord shal nouȝt be made [2] lasse of all gode.

11. Comeþ, ȝe men, and hereþ[3] me; y shal teche ȝou þe drede of our Lord.

12. Which is þat man þat wyl þat lif þat euer shal laste, and loueþ to se gode daies?

13. Defende þy tunge fram yuel, and þy lippes þat hij ne speke nouȝt treccherie.

14. Turne þe fram iuel, and do gode; secheþ pes, and folweþ it.

15. Þe eȝen of our Lord ben vp þe riȝtful, and his eren to here her praiers.

16. Þe semblant of our Lord for-soþe is vp þe doand iuel, þat he destruie þe mynde of hem up þerþe.

---

[1] MS. *ine*. [2] fol. 28*b*. [3] MS. *bereþ*.

---

3. —*Lord*: me: hye: in.
4. & of all my t. he delyuerid me.
5. ȝour: —*ne*.
6. cryd: & of all h. t. he d. hym.
*7. *þe dred.*] in þe cumpas of men dredyng: deliuer.
8. Tasteþ: swete: be: men.
9. Douteþ: *mis. n. n.*] þer is no

10. & men sechyng (*e* added over line).
11. *men*] chylder: here me +and.
13. —*ne*: no gyle.
14. seche (*e* over line): folow.
15. eres: —*here*.
16. For-soþe þe face: þe] men: lese.

* fol. 14.

EARLY ENGLISH PSALTER. PSALM 34 (35). 39

17. Þe ryȝtful criden, and our Lord herd hem, [& he deliuerd hem] of alle tribulaciouns.[1]

18. Our Lord is nere honde to hem þat ben trubled in hert; and he shal saue þe milde in gost.

19. Mani ben þe tribulaciouns[2] of þe riȝtful; and our Lord deliuered hem of hem ichon.

20. Our Lord kepeþ al her bones; on of hem ne shal nouȝt be de-fouled.

21. Þe deþ of synȝers is werst; and hij þat hated ryȝtful þyng shul trespassen.

[3] 22. Our Lord shal bigen þe soules of his seruaunts; and alle þat hopen in hym ne shul nouȝt trespassen.

[4] PSALM 34 (35).

1. Iuge, Lord, þe anoiand me; fiȝt oȝain þe fitand wiþ me.
2. Take myȝt and uertu, & aryse in helpe to me.
3. Shade þy uengeaunce, and close it oȝains hem þat pursuen me; saie to my soule, Ich am þyn helþe.
4. Ben hij confunded, and drede hij þat sechen my soule.
5. Ben turned oȝain and ben confounded þe þenchand iuels to me.
6. Ben hij made as poudre to-fore þe face of þe wynde; and our Lordes aungel be constreinand hem.
7. Be her waies made derk and slider, and our Lordes aungel pursuand hem.
8. For hij hidden to me by her wylle deþ of her wicked enticement; hij reproced my soule of idelshippe.

---

[1] MS. tribulacous with a stroke over the o and part of the u. [2] The stroke is over the u and part of the s. [3] fol. 29. [4] Ps. 35, MS.

---

17. hem+& he deliuered hem: alł+her.
18. neȝ to hem þat(!) of sturbled hert: meke.
19. echon.
20. —ne.
21. hateþ.
22. The English transl. is om.

34. 1. Deme, Lord, men noyinge me, ouercome men fiȝtyng aȝens me.
3. Schede+oute.
4. þat s.] sechyng.
5. Be+þay: be+þai: þe]men.
6. —be.
7. sleder.
*8. hid wyllfullych to me: reproued.

* fol. 14b.

9. Cum to my enemy þe gnare which þat he ne knoweþ, and þe takeyng þat he hid take hym, and falle he in-to þat ¹ich gnare.²

10. My soule shal gladen in our Lord, and shal ioien in his helþe.

11. Al myn wittes shal saien, Lord, who ys liche to þe?

12. Þou shalt deliuer þe mysais fram yuel of his enemis, þe nedeful and þe pouer fram þe rauissand hym.

13. Wicked witnesses arisen, asked me þynges þat ich ne knew nouȝt.

14. Hij ȝauen oȝain to me iuels for gode, barainesse to my soule.

15. And as hij were anoiand to me, y was cloþed in penaunce.

16. Y lowed my soule in fastyng; and my praier shal be turned in myn helpe.

17. Y pleised neȝbur as our broþer; and ich was lowed as man sori and waimentand.

18. Hij ben gladed oȝains me, and comen to-gidres; and turmentes ben assembled³ up me, and y ne wyst nouȝt.

19. Hij ben wasted, and hij ne ben nouȝt prikked; hij tempteden me, and hij⁴ vndernimmeden me wyþ vnder-nyminge, & ⁵gnaisted vp me wyþ her teþe.

20. Lord, whan þou shalt loke to me, stablis my soule fram her wickednes, myn on soule fram fendes.

21. Y shal shryue to þe in stedfaste hert, and hij⁶ shal herien þe for sinful folkᵗ.

22. Ne gladen hij nouȝt vp me, þat ben contrarious oȝains me; þat hated⁷ me wyþ wylle, and hij loren oþer twynquelin⁸ wyþ eȝen.

23. For hij spakᵗ peisiblelich to me, and hij spekand þouȝten trecherie in wraþe of þe erþe.

---

¹ fol. 29b. ² MS. graue. ³ MS. assemblamd (dotted out) assembled. ⁴ and hij twice in MS. ⁵ fol. 30. ⁶ i.e., y (ego). ⁷ MS. hateþ (expuncted) hated. ⁸ oþer tw. underlined with black and red ink.

---

9. grynne — which: —ne: þat same grynne.
12. mys.] nedeful.
13. arysyng: —ne.
14. —oȝain: godes.
15. when: an.] heuy.
16. h.] bosum) or help.
17. pleised+my: as a sory man.
18. c. tog.] moued: ass.] gaderd: —ne: wyst+yt.
19. wasted and hij ne] sparbled &: pr.+ or for-þouȝt: & scornyd me with scornyng: grente.
20. st.] sett.
21. for] among.
22. — Ne: ioie: hateþ me wylfullych & twynkeleþ with her eȝen.
23. peseablech: gyle.

24. Hij maden her mouthe large up me, and seiden, Alas, alas! our eȝen seȝen.

25. Þou seiȝe hem, Lord, ne holde þe nouȝt stylle; ne depart þou noȝt fram me, Lord.

26. Ha Lord, my God, arise, and ȝyf kepe to my cause in iugement.

27. My Lord and my God, iuge me efter þy[1] riȝtfulnes; and ne glade nouȝt þe wicked vp me.

28. Ne saien hij nouȝt in her hertes, Sorow, sorow,[2] [3]to our soule; ne saien hij nouȝt, We shal deuouren hym.

29. Wexen hij asshamed, and dreden hij to-gidres, þat gladen of myn iuels.

30. Ben hij cloþed wyþ confusione and drede, þat speken iuels up me.

31. Gladen and ioien hij þat wyl my riȝtfulnes, and saie hij, Bi our Lord alwaie heried; and hij þat willen þe pees of his seruaunt glade.

32. And my tunge shal þenchen þy riȝtfulnes and þy heryynge ich day.

[4] PSALM 35 (36).

1. Þe vnryȝtful seid, þat he ne trespasseþ nouȝt in hym seluen; þe drede of God nis nouȝt to-forn his eȝen.

2. For he did trecherouslich in his siȝt, þat his wickkednes be founden to hatyng'.

3. Þe wordes of his mouþe ben wickednes and trecherie; he nold nouȝt vnderstonde to do wele.

4. He þouȝt wickednes in his couche, he stode to al wai nouȝt gode; for-soþe he ne hated nouȝt wickednes.

5. Lord, þy mercy his in heuen, and þy [5]riȝtfulnes vn-to þe cloudes.

---

[1] MS. *my*. [2] The second *o* is added over line. [3] fol. 30*b*. [4] Ps. 36, MS.
[5] fol. 31.

---

24. *maden*] sprad: —*large*: *seȝen*] haþ see.
25. —*ne*: —*ne*.
26. *Ha Lord*] My Lord & : *ȝyf*] take: dome.
27. *deme*—*me*: *my*] þy: —*ne*.
*28. —*Ne*: *ne*] &.
29. —*to-gidres*.
31. *bi*] be: glade *before* þai þat.

32. all day.

35. 1. —*ne*: is.
2. gylefullych.
3. *tr.*] gyle: wolde: vndestonde (!): well.
4. gode+& : —*ne*.
5. Lor.

* fol. 15.

6. Þy riȝtfulnes ys as þe mounteines of God, þi mani iugementȝ as helle.

7. Þou, Lord,[1] shal saue men and bestes, as tou, God,[2] haþ multiplied þy mercy.

8. For-soþe mennes sones shul hopen in graces of þy mercy.

9. Hij shul ben drunken of þe plente of þin hous, and þou shalt ȝeue hem drynk[] of þe welle of de-litinges.

10. For at[3] þe is þe wille of liif; and we shul se liȝt in þy liȝt.

11. Shade for-þe, Lord, þy mercy to þe knowand þe, and þy riȝtfulnes to hem þat[4] ben riȝtful of hert.

12. Ne cum nouȝt to me þe vice[5] of pride, and þe honde of sinȝer ne stir nouȝt me.

13. Þer fel hij þat wirchen wickednes; and hij [ben] putt out, and hij ne myȝt nouȝt stonden.

[6]PSALM 36 (37).

1. Ne wil þou nouȝt filȝen in þe wicked; ne loue þou nouȝt þe doand wickednes.

2. For hij shul drien hastilich as hay, and hij shul fallen sone as worten of herbes.

3. Hope in our Lord, and do godnesse, and wonne in erþe; and þou shalt be fed in his riches.

4. Delite þe in our Lord, and he shal ȝeue to þe askinges of þyn hert.

5. Shewe þy way to our Lord, and hope in hym; and he shal do þy wylle.

6. And he shal lede þy riȝtfulnes as liȝt and þy iugement as middai; bi suget to our Lord, and praye to hym.

7. Ne wil þou nouȝt folwen in him þat prosperet in his waie, ne in man þat doþ wronges.

---

[1] Here the MS. has a þ, which is struck out.   [2] MS. astougod, followed by a þ, which is struck out.   [3] MS. þat.   [4] Here the writer has first written an h, but has struck it out.   [5] MS. voice.   [6] Ps. 37, MS.

---

6. domys.
8. men: in þe grace.
9. delites.
10. For at þe: well.
11. Schewe: þe kn.] men knowyng.
12. —Ne cum nouȝt to: vice: —ne: moue.

13. & þai & þai beþ put oute:—ne.

36. 1. —Ne: felow: þe d.] me[n] doyng euyl or.
4. to þe + þe.
*6. dome: bi] be.
7. —Ne: folow in (!) þat wele fareþ no in his way non in: wrong.

* fol. 15b.

EARLY ENGLISH PSALTER. PSALM 36 (37). 43

8. Ende fram ire, and forsak[t] wodeship ; and ne wyl þou nouȝt folwe ire, þa-tou be made wicked.

9. For hij, þat ben wicked, shal be don out of heuen; hij, þat seruen our Lord, shul han þe heritage of heuen.

10. And ȝit a litel vnder-stonde, and no synne (!) shal be in heuen; and þou shalt seche his stede, and þou shalt nouȝt finde it.

11. For-soþe þe mylde shul enerit þe heuen, and delyten in þe michelnes of ioie.

[1] 12. Þe synȝer shal pursuen þe riȝtful,[2] and shal gnaist up hym wyþ hys teþe.

13. Our Lord for-soþe shal scorne hym, for he seþ þat his ende come.

14. Þe synȝers made her manaces, and sheweden her iuels,

15. Þat hij deceyue þe suffrand and þe gode, þat [hij] folen þe ryȝtful of hert.

16. Her manaces entre in-to her soules, and be he[r] iuel to-broken.

17. Better[3] is lytel þynge wyþ ryȝt, þan mani riches wyþ synȝes.

18. For þe myȝtes of þe synȝers shal be defoulede ; our Lorde for-soþe helpeþ þe riȝtful.

19. Our Lord knew þe dedes of þe vnwemmed, and her heritage shal be wyþ-outen ende.

20. Hij ne shul nouȝt be confounded in tyme of vengeaunce, and hij shul be fulfild in daies of pines; for þe synȝers shul perissen.

21. For-soþe þe enemys of our Lord, as [4] sone as hij ben worþshipped and heȝed, hij shul fail [5] failand as smoke.

22. Þe synful shal borow and nouȝt ȝelden ; þe riȝtful for-soþe han mercy, and shal ȝelden.

---

[1] fol. 32.   [2] MS. *riȝtfus* (with a round *s*).   [3] MS. *Beiter*.   [4] fol. 32*b*.
[5] MS. *fall* (expunged) *fail*.

---

8. Sese : wodnes : —*ne*.
9. heuen+& : s*er*uye.
10. no*n* syn.
11. meke : enheryt—*þe*.
12. riȝtful : grent.
13. For-soþe *our* Lorde : schal cu*m*.
15. deseyue me[*n*] sufferyng+or þe pore : *þat folen*] & defule.

16. *he*] her.
17. Better : ryȝt+for to haue : riches+of synn*er*s.
18. defoilyd.
19. vnfilyd.
20. payne.
21. enhyed : defaylyng : smeche.
22. pay : haþ : pay.

23. For þe blissand our Lord shul en-herit þe heue*n*; and þe iuel sygg-and[1] to hym shul sholden fram hym.

24. Þe goynges of man shul be dresced to our Lord; and he shal wylle his waie.

25. Wha*n* þe ri3tful haþ fallen, he ne shal nou3t ben hirt; for our Lord laiþ his honde vnder hym.

26. Ich was 3onge, and by-come olde;[2] and y ne sei3 neu*er* þe ry3tful for-saken, ne his sede faile ioies.

27. Þe ry3tful ys m*er*ciful al day, and laneþ; and his sede shal [ben] in bliscynge.

28. Bowe fram 3uel, and do gode; and woneþ in þe world of worldes.

29. For our [Lord] loueþ iugement, and shal nou3t forsaken hys halwen; hij shul ben kept wyþ-outen ende.

30. Þe vnry3tful shul be punist, and þe sede of þe wicked shal p*e*risse.

[3] 31. Þe ry3tful for-soþe shul enherit þe erþe, and hij shul [wonen in þe] worlde of worldes up it.

32. Þe mouþe of þe ry3tful shal þenchen wisdam, and his tunge shal speke iugement.

33. Þe lawe of God ys i*n* his hert, and his goynges ne shul nou3t be put out.

34. Þe syn3er seþ þe ry3tful man, and secheþ to sle hym.[4]

35. Our Lord for-soþe ne shal nou3t for-sake þe ri3tful in þe hondes of þe sin3er; ne he ne shal nou3t da*m*pne him, as he haþ iugod[5] hym.

36. A-bide our Lord, and kepe his waye; and he shal a*n*he3e*n* þe, þat tou take þerþe in heritage; and þou shalt sen, wha*n* þe syn3ers shul p*e*risse.

---

[1] MS. *syngand*. (dotted out) *hym*.   [2] MS. *hold* (expuncted) *olde*.   [3] fol. 33.   [4] MS. *hi*m   [5] MS. *iu god*.

---

23. For me*n* blyssyng: *iuel siggyng: p*e*risch.
24. *goynges*] waies.
25. —*ne*: hurte+or harmyd.
26. & y wex elde: —*ne*: r.+ ma*n*: no*n* his sede sechyng his his brede or faylyng ioies.
27. leneþ: schal+be.
28. wone.
29. +Lorde: dome &+he.
31. For-soþe þe r.: schall+won in þe: *up it*] þ*er* vp.
32. dome.
33. wayes—*ne*.
35. For-soþe o*ur* L.—*ne*: *ne he ne*] & he: whe*n* he schal be demyd to hym.
36. Habyde: enhye.

* fol. 16.

37. Ich seiȝe þe wicked up-heȝed and vp-lifted as þe cedros of Liban.

38. And ich passed, and se! he nas nouȝt; ich soȝt hym, and his stede nas nouȝt yfunden.

39. Kep clennesse, and se euennes; for hij ben relikes to man þat his peisible.

40. Þe vnriȝtful forsoþe shul ben desparplist, and þe relikes of þe wicked shul dien.

41. [1] Þe helþe of þe ryȝtful ys of our Lord, and he his her defendour in tyme of tribulacion.

42. Our Lord shal helpen hem, and diliuer hem, and defende hem fram synȝers, for þat hij hopeden in hym.

[2] PSALM 37 (38).

1. Lord, ne wyþ-nyme [3] me noȝt in [þy vengeaunce, ne reproce me nouȝt in] þyn ire.

2. For þyn a-sautes ben ficched [4] to me, and þou confermed vp me þyn helpe.

3. Helþe nys nouȝt in my flesche [5] for þe charge of [þyn ire, þer nys no pes to my bones for þe charge of] myn synȝes.

4. For myn wickednesse ben ouergon myn heued, and as a greue charge hij ben greued up me.

5. Min helynges oþer helþes a-bouen roteden, and ben corrumped of þe charge of myn vncunninges.

6. Ich am made wroched (!) and croked vnto ende, and ich entred al day sorȝful.

7. For myn baches [6] ben fulfild of illusiouns; and helþe nys nouȝt in my flesshe.

---

[1] fol. 33b.   [2] Ps. 38, MS.   [3] MS. *wyþ myne*.   [4] Above the second *c* there is a stroke shaped like an horizontal comma.   [5] Instead of the *e* the MS. has a curved stroke after the *h*, such as is usually written as an abbreviation for *n*.   [6] MS. *uaches*.

---

37. se: enhied & rered vp: ceders of + þe.
38. was: was.
39. to a pesable man.
40. For-soþe þe v.: disparpled.
41. is—*of.*

37. 1. — *ne*: wiþnym: *ire*] vengaunce no reproue me noȝt in þin ire.
*2. prikkyd: confirmyd þin help vp me.

3. is: charge of + þine ire þer is no pes to my bones for þe charge of.
4. *greue ch. hij*] greuous chard(!) þat.
5. My helyd woundes beþ roten & corrupt for þe ch. of myn vncunnyng.
6. wrechid & ych am made cr. vnto + þe: soryfull.
7. lenden: dyssaytes: is.

* fol. 16b.

EARLY ENGLISH PSALTER. PSALM 37 (38).

8. [1] Ich [am] turmented, and ich am michel lowed; and ich cried fram þe sorweyng' of myn hert.

9. Lor,[2] al my desire is to-fore þe; and my waymentyng' nys nouȝt hid fram þe.

10. Myn hert his tribled in me; my uertu haþ forsaken me, and þe liȝt of myn eȝen, and þat nys nouȝt wyþ me.

11. Myn frendes and myn neȝburs com to-wardes me and stoden.

12. And hij þat weren by me stoden fer fram me, and hij þat souȝten[3] my soule made force.

13. And hij þat soȝten iuels to me speken uanites; and aldai hij þouten trecheries.

14. Ich for-soþe [as defe] herd nouȝt, and as doumbe nouȝt openand his mouþe.

15. And ich am made as man nouȝt herand and nouȝt hauand vndernimynges in hys mouþe.

16. For ich hoped in þe, Lord; Lord, my God, þou shal here me.

17. For y seid, þat myn enemys ne ioien nouȝt vp me, and spoken grete þynges vp me, þer-whyles þat my fete ben stired.

[4] 18. For ich [am] made radi in tourmentes, and my sorowe ys alway in my syȝt.

19. For ich shal tellen my wickednesse & þenche for my sinȝe.

20. Myn enemys for-soþe liuen, & ben confermed vp me; and hij, þat hateden me wickedlich, ben multiplied vp me.

21. Hij þat ȝelden iuels for godes, bakbytyng' me, for þat ich folwed godenes.

22. Ha Lord, my God, ne forsake me nouȝt, and ne depart nouȝt fram me.

23. Lord God of myn helþe, vnderstonde in-to myn helpe.

---

[1] fol. 34.   [2] MS. ffor.   [3] MS. þouȝten.   [4] fol. 34b.

---

8. +am: *ich am ..fram*] lowed gretlych ych rored for.
9. *For*] Lord: is.
10. sturblyd: is.
11. stode+or aȝens me.
12. *by*] next: *fer . . .*] afarre & made strengþe þai þat souȝt my s.
13. *Latin and English omitted.*
14. *Ich forsoþe*] & ych as dumbe defe(dumbe *being expuncted*): openyng noȝt his+his(!).
15. hauyng in his m. reprouynges.
16. —*lord.*
17. —*ne*: ioied: & þai spake.
18. +am: into tourmentynges.
19. *tellen*] schewe.
20. For-soþe m.e.: confirmyd.
21. euyl for gode bakbyted.
22. —*Ha*: —*ne*: —*ne*.
23. *vnderst.*] take hede.

EARLY ENGLISH PSALTER. PSALM 38 (39). 47

¹PSALM 38 (39).

1. Ich seid, Y shal kepen my vertuȝ, þat ich ne trespas nouȝt in my tunge.
2. Ich sett kepyng' to my mouþe, þer-whiles þat þe synȝer stode oȝains me.
3. Ich bi-com doumbe, and [was meked, and] helde me stylle fram godes; and my sorowe is newed.
4. Myn hert wex hote wiþ-inne me, and fur bigan to brenne in my þouȝt.
5. Ich spak' wyþ my tunge, Make, Lord, knowen to me myn endyng',
6. And þe numbre of my daies which it is, þat ich wite, what þynge me lackeþ.
7. Se! þou settest myn daies mesurable, and my substaunce as nouȝt to-fore þe.
8. For-soþe ich man² liuiand ys al manere of vanyte.
9. Man for-soþe in likenes [passeþ]; ac in vayn he hys tribled.
10. He gadered tresours, and he wote neuer to whom he shal gaderen hem.
11. And which is nou myn abydyng'? nouȝt our Lord? and my substaunce ys to þe.
12. De-fende me fram alle wickednesses; þou ȝaf³ me reproce to þe vnwis.
13. Y by-com dumbe, and ne oponed nouȝt my mouþe, for þou it made; do oway fram me mi⁴ synȝes.
14. Ich failed⁵ in blamynges for þe strengþe of þyn honde; þou reproceþ man for wickednes.
15. ⁶And þou madest his soule to stumblen as a lob; ich man for-soþe is trubled idelliche.

---

¹ Ps 39, MS. ² MS. am. ³ MS. h (dotted out) ȝaf. ⁴ MS. in.
⁵ MS. falled. ⁶ fol. 35b.

38. 1. —ne: with.
*3. bicom . . . godes] was dum & ych was meked & ych was still fram godenes: was made newe.
4. in my mynde fure schal berne.
5. Lord, make myn ende know to me.
6. And] & make know to me: know what fayleþ to me.
7. Lo.

8. am] man: —of.
9. For-soþe man in ymage passeþ bot: sturblyd.
10. gadreþ: note—neuer.
11. ab.+wheþer: to] at.
12. wykkydnes: reproue: +man.
13. ne] y: opend: in] my.
14. faylyd: strenkeþ: h. + &: reprouyd.
15. for-soþe ych man is sturblyd.

* fol. 17.

16. Here, Lord, myn orisou*n* and my praiere; take my teres[1] to þyn eren.

17. Ne for-sake me nou3t, for ich am synn*er* at þe and passand, as alle my fadres weren.

18. Grau*n*te to me, þat ich be wasshen of syne, to-fore[2] þat ich die; and ich ne shal nomore be dampned.

PSALM 39 (40).[3]

1. Ich abidand þe grace of our Lord a-bode my Lord; and he vnderstonde (!) me.

2. And he herd my p*r*aiers, and lad me out of þe stenche of uices and fram þe pynes of helle.

3. And he stablist my fete in stedfastnes, and dresced my goynges.

4. And he laide gode worde in my mouþe, dite to our Lord.

5. Many shul sen and douten and[4] hopen in our Lord.

[5] 6. Blisced be þe man, of which þe name of our Lord his his hope, and ne haþ don no uanites, ne fals wodnesses o3ains his lawe.

7. Lord, my God, þou dost many wou*n*dres; and þer nis non, þat is lich to þe in þy þou3tes.

8. Ich shewed and spak' þyn wondres vn-to men; and myn wordes ben multiplied wyþ-outen nou*m*bre.

9. Þou ne woldest sac*ri*fie non offrynge wyþ-outen vertu; þou madest for-soþe vnderstondyng' to me.

10. Þou ne askedest nou3t offrand for synne; þan seid ich, Se! y com to þe.

11. Wryten it is of me in þe comau*n*dement of þe lawe, þat ich do þy wylle; ha mi God, ich it wolde, and þy lawe amiddes myn hert.

---

[1] MS. *trese* (expuncted) *teres*.   [2] Twice *to fore* in MS.   [3] Ps. 40, MS.
[4] MS. *an hon* (struck out) *and*.   [5] fol. 36.

---

16. L. h.: *to*] w*i*th.
17. —*ne*: am+a.
18. *w.*] clene: —*ne*.

39. 1. habydyng: vnsterstode.
2. vices+or of þe wat*er* of wrechidnes: pay*n*nes.
3. sett.
4. put.

6. *ne haþ*] he haþ: wodnes.
7. My Lorde Godd: madest: *nis*] is.
8. *ben*] wer.
9. —*ne*: *s.*] sac*ri*fice: f.s. þou.
*10. —*ne*: cu*m*.
11. *com.*] heste: *ha . . wolde*] y wolde it (*it* is added over the line) my Godd.

* fol. 17*b*.

EARLY ENGLISH PSALTER. PSALM 40 (41).

12. Ich shewed þy ryȝtfulnes to many trew; Lord, y ne shal nouȝt defenden myn lippes; þou it wyst.

13. Y ne hyd nouȝt þy ryȝtfulnes in myn hert, ich seide[1] þy soþenes and þyn helþe.

[2]14. Ich ne hidde[3] nouȝt þy mercy and þy soþenes fram þe michel conseil of þe vntrew.

15. Ne do nouȝt, Lord, þy mercy fer fra me; þy mercy and þy soþenes alway han y-take[4] me.

16. For yueles, þat [no] noumbre is of, han i-cumpassed[5] me; my[6] wickednesses token me, and y ne myȝt nouȝt, þat ich seyȝe hem.

17. Þe wicked ben multiplied vp þe heres of myn heued; and myn[7] hert haþe for-saken me.

18. Plese it, Lorde, to þe, þat þou defende me; loke, Lord, for to helpe me.

19. Ben hii confounded, and waxen hij asshamed to-gideres, þat sechen my soule, þat hij don fram þe.

20. Ben hij turned oȝayn & asshamed, þat wyllen iuels to me.

21. Beren hij hastiloche[8] her confusion, þat saien to me, Alas! alas!

22. Alle þat sechen þe, hij shul gladen vp þe[9] and ioien; and saien hij euermore, þat louen þyn helþe, Be our Lord heried.[10]

23. Ich am for-soþe beggand and pouer; our Lord ys bisi of me.

24. Þou art myn helper and my defendour; ha my God, dwelle nouȝt.

[11]PSALM 40 (41).

1. Blisced be he, þat helpeþ þe nedeful and þe pouer; our Lord shal de-liuere hym fram iuels atte daye of iugement.

---

[1] *i* added over line. [2] fol. 36b. [3] MS. *bidde*. [4] MS. *haby* (or *haly?*) *take*; *b* and *y* are written very close together. [5] MS. *ham cump.*, or for *han cump.* without *i-?* [6] MS. *wyþ*. [7] *heued and myn* twice in MS. [8] *o* corrected from *y*. [9] MS. *me*. [10] MS. *heued*. [11] Ps. 41, MS.

---

12. r.+in a grete church : trew +men se : —*ne* : þou wyst it well.
13. —*ne*.
14. Y hyd : much : of vntrew men.
15. —*Ne* : *haby*] han.
16. euyl thynges þat+no : han closyd me my w. : —*ne* : *þat ich s.*] se.
17. w. + men : *of*] on.

18. Lord pl. it : —*for*.
19. *þat hij don*] to do it.
22. *hij shul . . . me*] be þai glade vp þe : ioie+þay : heryed.
23. F. s. ych am a beggar a. p. +&.
24. tary.

40. 1. þat+vnderstondeþ or : at þe : dome.

4

2. Kepe hym our Lord, and quike hym : he shal make hym blisced in erþe, and he shalt nouȝt ȝyf hym into þe pouste of hys enemys.

3. Our Lord be to hym helpe up þe charge of his sorowe; þou, Lord, turned alle his sharpenes in his sykenes.

4. Y seid, Lorde, haue mercy on me; hele my soule, for ichaue sinned to þe.

5. Myn enemis seiden iuels to me, whan he shalle dien, and his name shal peris.

6. And ȝif myn enemy entred in-to my hous, þat he seiȝe me, he spak' idel þynges; his hert gadered wickednes to hym.

7. He went out, and spak' in þat ich þynge.

8. Alle myn enemys grucched oȝains [1]me, and þouten iuels to me.

9. Hij stablisshe[d] þe wicked worde oȝayns me, þat his to wyte,[2] ȝyf he þat slepeþ arise nouȝt and go.

10. For þis man was of myn pes, in whom ich hoped; hij þat eten min loues, herieden vp me supplauntynge oþer puttyng'[3] out.

11. Haue þou, Lord, mercy on me, & arere me; and hij[4] shal ȝelden [hem] her mede.

12. Ich wist by þis þynge, þatou woldest me; for myn enemy ne shal nouȝt ioien up me.

13. þou for-soþe toke me for vn-loþ-fulnes, and confermed me in þy siȝt wyt-outen ende.

14. Blisced be our Lord, God of Israel, fram þe worled into þe worled[5]; be it don, be it don.

[6]PSALM 41 (42).

1. As þe hert de-siret to þe welles of waters, so de-sired my soule to þe,[7] Lord.

---

[1] fol. 37b. [2] MS. me (expuncted) wyte. [3] oþer putting is underlined. [4] i.e. y (ego).
[5] MS. worded. [6] Not numbered in MS. [7] After þe, a word is erased.

---

2. quike...] make hym qwyk & he schal noȝt ȝyf þet into þe power of h. e.
6. schuld se : þinges+and.
*9. sett—þe : wytt.
10. For+he : —suppl. oþer.

11. Lord haue m. : y schal ȝelde +hem.
12. —ne.
13. F. s. þou.
14. world : world.

41. 1. desireþ : desireþ.

† MS. hym (struck out) þe.   * fol. 18.

2. And my soule þrefe (!) vnto God, welle liueand, whan ich shal cum and apere to-fore þe face of God.

3. Mi teres were to me loues day and ny3t, þer-wyles þat man seid to me ich day, Where hys þy God?

4. Ich by-þou3t of þe þynges, and priked in me my soule; for hy[1] shal passen in-to þe stede of purgatorij ful of pines, ri3t vn-to heuen.

5. Þe soune of þe ioiand ys in þe voice of ioie and of shrift.

6. Ha þou my soule, why ertou sori, & why trubles tou me?

7. Hope in God, for y shal 3ete shriue vnto hym; he his helþe of my gost and my God.[2]

8. Myn soule is trubled vn-to my seluen; for-þy, Lord, y shal be þenchand on þe, God, of þe tur[n]ing of folk' of þe londe of Jordan and of þe folk' of þe littel hille of Hermon.

9. Helle blameþ þe fendes for þy deþ of þe croice.

10. Alle þyn lorde-shippes and þy techynges passeden up me.

11. In daie our Lord sent his mercy and on ny3t his confort.

[3] 12. Lord, þe oreison of my lif is to þe; ha Lord, y sai, þou ert my taker.

13. Whi hastou for3eten me, and whi am ich sory, þer-whiles þat myn enemy tourmenteþ me?

14. Þer-whiles þat my3tes ben frusced, myn enemys, þat trublen me, reproued me;

15. Þer-whiles þat hij seiden to me vuch daye, Were is þy God?

16. Ha þou my soule, whi ar-tou sori, and whi trubles tou me?

17. Hope in God, for i shal 3it schryue to hym; he his helþe of mi gost and my God.

---

[1] i.e. *y* (ego).   [2] MS. *my god and my gost*.   [3] fol. 38*b*.

---

2. —*And*: afyrsteþ (!) to Godd a lyfyng weH: *and*] y schal.
3. *þat man*] yt is.
4. *of þe*] þise: *pri*kkyd: *hy*]y: *pu*rgatorie: paynes into þe hous of Godd þat is into h.
5. of ioiyng: of ioiyng.
6. O: heuy: *stu*rbelistow.
7. 3yt: *vnto*] to: *God*] goste: *gost*] Godd.

8. *stu*rblyd to: be-þenche: *tu*rnyng: 1. folk+or.
9. blameþ—þe: *þy*] þe.
11. In+þe: *in*.
12. —*ha*.
13. to-whyls.
14. *my3tes ben fr.*] my bones or m. beþ broket† or proschyd: *stu*rbleþ.
15. say: by aH days.
16. O: *stu*rblestow.

† Above and between the *r* and *o* there is a stroke like a long comma.

¹ PSALM 42 (43).

1. Iugg¹ me, Lord, and defende my cause fram folk¹ nouȝt holy, and defende me fram þe wicked man and þe trecherous.
2. For þou art Gode, my strengþe; whi² puttestou me out? and whi goe ich sorwand, þer-whiles þat myn enemy tourmenteþ me?
3. Sende out þy lyȝt and þy soþenes; hij ladden me out, ³ and ladde men me in-to þy holi hylle and in-to þy tabernacles.
4. And y shal entre unto Goddes auter⁴; to God, þat makeþ glade my ȝingþe.⁵
5. Ha God, my God, y shal schryue me to þe in þe in-mast of myn hert; ha þou my soule, whi ertou sori, and why trublestou me?
6. Hope in God, for ȝete y shal shryue to hym; he is helþ⁶ of my gost and my God.

⁷ PSALM 43 (44).

1. Ha God, we herden wyþ our eren⁸; our fadres telden vs
2. Þe werke, þat tou wrouȝt in her daies and in olde daies.
3. Þyn honde desparplist þe folk¹, and þou settest hem; þou tourmentedest⁹ folkes, and puttedest hem out of here pride.
4. For hij ne shul nouȝt haue þerþe in swerde, and her myȝt ne shal nouȝt sauen hem,
5. Ac þy god-hede and þy myȝt and þe liȝt of þy face; for þou plesed to hem.
¹⁰ 6. Þou¹¹ þy-self art my God and my kyng¹, þat sendest helþes to Jakob.

---

¹ Ps. 42, MS.   ² MS. wiþ; or for wi?   ³ fol. 39.   ⁴ MS. goddessauter (ss on erasure).
⁵ MS. þingþe.   ⁶ MS. holi.   ⁷ Ps. 43, MS.   ⁸ MS. eȝen (dotted out) eren.
⁹ o added over line.   ¹⁰ fol. 39b.   ¹¹ MS. vn.

---

*42. 1. Lorde deme me.
2. Godd: whi putestow.
3. 2. out] fram: lad me to into þine: into] in.
4. Goddes auter: ȝouþe.
5. O þou Godd: inermast: o: sturblestow.
6. ȝyt schal ych: holi] helþe.

43. 1. O þou Godd: tolde.
3. disparplid — þe: turmendid (!) folk: put.
4. — ne: in] with: — ne.
5. Bot: godhode: þe] þi.
6. Vn] þou: God] kyng: kyng] Godd: sentest.

* fol 18b.

EARLY ENGLISH PSALTER. PSALM 43 (44). 53

7. Whe¹ shul chace oway our enemys þurȝ force in þe, and we shul despysen in þy name þe arisand oȝains us.

8. For y ne shal nouȝt hopen in my waityng'; and my swerde ne shal nouȝt sauen me.

9. For þou sauedest vs [fram hem þat turmented vs], and þou confounded hem þat hateden vs.

10. Whe shul ben heried in God al day, and whe shul shryue in þy name in þe worled.

11. For-soþe² þou puttedest us now oway,³ and confoundedest us; and þou, God, ne shal nouȝt go out in our vertuȝ.

12. Þou turnedest vs by-hynde rygge efter our enemis; and hij þat hated vs rauissed vs to hem selue.

13. Þou ladest vs as shepe of metes; and þou desparplist vs amonge folkes.

14. Þou seldest þy folk' wyþ-outen pris; and multitude nas nouȝt in chaungynges of hem.

15. Þou laidest us in liknes to folkes, stireing' of heued in folkes.

⁴16. Þou settest us repruse⁵ to our neȝburs, vndernimyng'⁶ and scorne to hem þat ben in our cumpas.

17. Aldai my shame is oȝains me, and confusion of my face haþ couered me.

18. Fram þe voice of þe reproceand and þe oȝains spekand, fram þe face of þe enemy and of þe pursuand.

19. Alle þes þynges comen⁷ up us; and we ne forȝate þe nouȝt, and we did nouȝt yuel in þy testament.

20. And our hert ne departed nouȝt oȝain-ward; and þou bowedest þyn bysties fram þy waie.

21. For þou lowed vs in stede of turment; and shadew of deþ couered vs.

---

¹ MS. *who*.   ² MS. *for foþe*.   ³ After *oway* follows an *e*, which is dotted out.
⁴ fol. 40.   ⁵ MS *depruse*.   ⁶ Here an *e* follows, but is dotted out.   ⁷ MS. *to men*.

---

7. *Who*] we: þe ar.] men rysyng.
8. —*ne*: —*ne*.
9. sauyd vs+fram hem þat turmentyd vs: þat h.] hatyng.
11. For-soþe: put: confundyd: —*ne*: schalt.
12. *byh. r.*] a-bache.
13. lad: disparpled.

14. & þer was no m.
15. steryng.
16. *depruse*] reproue: scornyng.
18. of man reprouyng & aȝene spekyng+&: —*and of þe*.
*19. come: —*ne*.
20. —*And*: —*ne*: paþes.
21. in+þe.

* fol. 19.

22. ȝyf we forȝate þe name of our Lord, and putten forþe our hondes to a strange God,

23. It is to witen, ȝif God shal nouȝt asken þes þynges; for he knewe þe hidynges of þe hert.

24. For we ben slayn al dai for þe; we ben holden bi as shepe of slaȝtter.[1]

25. Arise vp, Lord; whi dwellestou? arise vp, and ne put vs nouȝt oway in ending.

[2]26. Whi turnestou þy face oway? þou for-ȝetest our mesais[3] and our tribulacioun.

27. For our soule is lowed in poudre, and our wombe is deuoured to-gideres in þerþe.

28. Arise up, Lord, and helpe vs; and bigge vs aȝayn for þy name.

PSALM 44 (45).

1. Myn hert put out gode worde; y saye my werkes to þe kynge of glorie.

2. My tunge is penne of þe scriuayn swiflich (!) wrytand.

3. Fair artou, Christ, in fourme to-fore mennes sones; grace is shadde[4] in þy lippes; for-þy blisced God þe wyþ-outen ende.

4. Be þou girded wyþ þy myȝt, aldermyȝtfullichest, up þy folke.

5. Ȝyf entent godelich, and go forþe, and regne in þy cumlichenes and in þy fairnes,

6. For soþnes and softnes and riȝtfulnes; and þy pouste shal laden þe wonderfulliche.[5]

7. Þy manaces ben sharp; folk' shul [6]fallen vnder þe vnto þe hertes of þe kynges enemys.

---

[1] MS. scaȝtter. [2] fol. 40b. [3] MS. me fuis. [4] MS. sbadde. [5] Instead of the last e the MS. has a stroke as commonly used as an abbreviation for n. [6] fol. 41.

---

22. Lorde+Godd: put.
23. preuy þinges.
24. slaȝtter.
25. tarystow: —vp: —ne: in +þe.
26. mysays.
27. to-gyder in erþe.
28. bigge vs aȝ.] deliuer vs.

44. 1. p. o.] schewyd: ioie.
2. is+þe: swyftelych.
3. sbadde] chade: þerfor he blyssyd þe Godd.
4. moste myȝtfulyche.
6. softnes] mekenes: pouer: lede—þe.
7. scharp+&: into.

8. Ha God, þy sege is in þe worlde of worldes; þe ȝerde of drescing[1] is ȝerde of þy[2] kyngdome.

9. þou louedest riȝtfulnes, and hatest wickednes; þer-for God, þy God, anoint þe wyþ oil of ioie to-for þy felawes.

10. Myrre and gutt' and smel ben of þy uestment, of þy houses[3] of heuen, of which þe gode soules deliteden[4] þe in þyn honur.

11. þe quene stode at þy ryȝt half in gildan cloþyng, encompassed alabouten wyþ selcouþnesse.

12. Here þou, soule, and se, and bowe þyn ere, and for-ȝete þy fole þoȝtes and þe substaunces of þy fader.

13. And þe kyng shal couait þy[5] fairhede; for he is þe Lord, þy God, and [þe folk shul worþship hym].

14. [And þe sones of Tyre & alle þe ryche of] þe folk' shal praien þy semblant in ȝyftos.[6]

15. Alle his glorie wyþ-innen hym is of þe soule of God of grete ioies, couered a-boute wyþ meruai'lous þynge.

16. Maidenes shal be brouȝt to God efter hym, and hys next shul ben brouȝt to þe.

17. Hii shul ben brouȝt in-to gladnes and ioie, and shul ben brouȝt in-to þe ioie of God.

18. Sones ben born to þe for þy fadres; þou shalt stablisse hem princes vp alle þerþe.

19. For-þy þe folkes shul shriue to þe wyþ-outen ente (!) in þy world of wordles (!).

[8] PSALM 45 (46).

1. Our Lord is refut and vertu, helper in tribulacioun, þat founde vs to michel.

---

[1] MS. *deescing¹*. [2] MS. *his*. [3] MS. *bones*. [4] MS. *delitende*. [5] MS. *þe*.
[6] The verses 13 and 14 are written in one in the MS. [7] fol. 41b. [8] Ps. 45, MS.

8. O: dressyng is þe ȝerd of þi k.
9. louyd riȝt and hatyd: anoynetyd.
10. *sm.*] swete sm.: vp þi cloþing of þe houses: delityd.
11. riȝt hondes in glyt (!) cl. enclosyd a-boute wyþ diuersnes.
12. foly: substance.
13. þi fayrehode: and + þe folke schal wyrschip hym.

14. And þe sonnes of Tyre & all þe ryche of þe folke schal pray þi chere in ȝiftys.
15. *glorie*]ioie: meruolus þinges.
*18. *for þy*] to (*dotted out*) fore þe: sett.
19. folk: ende+&: þe: worldes.

45. 1. vertu + &: þat + haþ: muche.

* fol. 19b.

2. Þer-fore we shul nouȝt douten, þer-whiles þat þerþe shal be trubled; þe mounteins shul be born in-to þe hert of þe see.

3. Þe waters souned, and ben trubled; þe mounteins ben trubled in his strengþe.

4. Þe deluuþ[1] gladeþ þe hous of heuen, þe almyȝtful halwed Noe and his.

5. God [2] ne shal nouȝt be stired in-middes þys wonyngꞌ; God shal helpen hym erlich in þe morwenyngꞌ.

6. Men ben trubled, and kyngdoms ben lowed; God ȝaf his vengaunce, and þerþe is stired.

7. Þe Lord of vertuȝ ys wyþ vs; our taker ys God of Jacob.

8. Comeþ, and seþ þe werkes of our Lord, which he sett wonders vp þerþe.

9. Doand oway batail vnto þende of þerþe, he shal de-foule bowe and breke armes and brenne þe sheldes in þe fur.

10. Abideþ and seþ, for ich am God; y shal be heȝed in folkꞌ, and y shal be heȝed in erþe.

11. Þe Lord of vertu is wyþ us, þe God Iacob his[3] our taker.

PSALM 46 (47).

1. Ȝe alle folkꞌ, plaieþ wyþ hondes; gladeþ to God in voice of ioie.

2. For our Lord ys heiȝe, dredful, and michel kyngꞌ vp al þerþe.

3. He made folkes vnderlynges to us, and men he leid [vnd]er[4] oure fete.

4. He ches to vs hys herytage, [5] þe fairnes of Iacob, which he loued.[6]

5. God steȝ up in swete songe, and our Lord in uoice of trumpe.

6. Syngeþ to our Lord; syngeþ, syngeþ to our kyngꞌ, syngeþ.

7. For God his kyng of alle þerþe; singeþ wiseliche.

8. God shal regne vp men; God shal sitten vp his holi sege.

---

[1] Read duluuy? [2] fol. 42. [3] The MS. repeats wyþ after his. [4] MS. leider. [5] fol. 42b. [6] MS. loueþ.

---

3. —þe m. ben tr.
4. d.] grete flode: halowed+his tabernacle þat is.
5. —ne.
6. sturblid: mouyd.
8. þat haþ sett.
9. he] &: defuyle.
10. enhyed among: enhied: in +þe.

11. vertues: Godd+of: —wyþ.

46. 1. ioieþ with+ȝour: h.+&.
2. michel k. vp] grete aboue.
3. He cast vnder to vs nacions, & vnder our f. he layde men.
4. louyd.
5. in sw. s.] with ioie.
8. men+&: sege] sete.

9. Princes of folkes ben assembled wyþ God of Abrahαm;[1] for þe stronge goddes of þe erþe ben gretliche an-heȝed.

PSALM 47 (48).

1. Ou[r] Lord is michel [& worþi to be praysed] in þe cite of our God, in hys holy moυnteyn.

2. Þe mouɴt Syon is fouɴded in joie in alle þerþe; þe sides of þe norþe is þe cite of þe grete kyng'.

3. God shal be knowen in his house, as he shal take it.

4. For se! þe kynges of þe erþe[2] ben assembled; hij acordeden in on.

5. Hij sehen in swich manεre, and ben amεr-uailed; hij ben trubled and stired, dre[3]de toke hem.

6. Þer ben sorowes as of þe [berand] child; and þou [s]halt defoulen þe folk' of Thars in grete vengeauɴce.

7. We seȝen so as we herden in þe cite of our Lord; God founded hit wyþ-outen ende.

8. God, we han taken þy mercy amiddes þe holi fante of þi temple.

9. Ha Lord, eftεr þy name, so þyn heriinge ys in þe londe of erþe; þy lawe is ful of ryȝt-fulnes.

10. Deliten þe folk' of Syon, and ioieɴ þe children of Jude, Lord, for þy iugementȝ.

11. Cυmpasseþ Syon, and clippe it; telleþ to folk', hardened[4] in hert.

12. Sett ȝour hertes in his vertu, and ȝeueþ his ryȝtes, þat ȝe tel it to þe woniand in heueɴ.

13. For here is our God[5] wyþ-outen ende in þe worled of worldles (!); and he shal gouerne vs in heuens.

---

[1] Instead of the last a, the MS. has the usual abbreviation for ra. [2] *For se þe kynges of þe erþe* twice in MS., but the corrector has struck it out once. [3] fol. 43. [4] MS. *hardeneþ*. [5] MS. *lord* (expuncted) *god*.

9. Þe princes of folk beþ gadred.

47. 1. Our: grete+& worþi to be praysyd.
3. wheɴ.
*5. *sehen in sw. m. and*] seyng so: stυrbled: st.+&.
6. *þe*] a womaɴ beryng: schalt defoile.
7. *We seȝen . . . herden*] So as we herd, so we seiȝ iɴ þe cite of our Lord of vεrtus.
8. —*taken*: fonte.
9. O: þe erþe.
10. domes.
11. Goþe aboute, & beclipeþ it & t. in þe toures of it to folk herd þe hertes.
12. *ryȝ'les*] ryches: teℓℓ it *in* an oþer kynrεd þat is to hym dwellyng in h.

* fol. 20.

[1] PSALM 48 (49).

1. ȝe al men, hereþ þes þyn[2]ges; he[3] alle þat wonen in herþe, vnderstondeþ wyþ eren.
2. ȝe, al erþelich and mennes sones, ben to-gider in on riche and pouer.
3. My mouþe shal speke wisdome, and þe þouȝt of myn hert quaintise.
4. Y shal bowe myn ere in parabiles, and shal open in þe sauter myn purpose.
5. Whi shal ich doute in þe daie of iugement? þe wickednes of myn hele shal go a-bout me.
6. Hii, þat affien hem in her vertu and in þe mychelnes of her riches, gladen.
7. Broþer ne biggeþ, man shal raunsoun, he ne shal nouȝt ȝeuen to God his quemeyng.[4]
8. And for þe pris of his raunsoun he shal trauail wyþ-outen ende; and ȝete he shal liuen euermore.
9. He ne shal nouȝt se þe deþ, as he haþ sen þe wise dyand; þe vnwyse and þe fole shal perissen to-gidres.
10. And hij shal laten her riches vn-to stranges, and her biriels shul ben her houses wyþ[5]-outen ende.
11. Her tabernacles ben in kynde and kynde; hij shul clepen her names in her erþes.
12. And as man was in honur,[6] he ne vnderstode nouȝt;· he his liche to meres vn-wyse, and he is made liche to hem.
13. Þys her[7] way his sclaunder to hem; and efter hij shul plesen uiciouseliche[8] in her mouþe.

---

[1] Not numbered in MS.   [2] fol. 43b.   [3] i.e. ȝe.   [4] The MS. has a *q* with a stroke over it as is elsewhere used to abbreviate an *n*.   [5] fol. 44.   [6] MS. *homur*.
[7] MS. *ys* (expuncted) *her*.   [8] MS. *uicouseliche*; cf. *uicōse* in the Latin text.

---

48. 1. he] ȝe: in erþe.
2. men.
3. mynde: quayntenes.
4. ensaumples &+y.
5. dome: *go about*] enclose.
6. beleueþ or trusteþ — *hem*: gretnes.

7. ne b.] biggyþ noȝt: —ne: quemyng (*MS.* q *with an* e *over it*).
9. —ne: haþ sen] schal se: togeder.
10. strangers: hous.
11. londes.
12. honour: —ne: is likkynd to bestes.

14. Hij ben don in helle, as shepe ben to-gidres in flok¹;¹ and þe fende shal tourmenten hem.

15. And þe riʒtful shul lord-shippe vp hem in ioie; and her helpe shul bycomen olde fram her glorie in helle.

16. For-soþe God shal bige oʒain my soule fram þe pines of helle, whan he haþ taken me.

17. Ne doute þe nouʒt, whan man his made riche, and whan þe glorie of his hous his multiplied.

18. For whan he shal dyen, he ne shal nouʒt take al þynges; ne his glorie ne shal nouʒt descen²den wyþ hym.

19. For þe soule of þe gode shal ben blisced in his liue, and he shal reioys to þe whan þou hast wele don to hym.

20. Þe wicked shal entren unto þe progenie, uel, oþer, kynde,³ of his faders, and he shal se no liʒt wyþ-outen ende.⁴

21. As man whas in honur, he ne vnderstode nouʒt; he his likened to meres vn-whis, and he ys made liche to hem.

⁵PSALM 49 (50).

1. Our Lord, God of goddes, spak¹, and cleped þerþe.

2. Fram þe sonne arisyng¹ vn-to þe going¹ a-doune, þe spece of his fairnes is of Syon.

3. God shal comen aperteliche, our Lord; and he ne shal nouʒt be stylle.

4. Fur shal by-gynne to brenne in his siʒt, and grete tempest shal ben in his cumpasse.

5. He cleped þe heuen fram a-bouen, and þerþe for to iugen his puple.

6. He⁶ god, assembleþ ʒe to hym his halwen, þat ordeine his testament vp sacrifices.

---

[1] MS. *folk¹*.   [2] fol. 44b.   [3] The last three words are underlined with red ink.   [4] *Notabile* written in margin by a later hand.   [5] Ps. 48, MS.   [6] i.e. ʒe.

---

14. to-geder: flok.
15. *lordsh.*] haue lordschip: ioie.
16. paynes.
17. *Ne doute þe*] Drede þou: ioie.
18. —1. *ne*: 2. *ne*] no: ioie: —3. *ne*.
*19. reioie: *don to*] do.
20. in-to: *uel oþer*] or þe.

21. Whe[n]: —*ne*: was lykkynd to vnwyse bestes.

49. 2. *vnto ... adoune*] into þe fallyng.
3. —*ne*.
6. —*He god*: Gadreþ: ordeyneþ: sacrifice.

* fol. 20b.

7. And þe heuens shul tellen his riʒtfulnes; for [1] God his iuge.

8. Here ʒe, my folk[1] of Israel; and hy shal speken, and witnes to þe; y, God, ham þy god.

9. Y ne shal nouʒt repruue þe in þy sacrifices; þyn offrynges for-soþe ben alway in my siʒt.

10. Y ne shal nouʒt taken chalues of þyn hous, ne kiddes of þyn flokkes.

11. For alle þe wilde bestes of þe wodes ben myn, þe meres and þe oxen in þe mounteins.

12. Y knew alle þe foweles of heuen, and þe fairnes of þe felde is wyþ me.

13. ʒyf ich haue hunger, y ne shal nouʒt saie to þe; for þe world and þe fulnes of it is myn.

14. Ne shal ich nouʒt ete bulles flesshe, ne drynke kiddes blode?

15. Offre to God sacrifice of heryynge, and ʒeld to þe alderheʒest þyn uowes.

16. And clepe me in daie of tribulacioun; and y shal defende þe, and þou shalt worship me.

17. God for-soþe seide to þe synʒer, Whi tellestou my ryʒtfulnes,[2] and takeþ my testament by þy mouþe?

[3]18. Þou for-soþe hatedest[4] discipline, and þou kest my wordes by-hynde rygge.

19. ʒyf þou sest a þef, þou ran wyþ hym, and laid[5] þy porcioun wyþ spouse-breches.

20. Þy mouþe wex ful wyþ malice, and þyn tunge songe treccheries.

21. Þou sittand spak[1] oʒain þy broþer, and þou settedest sclaundre oʒains þe sones of þy moder; þou dest þes þynges, and ich helde me stille.

---

[1] fol. 45.   [2] The MS. has myʒtfulnes instead of my ryʒtfulnes.   [3] fol. 45b.
[4] MS. haddest.   [5] i added over line.

---

7. schew.
8. hy] y.
9. —ne: reproue: sacrifice.
10. —ne: no.
11. þe meres and þe] kyne &.
12. know: foweles] folkes.
13. haue h.] schal hungre: — ne: plenteusnes þer-of.
14. —Ne: ne] non.

15. alderh.þyn u.] hyest þi wonnes.
16. in+þe: wyrschip.
17. F. s. Godd: telestow my riʒtfulnes.
18. Fo (!) soþe þou hatyd lore —rygge.
19. seiʒ: ʒerne: put: wonteres.
20. was: of: spake gyle.
21. aʒens: put: son: dyd þise.

EARLY ENGLISH PSALTER. PSALM 50 (51).

22. Þou wendest wickedleche, þat y shal be lich to þe; y shal reproue þe of þy susposeing, and y shal stablis iugumen oȝayn þy face.

23. Ȝe þat for-ȝeteþ God, vnderstondeþ þes þynges, þat he ne dampne ȝou nouȝt, and þat þer be non þat defendeþ ȝou.

24. Sacrifice of heryyng[1] shal honour me; and þer is þe waie þer y shal shewen to hym þe helpe of God.

[1] PSALM 50 (51).

1. Ha mercy on me, God, efter þy mychel mercy.
2. [2] And efter þe mychelnes of þy pites do way my wickednes.
3. Whasshe me more of my wickednes, and clense me of myn synne.
4. For ich knowe[3] my wickednes, and my synne ys euermore oȝains me.
5. Ich haue synned to þe alon, and ich haue don iuel to-fore þe, þa-tou be made ryȝt-ful in þy wordes, and þatou ouercum whan þou art iuged.
6. Se! for ich am conceiued in wickednesses, and my moder conceiued me in synnes.
7. Se! for þou loued soþenes; þe vncerteyn þynges and pryue of [þy] wisdom þou made to me apert.
8. Þou sprengest me, Lord, wyþ þy mercy, and y shal be made clene; þou shalt purifie[4] me, and y shal be made whyȝte vp snowe.
9. Þou shalt ȝeue ioie and gladnes to myn heryng[1], [5] and þe mylde dedes of my hert shul gladen.
10. Turne þy face fram myn synnes,[6] and do oway al myn wickednes.
[7] 11. Ha God, make in me clene hert, and newe þou a ryȝt gost in myn hert.

---

[1] Ps. 49, MS.   [2] fol. 46.   [3] MS. knewe.   [4] MS. purisie, with a long s.
[5] MS. beryng[1].   [6] MS. synmes.   [7] fol. 46b.

---

22. wende + wykkydnes or: supposyng: put dome.
23. for-ȝete: þis: — ne: defende.
24. sacrif.] þe s.

50. 1. Godd haue m. on me: grete.
2. gretenes: mercyes: do away.
3. More-ouer wasch me fram: fram.
*4. know.

5. made r.] iustified: schalt deme.
6. wykkydnes.
7. preuy of+þi: opyn to me.
8. Lord þ. sprenged me: wasch: whytter þan.
9. heryng: meke.
10. synnes.
11. O: m. cl. h. in me & make new a riȝte g.

* fol. 21.

12. Ne putt me nouȝt fram þy face, and ne do nauȝt o-way fram me þyn holy gost.

13. Ȝelde to me gladnes of þyn helþe, and conferme me wyþ þyn holy gost.

14. Y shal techen þe wicked þyn wayes, and þe wicked shul ben conuerted to þe.

15. Ha þou God, God of myn helþe, deliuer me of sinnes,[1] and my tunge shal gladen þy ryȝtfulnes.

16. Lord, þou shalt open myn lippes, and my mouþe shal tellen þyn heryyng'.

17. For ȝyf þou hade wolde, ich hade ȝeuen sacrifice; forsoþe þou ne shalt nouȝt deliten in sacrifices.

18. Trubled gost[2] is sacrifice to God; þou, God, ne shal nouȝt despisen þe hert sorowful and meke.

19. Do blisfullich, Lord, to þy chosen in þy gode wille, þat þe gode be confermed in heuens.

20. Þan shal tou take [3] sacrifice of ryȝt, seruice, and honours; hij shul þan setten godenesses to-fore þy throne.

[4] PSALM 51 (52).

1. Ha þou wicked, whi gladestou in malice, þat art myȝtful in wickednes?

2. Al day seid þy tunge vnryȝtfulnes; þou dost treccherie as a rasour sharp sauaand (!).

3. Þou louedest malice up blisfolhede, more to speken wickednes þan euennes.

---

[1] MS. fines. [2] MS. gᵒd. [3] fol. 47. [4] Ps. 50, MS.

---

12. —Ne: —ne.
13. Latin and English omitted.
14. turned.
15. O: synnes: gladen] wyrschip.
16. t.] schewe.
17. Fo(!): —ne.
18. A sturbled goste: þou . . . despisen] Godd dispise þou noȝt.

19. L. do beniglich(!): confirmyd: heuen.
20. godnes: trone.

51. 1. O: ioiestow.
2. þouȝt: as a scharp rasour þou did gyle.
3. vp bl.] more þan mekenes &.

EARLY ENGLISH PSALTER. PSALM 52 (53).

4. þou louedest [alle] trubland wordes in fibel tunge.

5. Þer-for shal God destruen þe on ende, and shal draw þe vp bi þe rotes out of þy¹ tabernacle and þy rote fram þerþe of liueand.

6. Þe ryʒtful shul sen þe iuels of þe wicked, and hij shul douten hem; and hij shul leʒen vp hym, and shul sayen, Se þe man þat ne sett nouʒt God his helper.

7. [B]vt he hoped in þe multitude of his riches, and he was michel worþ in his vanite.

8. ²Ich am in Godes hous as oliue fructifiand, ich hoped in þe mercy of God wyþ-outen ende in heuens.

9. Y shal shryue to þe in þe world, for³ þou it madest; and y shal abyde þy name, for it ys gode in þe syʒt of þyn halwen.

⁴PSALM 52 (53).

1. Þe vnwys⁵ seid in his hert, God nis nouʒt.

2. Þe wicked ben corrumped and made loþeliche in⁶ wickednesses; þer nys non þat doþ gode.

3. God loked fram heuen vp mennes sones, þat he se, ʒyf any be vnderstondeand oþer sechand God.

4. Al louteden⁷ to-gidres fram godnes; hij ben made⁸ inprofitable; þer nys non þat doþ god, þer nys non vn-to on.

5. Ne witeþ nouʒt hij alle, þat wirchen wickednesses, þat deuouren my folk' as mete of brede?

6. Hij ne cleped nouʒt God; þer hij tre[m]bleden for drede, þer no drede nas.

⁹7. For God wasted þe bones of hem þat plesen to men; hij ben confounded, for God haþ despised hem.

---

¹ MS. þe.   ² MS. fol. 47b.   ³ MS. twice *for.*   ⁴ Ps. 51, MS.   ⁵ MS. *wn* (struck out) *vnwys.*   ⁶ MS. *and.*   ⁷ *o* corrected from *e.*   ⁸ MS. *maden.*   ⁹ fol. 48.

4. louyd all wordes of casting doune in gyleful tung.
   5. on] into þe : þi t.
   6. drede : *hym*] hem : — *ne* : helpe.
   7. Bot :—þe : worþi.
   8. as an olyf beryng frute.

52. 1. is.
*2. *and wick.*] in her studes or in her wykkydnes : is : gode+þer is noʒt to one.
   3. or.
   4. All þay lowtyd to-gyder f. godenes+& : made vnprofitable : is : is noʒt to one.
   5. wit : wykkydnes+&.
   6. —*ne* : —þer : *tr.*] were agast : was.
   7. her bones þat plesed.

fol. 21b.

8. Who shal ȝyf of Syon helþe to Israel? whan our Lord haþ[1] tourned þe wrocchedhede of his folk', þe kynde of Iacob shal gladen, and þe folk' of Israel shal ioyen.

[2] PSALM 53 (54).

1. Ha God, make[3] me sauf in þy name, and iuge me in þy uertu.
2. God, here my praiere, and take in þyn eren þe wordes of my[4] mouþe.
3. For strange arysen oȝains me, and stronge soȝt my soule, and ne sett nouȝt God to-forn her syȝt.
4. Se! for God helpeþ me, and our Lord is taker of my soule.
5. Turne oway iuels fro myn enemys, and departe hem in þy soþenes.
6. Y shal sacrifye to þe wyþ gode wylle, and shryue to þy name, Lord; for it is gode.
7. For þou deliuered [5] me of ichan tribulacioun, and myn eȝe despised vp myn enemys.

[6] PSALM 54 (55).

1. Ha God, here myn oreisoun, and ne despise þou nouȝt my praiere; vnder-stonde to me, and here me.
2. Ich am made sori in my haunteyng, and am tribluled (!) fram þe voice of myn enemy, and of þe tribulaciouns of þe sinȝers.
3. For hij bowed wickednisses to me, and hij were derend to me in ire.
4. Myn hert his trubled in me, and drede of deþ fel vp me.
5. Drede and quakeyng comen vp me, and derknesses couered me.
6. Who shal ȝyf me þe ȝyftes of þe holi gost? and y shal fleȝe to heuen and resten þer?

---

[1] MS. had. [2] Ps. 52, MS. [3] MS. maked. [4] MS. þy. [5] fol. 48b.
[6] Ps. 53, MS.

---

8. haþ: wrechydnes.

53. 1. O Godd make: deme.
2. with: eres: my.
3. straunge menaros: str.+men:
—ne.
4. Lo.
6. s. wylfullych to þe.

7. ichan] aH.

54. 1. O: —ne: —þou.
2. vsyng & y am sturbled: tribulacyon: synner.
3. wykkydnes: heuy.
4. sturblyd.
5. derknes.

EARLY ENGLISH PSALTER. PSALM 54 (55).

7. Se! ich fleand fram God wyþ-drowe me fram hym, and ich woned in iuels.

8. Ich abode hym þat made me sauf of my litelhede and of þe persecucioun of þe gost.

9. Ouer-þrawe hem, Lord, [1] and de-parte her tunges; for ich seiȝ wickednes & oȝain-sigging in þe cyte.

10. Wickednes shal cumpasse hym day and nyȝt vp his walles, and trauail and vnryȝtfulnes amiddes of hym.

11. And usure and trecherie ne failed nouȝt in his waies.

12. For ȝyf myn enemy had missaid[2] me, for-soþe ich had suffred.

13. And ȝif he, þat hated me, had spoken gret þynges vp me, par-chaunce, ich had hid me fram hym.

14. Soþeliche þou, God, art man of on hert, and my lader and my knower.

15. Þou man, þat tou-gadres[3] wyþ me toke swete metes: we ȝede in in Goddes hous wyþ on assente.

16. Cum þe deþe vp þe yuel, and descenden hij into helle al liueand.

17. For wickednisses ben in her woninges in-middes of hem.

18. Ich for-soþe cried to our Lord, and our Lord saued me.

19. Y shal tellen at euen and at morwen and at mydday, and y shal nempnen þe heryyng‘ [4] of God; and he shal here my voice.

20. He shal bigge oȝain my soule in pees fram þe wicked, þat comen nere me þurȝ iuel; for hij were wyþ me a-monges many gode.

21. God shal heren me and lowen hem, þe which is to-fore þe wordles.

22. For chaunge nis nouȝt to hem of her iuel lif,[5] and hij ne drad nouȝt God; he putt forþe his vengeaunce in-to ȝeldyng‘.

---

[1] fol. 49.   [2] Second *i* added over line.   [3] *tou gra* (*gra* is, however, expuncted) *gadres*.
[4] fol. 49*b*.   [5] *iuel lif* twice in MS.

---

7. And ych with-drow me fram him flying fram God.
8. fram my litylhode.
9. se: in+in.
*10. enclose.
11. gile: —ne.
12. y schuld had (!) suffyrd.
13. par-auentur.
14. For-soþe: —man: knowen.

15. Þou man toke sw. m. to-gadres w. me.
16. Cum—þe: wykkyd+men: fall.
17. wykkydnes beþ.
18. For-soþ ych.
19. at morow atte mydday & atte euen: schw (!).
20. among.
22. is: —ne.

* fol. 22.

23. Hij defouled his testament, and hij ben departed fram þe ire of his myȝt; and his hert neȝed ire oȝayns hem.[1]

24. Hys wordes ben molist up oile, and na-for-þa (!) hij ben dartes.

25. Man, cast þyn hert up our Lord, and he shal norisen þe; he ne shal nouȝt ȝeuen euermore meltynge to þe ryȝtful.

26. Þou, God, for-soþe shalt laden hem into þe pitte[2] of deþ.

27. Men defouled wyþ[3] dedelich synne and þe trecherous[4] ne shul nouȝt han half her daies; for-soþe, Lord, ich shal hope in þe.

[5]PSALM 55 (56).

1. Haue mercy on me God, for man haþ defouled me; þe fende trubled me, feȝtand alday oȝayns me.

2. Myn enemys defouled m[e] alday, for many were feȝtand oȝains me.

3. Y shal drede þe fram þe heȝt of þe daye; y for-soþe shal hope in þe.

4. Hij[6] shal hery my wordes [in God, ich hoped in God; y ne shal nouȝt dreden,] what manes flesshe doþ to me.

5. Alday þe wicked acurseden myn wordes oȝains me; alle her þoutes ben in iuel.

6. Hij shul wonen in helle, and þer hij shul hiden hem; and hij shul kepen mi d[e]-fouleingˡ.[7]

7. As hij tempteden my soule, for nouȝt þou shalt make hem sauf; and þou shalt bringˡ to nouȝt þes folkes in þyn ire.

8. Ha God, ich telde my lyf to þe; þou laidest min teres in þy syȝt.

9. As in þy bihest shul þan [8]myn enemys be turned oȝain-ward.

10. In wat daye þat ich cleped to þe, se! ich am aknow[9] þat þou art my God.

---

[1] MS. hym.   [2] Or pute.   [3] wyþ twice in MS.   [4] trecherorousus, MS.
[5] Ps. 54, MS.   [6] i.e., y (=ego).   [7] MS. mid fouleingˡ.   [8] fol. 50b.
[9] Last word of the line. The expression is miswritten for ichaua know, ich haue knowen, cf. ich haua songen, Ps. 70, 25.

---

23. diffoiled : be : n.] broȝt neȝe: hem.
24. softer þan : neþeles.
25. —ne.
26. F. s. þou Godd : put.
27. Men of synnes & gyleful men schal.

55. 1. defoilid : haþ sturblyd.
2. defoilid : m] me.

3. & for-soþe y.
4. Hij] y : wordes + in Godd ych hopid in Godd y schal noȝt drede.
6. my defoulyng.
7. þise folk.
8. O : schewd : sett.
9. shul ... enemys] myn enemys schal þan.
*10. clepe : lo : haue know.

* fol. 22b.

EARLY ENGLISH PSALTER. PSALM 56 (57). 67

11. Y shal herien worde in þe, God, y shal heryen worde in þe, Lord; ich[1] hopede in þe, God; y shal nouȝt drede, what man doþ to me.

12. Ha God, þy desires ben[2] in me, for which y shal ȝelde to þe heryynges.

13. For þou deliuered my soule fram helle and myn fete fram slydynge, þat ich plese to-fore God in þe lyȝt of hem[3] þat ben saued.

[4] PSALM 56 (57).

1. Haue mercy on me, God, haue mercy on me; for my soule affieþ in þe.

2. And ich shal hope in þe myȝt of þy grace, þer-whiles þat my wickednesses passe.

3. Y shal crye to þe God alderheȝest, to God þat did wele to me.

4. He sent his sone fram heuen, and deliuered me out of helle, and ȝaf[5] in [6]reproceinge þe defouland me.

5. God sent fram heuen his mercy and his soþenes, and deliuered my soule fram sharpnes of tourmentes of fendes; and ich dwelled trubled.

6. Mennes sones han her werkes hard and sharp, and her tunges[7] ben[8] sharp swerdes.

7. Be þou, God, anheȝed vp þe heuens, and þi glorie in[9] alle erþe.

8. Mennes sones diȝten gnares to myn fete, and tempted my soule.

9. Hij daluen a diche to-fore my face, and fellen hem seluen þer-inne.

10. Myn hert ys diȝt to þe, God, myn hert is diȝt; and y shal synge, and sai a salme.

11. Þou my glorie, arise þou; sautrie[10] and harpe, arise; y shal aryse in þe morwenynge.

12. Y shal schryue to þe, Lord, in folkes, and saie to þe a songe in men.

---

[1] MS. *ich ich*. [2] MS. *len?* [3] MS. repeats *þat ich plese to-fore god in þe lyȝt of hem*. [4] Ps. 55, MS. [5] Before *ȝaf* the MS. has *ha*, which has been struck out. [6] fol. 51. [7] After *tunges* a superfluous *and* follows. [8] Here *hard* is expuncted. [9] MS. *and*. [10] *i* added over line.

---

11. *Y*] Lord y.
12. —*Ha*: beþ: schald.
13. *helle*] þe deþ of hell.

56. 1. Lord: trusteþ.
2. wykkydnes.
3. Godd hiest: well.
4. into reproue men defoilyng.

5. sturblyd.
6. Men: tunges—*and*.
7. enhyed vp—þe: ioie in all þe erþe.
8. Men sonnes dyȝtyd grynnes.
9. delue.
11. ioie: sauter.
12. *in men*] among folkes.

6 *

13. For þy mercy his heried vn-to þe heuens, and þy soþenes vn to þe cloudes.

[1]14. Be þou, God, anheȝed up þe heuens, and þy glorye in al erþe.

[2]PSALM 57 (58).

1. Ȝyf ȝe speke in alle þynges[3] ryȝt, ȝe mennes sones, iugyȝt ryȝtfullich.

2. For ȝe wirchen wickednesses in our hertes in erþe; ȝour hondes wirchen vnryȝtfulnes.

3. Þe synȝers ben aliened fer fram þe wombe; hij erreden fram þe wombe; hij spoken fals þynges.

4. Her wirship is efter þe wickednes of þe serpent, as of aspide def and stoppand his eren.

5. Þe which ne shal nouȝt here þe voice of þe charmeand, and of þe makand uenym charmeand wiselich.

6. God shal de-foulen her teþe in her mouþe; our Lord shal breke þe uttemast iuels of þe wicked.

7. Hij shul by-comen noȝt as water ernand; our Lord shal shewe his myȝt, þerwyles þat hij ben made[4] vnstable.[5]

8. Þe wicked shul ben wasted as wax þat melteþ; þe [6]wreche of God fol vp her werkes, and hij ne seiȝ noȝt her saueour.

9. Er þat ȝour synnes vnderstonde þe dampnacioun euerlastand, þe fur of vices shal deuoren hem as liueand in ire.

10. Þe ryȝt-ful shal gladen whan he seþ þe vengeaunce, and he shal wasshen his hondes in þe blode of þe synȝer.

11. And man shal saie for-soþe, Ȝyf frute be to þe ryȝtful, for-soþe God is iugeand hem in erþe.

---

[1] fol. 51b.   [2] Ps. 56, MS.   [3] y on erasure.   [4] After *made* an *n* is erased.
[5] v on erasure.   [6] fol. 52.

---

13. *heried*] made grete: vnto— þe.
14. vp heuens: ioie vp.

57. 1. For-soþe ȝyf ȝe speke riȝt-lych in all þ.: mensonnes demeþ.
2. wickydnes: our] ȝour: erþe+ &.
3. 2. wombe+&.

4. *wirsh.*] wodeschip: *wickedn*] likenes: *as . . . st.*] & of þe defe aspyde stoppyng: eres.
5. —*ne*: þe venum maker.
6. ottermast.
7. ȝernyng: þerwyles] to.
*8. fell: —*ne*.
9. Or: þe] ȝour.
11. demyng.

* fol. 23.

PSALM 58 (59).

[1]PSALM 58 (59).

1. Ha my God, defende me fram myn enemis, and deliuere me fram þe ariseand oȝains me.

2. Defende me fram wirchaund wickednes, and saue me fram men defouled wiþ dedelich sinnes.

3. Se, for hij token my soule; þe stronge fel oȝains me.

4. Ne my wickednes, Lord, ne my sinne; ich[2] ran wiþ-outen wickednes, and dresced þis worde.

5. Aryse, Lord, in myn oȝain-erning, and se; and þou, Lord, art [3]God of uertuȝ, God of Israel.

6. Ȝif entent to uisiten al folkes; ne haue þou nouȝt mercy on alle þat wirchen wickednes.

7. Hii shul ben turned at euen, and shul suffren hunger as hundes; and hij shul cumpassen þe cite.

8. Se, hij shul speken in her mouþe, and sharpnes of wordes his in her lippes; and hij shul saien, Who herd it?

9. And þou, Lord, shalt scornen hem, and þou shalt bringe to nouȝt alle folkes.

10. Y shal kepe to þe myn strengþes, for God is my taker, my God; his mercy shal come to-fore me.

11. God shewed miȝt to me vp myn enemys; Lord, ne sle[4] hem nouȝt, þat þe folk ne forȝete me nouȝt.

12. De-part hem in þy uertu; and þou, God, my defendour, do hem oway fram yuel.

13. For þe trespas of her mouþe and þe worde of her lippes ben þe wycked[5] taken in her pride.

14. And of her waryinge and of her lesyng hij shul ben shewed in [6]her endyng.

---

[1] Ps. 57, MS.   [2] Here *ram* is expuncted.   [3] fol. 52b.   [4] MS. *she.*
[5] MS. *kycked.*   [6] fol. 53.

---

58. 1.—*Ha* : *defende*] deliuer : þe] men.
   2. þe] men : men ... sinnes] synful men.
   3. Lo : soule+&.
   4. *Ne*] Noþer : *ne*] no : synne +bot : ȝerne.
   5. in-to my course.
   6. visytyng : *ne*] &.
   7. atte : go abowte.
   11. —*ne* : sle : —*ne*.
   13. *lippes*] mouþe : wykkyd takyng.
   14. werying.

70   EARLY ENGLISH PSALTER. PSALM 59 (60).

15. And hij ne shul nouȝt ben saued in þe ire of endeing¹; & wyten hij þat God shal lordship Iacob sones and þe cuntres of þerþe.

16. Hij shul ben departed at euen, and hij shul suffren hunger as hundes, and hij shul gon a-boute þe cite.

17. For-soþe y shal syngen þy strengþe, Lord, and erliche heȝen in þy mercy.

18. For þou art made my taker and my socour in dai¹ of my tribulacioun.

19. Ha my helper, y shal synge to þe, for þat þou, God, art my taker, my God, my mercy.

²PSALM 59 (60).

1. Ha God, þou hast put us oway fram þe, and þou hast destriued us; þou art wroþ, and þou haddest pite of us.

2. Þou stired þerþe, and trubled it; hel þe³ contriciouns of it, for it is stired.

3. Þou shew[ed]est hard þynges to þy folk¹ for synne, and þou⁴ ȝaf us a drink¹ of þe biternes of prikkyng¹.

⁵4. Þou haf⁶ tokenyng¹ of wisdom to hem þat dreden þe, þat hij shuld fle fram þe corrupcioun of synne.

5. Þat þyn loued ben deliuered fram iuel, make me sauf for þy ryȝthalf, and here me.

6. God spak¹ in his halwe, Y shal delyten, and y shal departen driehede, and y shal meten þe ualaie of tabernacles.

7. Galaad ys myn, and Manasses is myn, and Effraim is þe strengþe of myn heued.

8. Judas ys myn kynde, Moab is þe enterete of myn hope.⁷

---

¹ MS. *sai* (with a long *s*). ² Ps. 58, MS. ³ MS. *helþe*. ⁴ Here *ha* has been expuncted. ⁵ fol. 53*b*. ⁶ i.e. ȝaf. ⁷ MS. *hopie*, of which the *i* is dotted out.

---

15. —*ne*: *lordship ... and*] haue lordeschipe of I. sonnes & of.
16. atte.
17. enhyȝe—*in*.
18. day.
19. O : my Godd+&.

*59. 1. —*Ha*: destruyd: on.
2. *trubled*] sturbled : hele þe : mouyd.

3. shewed: *pr.*] compunccion.
4. *haf ... shuld*] ȝaf to men dredyng þe holynes of wysdome þat þay drede þe & þat þay.
5. with þi riȝt honde.
6. *in*] by : drynes.
7. M.—*is*.
8. kyng+& : *e.*]holenes.

* fol. 23*b*.

9. Y shal shewe my ve*n*geau*n*ce in Ydume; st*r*ange be subiectes to me.

10. Who shal lade me in-to a cite warnist, who shal lade me in-to Ydume?

11. Nouȝt þou, God, þat put us away fram þe fende, þou, God, ne shal nouȝt gon out in our v*er*tuȝ?

12. Ȝyf us, Lord, helpe of tribulac*i*ou*n*, for helþe of man is ydel.

13. We shul do u*er*tu in God, and he shal brynge to nouȝt þe t*ru*¹bland vs.

²PSALM 60 (61).

1. Here, God, my p*r*aier, and understounde myn oryson.

2. Ich c*r*ied to þe fram þe cu*n*tres of þerþe, þerwhiles þat myn hert was anoied; þou heȝedest me in stablenes.

3. Þou laddest me out, for þou art made myn hope; þou art tour of stre[*n*]gþe fram þe face of þe ³ enemy.

4. Y shal wonen in þy tabernacle in þe worldes; y shal be defended in þe couering' of þy mercyes.

5. For þou, my God, herdest myn oreison; þou ȝaf heritage to þe dredand þy name.

6. Þou shal casten dayes up þe daies up þe kynge, and his ȝeres ⁴ vn-to þe daye of kynde & kynde.

7. He woneþ wyþ-outen ende in þe syȝt of God; who shal sechen his mercy and hys soþenes?

8. Y shal saye þus a songe to þy name in þe world of⁵ world, þat ich ȝelde [myn] a-vowes fram daie to daie.

---

¹ fol. 54.   ² Ps. 59, MS.   ³ Here an *n* has been expuncted.   ⁴ *s* corrected from *g*.   ⁵ Here follows *wol*, which however is expuncted.

---

9. straungers beþ sugettes.
10. *warn.*] ywarnyd &.
11. *Nouȝt*] Wheþer noȝt: —*ne.*
12. ma*n*nes helþe is vayne.
13. þe *trubl.*] me*n* stu*r*belyng.

60. 1. understonde+to.

2. þ*erwhiles* þat] to: & þou hydest.
3. hope+&: strengþe.
4. scha (!).
5. orysun+&: þe] men.
6. of þe kyng: into.
8. þus a] so: ȝelde+my*n*.

PSALM 61 (62).

1. Ne shal nouȝt my soule be ¹vnder-lout to God? for in hym hys myn helþe.

2. For he ys my God and myn helþe & my taker; y ne shal no more dreden.

3. Þer-whyles þat ȝe fallen into holy chyrche, ȝe al sle þe in-nocent liggand to hym, as to a wal þat þe morter [is] putt out.

4. Þe wicked for-soþe þouȝten to putt oway my god dede, and ich vnderstode her pryuetes; hij blisced me wyþ her mouþe, and waried me wyþ her hert.

5. Ha þou my soule, be þou subiecte for-soþe to God, for of hym ys my suffraunce.

6. For þat he is my God, my saueour, myn helper, y ne shal nouȝt passen out of his comaundement.

7. Myn helþe is in God and my glorie; God ys þe wille of myn helpe; and myn hope is in God.

8. Ha, he² alle assemble of folk⸱, hopeþ in hym, heldeþ out to-forn hym your hertes; God ys our helper wyþ-outen ende.

³9. For-soþe mennes sones ben idel, mennes sones ben liȝers in balaunces, þat hij deceiuen of idelnes in þat ich þynge.

10. Ne wyl ȝe nouȝt hopen in wickednes, and ne wil ȝe nouȝt couaite rauyns; ȝyf riches flowe to you, ne wil ye nouȝt sett your hert to hem.

11. God spak⸱ o-nes to þynges, ich herd hem, for þat þe myȝt of God is; and, Lord, to þe is mercy, for þou shalt ȝelde to ichon efter his werkes.

---

¹ fol. 54b. ² i.e. ȝe. ³ fol. 55.

---

61. 1. —*Ne*: *vnderl.*] suget.
2. —*ne*: drede no more.
3. To-whyls: *into*] aȝens man or: a+bied: *morter is put away.
4. F. s. þe w.: her p. ych vnderstode: *cursyd.
5. O: suget—*for soþe.*
6. sauyour+&: —*ne.*

7. ioie.
8. *Ha he*] ȝe: *congregacion* of pepyll: *heldeþ*] schedeþ.
9. men: men: balance: desayue: —*ich.*
10. —*Ne*: *ne wil ... rauyns*] couayte ȝe noȝt raueynes: —*ne.*
11. ons þise two þinges.

* fol. 24.

PSALM 62 (63).

1. Ha God, my God, ich wake to þe of lyȝt.
2. My soule coueited¹ to be wyþ þe, and my flesshe to þe ful many-fold.
3. In wylde lond and out of way an² drye in swyche manere, ich shewed me to þe [in] holy þynge, þat ich seiȝe þy vertu and þy glorie.
4. For þy mercy is better vp lybbeinges; myn lippes shul heryen þe.
5. Se, y shal blisce þe in my lyf; and in þy name³ y shal lift up myn hondes.
6. Be my soule fulfyld ⁴as of flour and of grece; and my mouþe shal heryen þe [wyþ] lippes of gladnes.
7. So was ich þenchand on þe up my bedde, y shal þenche on þe in þe morwenyng¹; for þat þou was myn helper.
8. And y shal gladen in þe coue[r]ing of þy mercies, my soule haþ drawen efter þe; þy ryȝt syde toke me.
9. For-soþe þe wicked tempted my soule in vayn, and hij shul entren in-to þe deppest of þe erþe; so hij shul be ȝeuen in-to sharpenes of vengeaunce, so⁵ shal hij ben att þe parties of fendes.
10. þe kynge for-soþe shal ioien in God, alle þat hopen in hym shul ben heried; for þe mouþe of þe spekand wicked þynges ys stopped.

⁶PSALM 63 (64).

1. Here, God, my praier, whan ich praie; defende my soule fram þe drede of þe enemy.
2. þou defendest me fram þe felawe-shippe of þe wicked, fram þe multitude of þe wirchand wickednes.

---

¹ MS. *couerted*. ² i.e. *and*. ³ Here follows an erasure of three letters.
⁴ fol. 55b. ⁵ Here follows an *h*, which has been dotted out. ⁶ Ps. 61, MS.

---

62. 1. O : fram.
2. couayteþ.
3. an . . . . manere] & dry þus : þe+in : ioie.
4. lyues.
6. As myne s. is f. with fatnes & plenteusnes—and: þe+with.
7. beþencher of.

8. coueryng: dr.] drow: syde] honde.
9. tempyd (!): ȝefe into+þe.
10. F. s. þe k.

63. 1. praye+&.
2. defendid: feleschyp: wickyd +&.

[1]3. For hij whetted her tunges as swerde; so hij maden her manaces þyngˑ bytter, þat hij turmenten þe vnwemmed in hidels.

4. Hij shul turmenten hym sudeinlich,[2] hij shul nouȝt dreden[3]; hij fastened to hem iuel worde of me.

5. Hij telden þat hij hidden falsnisses, and saiden, Who shal sen hem?

6. Hij soȝten wickednisses; þe sechand faileden in her secheyngˑ.[4]

7. Þe man ryȝtful shal neȝen to holi hert, and God shal ben heȝed.

8. Þe turmentes of þe wicked ben made her deþ, and her tunges ben made vnstable oȝains hem.[5]

9. Alle gode men þat sehen[6] hem in her malices, weren trubled; and ich man drad hem.

10. Þe gode telden þe werkes of God, and vnderstonden his[7] dedes.

11. Þe ryȝtful shal gladen in our Lord, and he shal hopen in hym; and al ryȝtful of hert shul ben heried.

[8]PSALM 64[9] (65).

1. Ha God, heryyngˑ by-comeþ þe in Syon; and to þe shal bowe[10] be ȝolden in Jerusalem.

2. Here my praier; icha flesshe schal come to þe.

3. Þe wordes of þe wicked vailed more vp vs; and þou shal be mercyful to our wickednesses.

4. Blisced be þe[11] man þat þou ches and toke; he shal wonen in þyn hallis.

5. We shul be fulfild of þe godes of þyn hous; and þi[12] temple ys holy, wonderful in euennesse.

---

[1] fol. 56. [2] MS. sudenilich. [3] hij shul nouȝt dreden twice in MS. [4] MS. sechenyng. [5] MS. me. [6] Probably only a blunder instead of seȝen. [7] his is followed by an h, which is expuncted. [8] fol. 56b. [9] Ps. 62, MS. [10] Blunder for vowe. [11] þ on erasure. [12] MS. þe.

---

3. manes *a bytter þing: þe vnfiled man in priuetes.
4. sudanlych.
5. grynnes or falsnes &+þay.
6. sechenyng] secheyng.
7. r. man: cum to+an: enhied.
8. me] hem.

9. seȝg: malesses: sturbled.
10. gode+men: vnderstode.

64. 1. O: be-semeþ: vow: ȝeld.
2. Here+Godd: ych mannes kynde.
3. wykkydnes.
5. þi t.

* fol. 24b.

6. Ha God, our helþe, here¹ us; þou art hope of alle þe cuntres of þerþe and fer in þe see;

7. Makand redy þe mounteins in þy vertu, girt wyþ myʒt; þat trubleþ þe depnes of þe see, þe soune of hys flodes.

8. Alle þe men þa[t] wonen in cuntres, shul ben trubled, and shul dreden of þyne toknes of þe out-going of morwen; and þou shalt deliten in þe euenyngᵗ.

9. Þou uysited þerþe, and made it fayre, and multiplied, for to make it ryche.

² 10. Þe flude of God ys fulfild of waters; þou, God, made radi her ernyngᵗ. for so ys his makyngᵗ rady.

11. Fylland hys ryuers,³ multiplie þou his buryon; he shal delyten in hys guters ekand.

12. Þou shalt blisce to þe time of þe ʒere of þy de-bonairte; and þy feldes shul be fulfild of plente.

13. Fair þynges of þe wyldernes shal by-comen fat, and þe woniand in þe mounteins shul ben fulfild of ioie.

14. Þe rammes⁴ [of shepe ben cloþed wyþ flese, & þe valeys shul] waxen ful wyþ wheten; folkᵗ shul crien and saien heriyngᵗ for ioye.

⁵PSALM 65 (66).

1. Ha alle þe londe, ioie to God, and saie songe to his name; ʒyf glorie to his⁶ heryynge.

2. Saiþ to God, Ha Lord, what þyn werkes⁷ ben dredeful; þyn enemys shul liʒen to þe in þe multitude of þy uertu.

3. Alle þerþe anoure þe, God, and synge to þe, and saie ⁸ songe to þy name.

---

¹ MS. *hele.* ² fol. 57. ³ MS. *ryūeils.* ⁴ MS. *raynes.* ⁵ Ps. 63, MS.
⁶ *God ... glorie to his* twice in MS. ⁷ MS. *wer werkes.* ⁸ fol. 57b.

---

6. O: *helþe*] heþ (!): *hele*] here.
7. gyrd: sturbleþ.
8. þa] þat: sturbled: tokenes— *of*: of þe+þe.
9. viset: made—*it.*
10. ʒernyng.
11. ryuers: burgunnynges + & : encresyng.
12. blys—*to*: —*of þy*: debonourte.

13. þe *won.*] men dwellyng: hylles.
14. þe ... *wheten*] þe rammes of schepe beþ cloþd with flese & þe valeys schall wex full of whete.

65. 1. *Ha ... ioie*] All ʒe men in þe world ioie ʒe: saiþ: ʒeuyþ ioie.
2. Say: o.
*3. anoureþ—þe.

* fol. 25.

4. Comeþ and seþ þe werkes of God dredeful in counseiles vp mennes sones;

5. Þat turneþ þe see in dryhede: hij shul passen þe flode on fote; þer shal we glade in hym.

6. Þat lord-shipeþ [wiþ-]outen ende in his vertu: his eȝen loken vp men; hij þat made[1] hem asper, ne be nouȝt heȝed in hem-seluen.

7. Ȝe folk', blisceþ ȝour God, and makeþ þe voice of his praiere herd;

8. Þat sett my soule to lif and ne ȝaf nouȝt my fete in styryng'.

9. For þou, God, proued us; þou assaid us wyþ fur as siluer is proued.

10. Þou laddest us in-to a gnare, and laidest tribulacions on our rygge, and settest men vp our heuedes.

11. We passed by fur and water, and þou laddest us into coleyng.[2]

12. Y shal entren in-to þyn hous in offrendes, and y ne shal ȝelde to þe myn avowes,[3] þat myn lippes distincted to þe.

13. And my mouþe spak' in my tribula[4]cioun.

14. Y shal offren to þe merȝþ offrendes wyþ encens[5] of shepe, and y shal offren to þe oxen wyþ kyddes.

15. Ȝe alle þat drede God, comeþ and hereþ; and y shal tellen ȝou hou many godes he did to my soule.

16. Ich cried to him wyþ my mouþe, and y gladed vnder my tunge.

17. Ȝyf ich seiȝ wickednes in myn hert, our Lord ne shal nouȝt here me.

18. For-þy God herd me, and vnderstode þe voice of my praier.

19. Blisced be God, þat ne did nouȝt oway myn orysoun ne hys mercy fram me.

---

[1] Here men follows, which is dotted out. [2] MS. toleyng. [3] MS. abowes.
[4] fol. 58. [5] MS. entens.

---

4. seþ] sayþ.
5. into drynes.
6. þat lordsh.] He þat lordschipeþ with: scharp: —ne: enhied.
8. —ne: into steryng.
9. proued us+&: is assayd.
10. gryn.
11. refreschyng.

12. offerynges: —ne: auowes: distinkt.
14. offrie: merȝþ] þe best: offerynges: incense: offrye.
15. — God. 16. ioied.
17. se: —ne.
18. þer-for.
19. —ne: ne] no.

PSALM 66 (67).[1]

1. God haue mercy on vs, and blisce vs, and lyȝt hys face vp us, and haue mercy on vs;

2. Þat we knowe þy waie in erþe, by þyn helþe in alle men.

3. Shryue to þe, God, þe folk; shryue to þe alle folk.

4. Deliten þe folk and gladen; for þou iugeþ þe folk' in[2] euenhede, and dresceþ þe folk' in erþe.

5.[3] Shryuen, God, þe folk to þe, shryuen to þe alle folkes; þerþe ȝaf hys frut þurȝ hys grace.

6. God, our Lord, blisce ous; blisce vs, God, and dreden hym alle þe cuntres of þerþe.

PSALM 67 (68).[4]

1. Arise, God, and be hys enemys wasted; and flen hij þat hated him fram his face.

2. De-failen hii, as smoke faileþ; as wex melteþ[5] fram þe face of þe fur, ryȝt so perissen þe synȝers fram þe face of God.

3. And eten þe ritful þe frutes of lyf, and gladen hij in þe siȝt of God, and delyten hij in gladnes.

4. Syngeþ to God, and says a[6] songe to hys name; makeþ way to hym þat steȝe vp þe doungoing of þe sunne; Lord hys his name.

5. Gladeþ ȝou in hys syȝt; hij þat iugen þe innocens shul ben put oway fram þe face of hym, fader of faderles and iuge of widues.

6. God is in hys holy heuen, God þat doþ þe gode wonen on hys[7][8] custum in hys hous;

---

[1] Ps. 64, MS.   [2] Here follows *he*, which is expuncted.   [3] fol. 58b.   [4] Ps. 65, MS.   [5] MS. *meltel*.   [6] MS. *and*.   [7] fol. 59.   [8] This is a corrupt form of the genitive *onis*.

---

66. 1. alyȝt.
2. *by*] & be : among.
3. Godd, be þe f. schryfe to þe, & alł f. be schryfe to þe.
4. Glade : ioie : demest : euenhode.
5. Godde schryue þe folk to þe, & alł folk Godd schryue to þe : þurȝth þi.

67. 1. flye : hateþ.
2. *as smoke faileþ*] a smeke (!) fayleþ & : melteþ.
3. frute: *delyten*] ioie.
4. *says and s.*] sayþ a songe : stieþ.
5. demeþ : faderles + chyldren : of þe wedous.
*6. *on hys*] of on.

* fol. 25b.

7. Þat ladeþ out þe bonden in strengþe, also hem þat stenchen, which þat wonien in biriels.

8. Ha God, as tou¹ went out in þe syȝt of þy folkͥ, as tou¹ passed in sharpnesses of peines,

9. þe erþe hys styred; for þe heuens dropped þurȝ þe grace of þe face of þe² God of Synay, of þe face of God of Israel.

10. Ha God, þou shalt depart wilful raine to þerþe, and it is made vnstable; þou for-soþe madest it.

11. Þyn bestes shul wonen þer-in; ha God, þou madest rady to þe pouer in swetnes nedful þynges.

12. Our Lord shal ȝeuen worde to hem þat tellen forþe þe gospeles þourȝ mychel vertu.

13. Ha kyngͥ of vertu of loued of loued, of þe grace of þyn hous to departen þe spuyles.

14. Ȝyf þat ȝe liuen³ bitwix þe lawes of þe olde testament ⁴and þe new, þe wil of þe [olde is] seluered, þat his to saie fainteliche made; bot þe lawe of þe last testament, þat hys, þe nywe, ben in palenes of gold, þat hys to saye, ben att þe wyl of God.

15. Þer-whiles þat þe fader of heuen iuge vp þat lawe, þc folkͥ kepand her souless hul ben made whyte as snowe in þe heuen, þat hys, Goddes⁵ hous ful of ioies.

16. Þe heuen ys ful of ioyes, þe heuen ys plentiuous; ha ȝe folkͥ, where-to loke ȝe in-to þe heuens ful of ioies?

17. Þe heuen in which it is wele likeand to God to wonen in it; for our Lord shal whonen þer wyþ-outen ende.

18. Þe wonyng of God hys .x. þousand multipliand þousandes of gladand; our Lord ys in⁶ hem in hys trone and in hys holy wonynge.⁷

---

¹ MS. astou. ² þe added over line. ³ MS. finen. ⁴ fol. 59b. ⁵ MS. gogged.
⁶ Here hys follows, which, however, has been dotted out. ⁷ The loop at the g has been erased and an e written instead.

---

7. in] with: —which: woneþ.
8. O: hastow: astow: scharpnes.
9. —face: Synay+and.
10. O: for-soþe þou made.
11. — ha.
13. O: þe grace] faire grace: forto: spoles.

14. lyf be-twene: seluered] olde Godd is syluerd: pallour.
15. þat lawe] þe law: Goddes hous+hous.
16. plentiful: o.
17. heue (!).

EARLY ENGLISH PSALTER. PSALM 67 (68). 79

19. Þou, Lucifer, steȝe on heȝe, and toke wrechedhede in fallyng into helle; þou toke vp-braydynges of men.

20. For hi, þat bi-leued nouȝt in God, our Lord, ne woned nouȝt þer.

[1] 21. Blisced be our Lord in þys daye; ich daie þe Lord of our helþes shal maky vs prospre waye.

22. God ys our God to make us sauf; and þe passion of þe deþ of our Lord ys of our Lord.

23. God for-soþe shal breken þe pouste of hys enemys and þe strengþe of þe fairhede of þe goand in her trespasses.[2]

24. Our Lord seide to þe folk' of Basan, Y shal turnen þe, y shal turnen þe into þe vengeaunce of slaȝter,

25. Þat þy fote be dipped in blode, and þe tunge of þyn houndes be dipped of it as þyn enemys.

26. Ha God, men seȝe þyn dedes, hij seȝen þe dedes of my God, my kyng', þat his in holy heuen.

27. Þe princes ioient com to-fore to þe syngand[3] amiddes ȝounlinges tabores.

28. Ȝe men, blisceþ God in chirches, to our Lord of þe mercy of hys folk' of Israel.

29. Þer hys Beniamyn, þe ȝong' man, in passyng' of þouȝt.

30. Þe princes of Iuda[4] ben her ladres, þe princes of Zabulon and þe princes of Neptalym were þer.

31. Ha God, sende grace to þy vertu, and conferme þys þynge, þat tou wirches in vs; þat hys to wyten, þat[5] tou be born þat we may be sauyd[6] þurȝ þe.

32. In þy temple of Ierusalem shal kynges offren to þe ȝyftes.

---

[1] fol. 60.   [2] ss on erasure.   [3] MS. synigand.   [4] of iuda of juda in MS.
[5] MS. þan.   [6] MS. said.

---

19. styed : wrechedhode : hell +& : reproues.
20. our] hour : —ne.
21. ich] & ech : make vs a gode way.
22. to make] of makyng.
23. pouer : enenemys (!) : fayrenes : þe] men : trespas.
25. of it as] þer-of as of.
26. O : seȝe] se.
27. ioynyd : syngyng : ȝong-lynges tabouresters.
*30. leders : Nyptalym.
31. O : confirme : wychest (!) : þan] þat : said] sauyd.

* fol. 26.

33. A gaderyng to-gidres of stable folkⁱ, þat ben in þe law of our Lord, blameþ þe sacrifice of ydolatr*ie*s, þat hij þat ben of ryʒt byleue shete out of her cu*m*painie hem þat maken mau*m*-metr*ie*s.

34. Ha God, waste þe folkⁱ þat wyl batails;¹ legats shul cu*m*en out of Egipte sleand þe Echiopenes; Echiepeiens shul fallen in seruage vnder þe Egipciens for her synne.

35. Ha ʒe folkⁱ of kyngdomes of erþe, syngeþ to God, syngeþ to our Lord.

36. Syngeþ to God, syngeþ; þat steʒe vp heue*n* of he²ue*n* at þe est.

37. Se, he shal ʒeue to hys voice voice of vertu; ʒeueþ gl*o*rie to God vp Isr*ae*l; hys heryng and hys vertu ys vp þe cloudes.

38. God is wonde-ful (!) in hys halwen, þe God of Isr*ae*l; he shal heue³ vertu and strengþe to hys folkⁱ; blisced be God.

⁴PSALM 68 (69).

1. Ha God, makⁱ me sauf; for temptaciou*n*s entred vn-to my soule.
2. Ich am ficched in þe gnarc of synʒe, and substau*n*ce nis nouʒt.
3. Ich come to riches of þe world, and cuuaitis⁵ ablynt me.
4. Ich trauailed cr*i*and, my chekes⁶ ben made wery, myn eʒen failed, þer-whiles þat ich hoped in my God.
5. Hij þat hated me wyþ wylle ben multiplied oʒa*i*ns myn heued.
6. ⁷Myn enemys þat pursued me wro*n*gfullich ben conforted; ich ʒelde hem þan þe⁸ þynges þat ich ne bi-na*m*⁹ hem nouʒt.
7. Ha God, þou wost myn vncona*n*dnes, and my trespasses ne ben nouʒt hid fram me.
8. Lord, ne be*n* hij nouʒt aschamed i*n* me þat abiden þe, Lord of vertuʒ.

---

¹ MS. *latails*. ² fol. 61. ³ Instead of *ʒeue*. ⁴ Ps. 66, MS. ⁵ MS. *ciruaitis*.
⁶ MS. *cheked*. ⁷ fol. 61*b*. ⁸ MS. þe þe. ⁹ MS. *nebi ram*.

---

33. *shete*] put: cu*m*pany: mau-metries.
34. O: batayles: Ethiopenes Ethiopenes.
35. O.
36. —2. *syngeþ*: styeþ: atte est.
37. ioie: heryng.
38. wonderful: ʒeue.

68. 1. O: —*me*.

2. fest: gryn*n*: is.
3. couatice ablent.
4. chekes: —þat: hepid (!).
5. *w.w.*] wylfullych: beþ+beþ: mult.+aboue þe heres of my*n* heued or.
6. þe þe] in: —*ne*.
7. O: wote: vncu*n*nyng: —*ne*.
8. —*ne*: habydeþ.

9. Lord, God of Israel, hij þat sechen þe ne be nouȝt counfounded vp me.
10. For ich suffred for þe reproces, confucioun couerd my face.
11. Ich am made strange to my breþer and pilgrime to þe childer of my moder.
12. For þe loue of þyn hous susteined me, and þe repruces[1] of þe repruceand þe fellen vp me.
13. And ich fasted for þe helþe of my soule, and þat hys made to me[2] in reproceing' þurȝ mani.
14. And ich made þe haire my cloþyng', and ich am made to hem into p[ar]ables.
15. And þe pouer þat were in her pouerte spaken oȝains me; and þe riche [3]þat diden her glotenie maden o me fables.[4]
16. For-soþe, Lord God, ich helded my praier in þe time of þy[5] quemeing.
17. Here me for þe[6] michelnes of þy mercy and þe soþenes[7] of þyn helþe.
18. Defende me fram synȝe, þat y ne be nouȝt fastened þer-in; deliuer me fram hem þat hated me, and fram þe temptaciouns of fondes (!).
19. Þe pines of helle ne turment me nouȝt; ne depenes[8] ne dou-oure me nouȝt; ne þe fende ne destreingne nouȝt on me his mouþe.
20. Here me, Lord, for blisful ys þy mercy; loke to me efter þe mychilnes of þy pytes.
21. And ne turne nouȝt[9] þy face fram þy childe; here me hastilich, for ich am trubled.
22. Ȝyf kepe to my soule, and deliuer it of synȝe, and defende me oȝain myn ene-mys.
23. Þou wost my reproceyng and my confisioun (!) and my shame.[10]

---

[1] There is a horizontal stroke through the lower part of the p.   [2] MS. come.
[3] fol. 62.   [4] MS. fabled.   [5] MS. my.   [6] for þe repeated in MS.   [7] þ on erasure.   [8] Second e added over line.   [9] o corrected from a.   [10] MS. shante.

---

9. —þe ne.
10. reproues+&: confusion.
11. broþerin: chyldren.
12. reproues of men reprouyng.
13. And ich ... soule] & ych helyd my soule with fastyng: come] to me: reproue per (!).
14. here: parables.
15. pouert: of me fables.
16. put oute m. pr.+to þe: þi quememyng (!).

17. gretenes.
*18. —ne: of þe fendes.
19. paynes: —ne: me ... dououre]: noȝt me no þe depnes deuour: no: ne destreingne nouȝt] distrue me noȝt or constreyne.
20. mekefull.
21. —ne: —nouȝt: sturbled.
22. aȝens.
23. wote: reprouyng: confusion: schame.

* fol. 26b.

24. Alle þat trublen me, ben in þy syȝt; my hert abode reproce and [1]me-sayes.

25. And ich susteined reproces þat were made sori; and he nas nouȝt, and hy [2] ne fond nouȝt hym þat conforted hym.

26. And þe wicked ȝauen to me iuel for gode, and in my nede hij compassed me wyþ reproceynges.

27. Be her malice made in dampnacion to-fore hem, and in ȝeldyng' and [3] in sclaunder.

28. Ben her eȝen [4] made derke, þat hij ne seiȝ nouȝt, and her rigge alwaies into croked þynges.

29. Helde vp hem þyn yre, and þe vengeaunce [5] of þyne yre take hem.

30. Be her wonyng made wylde; and þer ben non þat wone in her tabernacle.

31. For hi pursuden hym þat tou smote, and hij laiden sorow up sorow of hys woundes.

32. Sett wikkednes vp her wickednes, þat hij ne entren nouȝt in-to þy ryȝtfulnes.

33. Ben hij don out of þe boke of liueand, and ben hij nouȝt wryten wyþ þe ryȝtful.

34. Ich am pouer and sorow[6]and; ha God, þyn helþe toke me.

35. Y shal hery þe name of God wyþ songe; and y shal heryen hym wiþ heryyng'.

36. And þat þyng' shal plesen to God vp sacrifice of a ȝonge chalf bryngand out hornes and clees.

37. Sen þe pouer and gladen; secheþ [7] our Lord, and our soule shal liuen.

38. For our Lord herd þe pouer, and he despised nouȝt þe cheson.

39. Hereen hym þe heuens and erþe, þe see and alle þynges crepand in hem.

---

[1] fol. 62b.   [2] MS. hene.   [3] Here a y follows in the MS., which spoils the sense.   [4] Here make has been dotted out.   [5] MS ven vengeaunce.   [6] fol. 63.   [7] þ on erasure.

---

24. sturbleþ: reproues: mysays.
25. reproues: was: hene ne] y: conforte me.
26. enclosed: reproues.
27. —y.
28. —ne: se: in crokednes.
29. Schede.
30. be þer: tabernacles.
31. þat] &.
32. —ne.
33. ryȝtf.+men.
34. —ha.
37. glade+þay: seche: ȝour.
38. chosyn.
39. Heryeþ: —þe: —þe.

40. For God shal make sauf þe folk[1] of Syon, and þe seges of heuen shul ben fulfild.

41. And hij shul wonen þer, and hij shul purchasen it in heritage.

42. And þe sede of his seruauntes shal haue it; and hij þat louen his name shal wonen þer-inne.

[1]PSALM 69 (70).

1. ȝeue kepe, God, to my helpe, and haste þe, Lord, to helpe me.
2. Hij þat tempten my soule ben to-gidres confounded and asshamed.
3. [2]Hij þat willen [me] iuels ben turned oȝainward, and ben asshamed.
4. Hij þat sayen to me, Sorow! sorow! ben hij turned by-hynde rygge[3] and asshamed as sone.
5. Hij þat sechen þe, glade[4] and [in] þe ioie; and sayen hij alway þat louen þyn helpe, Be our Lord heried.
6. Ich am for-soþe nedeful and pouer; Lord, helpe þou me.
7. Þou art min help and my delyuerour; Lord, ne[5] dwelle þou nouȝt.

[6]PSALM 70 (71).

1. Lord, ich hoped in þe; ne be y nouȝt confounded wyþ-outen ende; deliuer me, and defende me fram iuel in þy ryȝtfulnes.
2. Bowe to me þyn ere, and saue me.
3. Be þou to me defendour in God and in stede warnist, þat tou make me sauf.
4. For þou art made my fastenynge and my socour.
5. Ha my God, defende me fram þe honde of þe synȝer, and fram þe honde doand oȝains þe lawe, and of þe wicked.

---

[1] Ps. 67, MS. being expuncted.   [2] fol. 63b.   [3] MS. rynge.   [4] MS. gladen, the n, however, being expuncted.   [5] MS. me.   [6] Ps. 68, MS.

---

40. þe seges] setes.
41. gete it by h.

*6. F. s. ych: hepe (!).
7. delyuerer: —me.

69. 1. Godd take kepe.
2. tempe (!): conf. to-gyders.
3. wyll me euyll: be þay asch.
4. byhynde .. sone] bacheward & a. on one.
5. & —[in] þe.

70. 1. —ne.
2. saue—me.
4. —made: fastnes: refute.
5. O: honde doand oȝ. þe] doyng aȝens þi (!).

* fol. 27.

6. For, Lord, þou art my paciencie(!), [1]and þou art, Lord, myn hope fram myn ȝouþe.

7. In þe ich am confermed of þe wombe, and þou art my defendour.

8. My songe is [2] euer in þe; ich am made wonder to many; and þou art stronge helper.

9. Be my mouþe fulfild of hereyng¹, þat ich synge alday þy glorie and þy gretnes.

10. Ne cast me nouȝt oway in time of elde, and ne forsake me nouȝt, whan my uertu failleþ.

11. For myn enemys saiden to me, and hij þat kept my soule made conseil in on;

12. Saiand, God haþ for-saken hym; pursueþ him, and takeþ hym, for þer nys non þat defendeþ hym.

13. Ne be þou nouȝt, God, fer fram me; ha my God, loke into myn[3] helpe.

14. Ben þe bacbitand my soule confunded, and failen[4] hij; ben hij couerd wyþ confusyon and shame, þat sechen iuel to me.

15. Ich for-soþe shal hope in þe, and [5]y shal grant to þe my uoice vp alle þyne heryyng¹.

16. My mouþe shalle shewe þy ryȝtfulnes, and ich daie þyn helþe.

17. For ich ne knew no lettrure; y shal entren in-to þe myȝttes of our Lord; ha Lord, y shal þenchen of þyn onliche riȝtfulnes.

18. God, þou tauȝtest me fram my ȝouþe, and vnto now y shal tellen forþ þy wonders.

19. And vnto vlde and elde, God, ne forsake[6] þou me nouȝt,

20. Þer-whiles þat ich telle þyn helpe to ich a kynde þat hys to comen.

21. Ha, God, þou shewest þy myȝt and þy ryȝtfulnes vn-to þe heȝest þynges, þat tou madest grete and wonderful; ha, God, who his liche to þe?

---

[1] fol. 64. [2] *is* added over line. [3] MS. twice *God fer . . . myn*. [4] MS. *fainlen*. [5] fol. 64b. [6] *a* corrected from *o*.

---

6. paciens.
7. confirmyd: wombe + of my moder wombe.
8. art + a.   9. herying: ioie.
10. —*Ne*: age: —*ne*.
11. *hij þat*] þat (*added over line*) þai.
12. forsake hym + þat: is.
13. —*Ne*: —*ha*.

14. fayle: euyls.
15. F. s. y.
16. scwe (!).
17. —*ne*: þi myȝtes: —*ha lord*: on.
18. w. + & (!).
19. age & age: —*ne*.
20. *ic ha*] ech.
21. O: shewyd: —*ha*.

22. Hou many tribulaciouns, many and wicked, shewedestou to me? and þou turned quiked me; and þou laddest me eft fram þe dep-nes of þerþe.

23. Þou multiplied þyn heryynge, and þou turned conforted me.

[1] 24. For y shal shryue to þe in wordes of songe þyn soþenes; ha God, y shal syngen to þe in harp, þou art þe holi of Israel.

25. My lippus shul gladen whan ich haua(!) songen to þe, and al-so my soule, þat tou bouȝt oȝain.

26. Bote my tunge shal þenchen alday þy riȝtfulnes, as hij, þat sechen me with [2] iuel, han ben counfounded and asshamed.

[3] PSALM 71 (72).

1. Ha God, ȝyf þo [4] þy iugement to þe kyng' and þy riȝtfulnes to þe kynges sone,

2. To iuge þe folk' in ryȝtfulnes and þe rebels to þe [in] iugement.

3. Take þe gode pees to folk' and þe [ryȝtful] ryȝtfulnes.

4. He shal iugen þe rebels of þe folk', and shal make sauf þe gode childer of þe rebels, and he shal meken þe fals chalangeours.

5. And þe ryȝtful shul dwellen wyþ God and to-fore his trone in kyndes of kyndes.

6. He shal descenden as rain into floes and as droppinges droppand on þerþe.

[5] 7. Ryȝtfulnes and waxing of pees shal arisen, to þat þe soule of Crist be don oway fram hys body.

8. And he shal lord-ship fram þe see [to þe see], and fram þe flode vnto þe termes of þe world.

---

[1] fol. 65. [2] MS. wich. [3] Ps. 69, MS. [4] MS. þou, the u being expuncted with two dots. [5] fol. 65b.

---

22. schewstow: eft] eftson.
24. —ha.
25. haue: —oȝain.
26. wich] with.
71. 1. —Ha: þou: dome.
2. deme: rebeli to þe in dome.
3. & þe+riȝtful.
*4. deme: chalagours (!).
5. in kynde.
6. into a flees: dropes droppyng.
7. plenteousnes: —oway: hys] þe.
8. haue lordeschip: se+to þe se.

* fol. 27b.

9. þe Echiopes[1] shul fallen to-for hym, and his enemis shul likken þerþe.

10. þe kynges of Thars and yles shal offren to hym ȝyftes; þe kynges of Arabum and of Saba shul bryngen to hym ȝyftos.

11. And alle kynges shal anouren hym, and alle men shul seruen hym.

12. For þat he deliuered þe pouer fram yuel of þe myȝtful, and þe pouer, to wham nas no helper.

13. He shal spare þe pouer and þe mesais, and make sauf þe soules of þe pouer.

14. He shal raunsoun her soules fram vsures and wickednes; and her name shal be worþshipful to-forn him.

15. And he shal lyue, and hym shal bi ȝeuen of þe seruice of gode; and hij shul worþship hym alway þer-of and blisccn hym aldaye.

16. Stablenes shal be in erþe amonge þe gode of þe world; þe frut of þe world shal wexen atte Goddes wille, and þe werkes of þe ryȝtful shul florissen in heuen as hay of þerþe.

17. Be his name blisced in heuens; hys name shal lasten to-fore þe sunne.[2]

18. And alle þe kyndes of þe erþe shul ben blisced in hym, alle folk' shul heryen hym.

19. Blisced be our Lord, God of Israel, þat doþ wondres al ou-liche.

20. And be þe [3] name of his maieste blisced wyþ-outen ende; and alle þerþe shal be fulfild of his maieste; be it don, be it don.

[4] PSALM 72 (73).

1. Hou gode his þe God of Israel to hem þat ben ryȝtful of hert.

2. Myn fete for-soþe ben nere stired; myn ouȝt[5]-goinges ben neȝe helded out.

3. For ich loued þe vp wicked, seand pees of synȝers.

---

[1] The second *e* is added over the line.   [2] MS. *sunme*.   [3] MS. *þy*.   [4] Ps. 70, MS.
[5] MS. *my nouȝt*.

---

9. Ethiopens.
10. Tarsis.
11. honour: seruy.
12. —þat: fram+þe: was: helpe.
13. misays.
14. her] he: vsureres &+fram: worschypfull.
15. be ȝif: wyrschyp.

16. atte] at.
17. dwel: sunne.
20. þy] þe: fulf.] blyssyd.

72. 1. —þe: —of Israel.
2. F. s. my f.: —nouȝt: neȝh sched out.

4. For abidei*ng*¹ nis nouȝt *in*¹ her deþ, and fastenyng¹ nys nouȝt in her pines.

²5. Þe ryȝtful ne ben nouȝt in t*r*auail of þe wicked, ne wyþ wicked me*n* ne shul hij nouȝt ben turmented.

6. For-þy helde pride hem; and hij ben cou*e*rd wyþ her wickednes and vndebonerte.

7. Her wickednes ȝede forþe as of grees; hij shul be born in-to þe tale*n*t of her hertes.

8. Hij þouȝten and spake wyckednisses, and hij spak wickednesses o*n* heȝt.

9. Hij sett her mouþe to þe heue*n*, and her tunges passeden in herþe.

10. For-þy shul my folk¹ be turned here, and ful daies shul be fou*n*den in he*m*.

11. And þe wicked seiden, Hou is God, and ȝif wisdom be on heȝt?

12. Se þes synȝers³; a*n*d þe wexand in þe world hadden riches.

13. And ich seide, For-þy ich made mi*n* hert ryȝtful wyþ-outen acheson, and ich wesshe myn hondes amonge þe vnwe*m*med.

14. And ich was turmented al daye, and my chastisynge was in þe morowen*in*g.

15. Ȝyf ich seid, Y shal tellen in þys man*er*, se, ich ⁴repr*u*ued þe in kynde of þyn chosen.

16. Ich wende þat ich knewe hym in þat trauail is to-fore me,

17. Þer-whiles þat ich entre in-to þe sa*nc*tuari of God and vnder-stonde⁵ in her endynges.

18. For-soþe þou sett þe wicked for trecheries; þou cast hem oway, þer-wyles þat hij were anheȝed.⁶

---

¹ MS. *and*. ² fol. 66*b*. ³ *y* corrected from *u*. ⁴ fol. 67. ⁵ Here follows *and*, which is expuncted. ⁶ MS. *andheȝed*, with the first *d* dotted out.

---

4. is: 1. *and*] *in*: is: peynes.
5. —*ne*: no: *ne* .. *hij*] þay schal.
6. pride helde: vnbonerte.
8. wykkydnes: wykkydnes *in* heȝht.
9. —þe: tung past in erþe.
10. þ*er*-for.
*12. incresyng: p*er*chast.

13. þ*er*-fore: cause: innocentes.
14. chasteseyng: mornyng.
15. *in* þ. *m*] þus: lo: reproued: —*in*.
17. þ*er*-*whiles*] To: *endynges*] last endes.
18. gyles: —*hem*: to-whyls— þ*at*: arered.

* fol. 28.

19. Hou ben hij made in desconforte? hij shul faillen sudeinliche, and shul perissen for her wickednes.

20. Lord, as sweuen of men risand oʒains þyn heuen, þou shalt bringen her ymage to nouʒt.

21. For myn hert is enflamned, & myn kidnares[1] ben chaunged; and ich am b[r]ouʒt to noʒt, and ich ne wist it nouʒt.

22. Ich am made atte as a mere wyþ-outen resoun, and ich am a[l]way wyþ þe.

23. Þou held my ryʒt honde, and þou laddest me in þy wille, and þou toke me wyþ glorie.

24. For wat þynge ys to me in heuen, and what wolde ich of þe up þerþe?

25. [2]My flesshe failed, and myn hert; þe Gode of myn hert, and my part hys wyþ God wyþ-outen ende.

26. For se, hii þat ben alloined þan fram þe shul perissen; þou lest alle þat don hordom wyþ-outen þe.

27. For-soþe god þyn[g] it is to me to draw[3] to God and sett myn hope in our Lord,

28. Þat ich shewe alle þyn prechynges in þe passyngᵗ of þe soules of þe saued.

PSALM 73 (74).

1. Whi, Lord, put þou us out on ende? þyn ire ys wroþe vp þe men of þe world?

2. Be þou by-þenchand of þy gaderyngᵗ, þat tou[4] hate-dest fram þe bygynnyngᵗ.

3. Ha God of heuen, þou bouʒt oʒain þe synʒes of mannes kynde, in which heuen þou wonest in þat kynde.[5]

4. Lyft[6] þyn hondes oʒain þe pride of þe wicked on ende; hou michel his þe weried enemy in holy þynge!

---

[1] The r differs in shape from either of the usual forms of that letter in the MS., and almost looks like an i with an accidental dot at the right side of the upper end.   [2] fol. 67b.
[3] MS. toward.   [4] Here follows hadd, which is however expuncted.   [5] MS. kymde.
[6] ft on erasure.

---

19. into.
20. Lor: dremyng.
21. inflammyd: kydners: broʒt: —ne.
22. at þe: beste: alway.
23. ioie.
24. —what.

26. lo: aloyned: loste: fornicacion.
27. gode—þyn it: toward] to draw.
73. 1. into þe ende.
2. hatedest] hadd.
3. O: kymde] kynde.
4. into þe ende: wer.] wickyd: holynes.

EARLY ENGLISH PSALTER. PSALM 73 (74). 89

5. And hij þat hated þe, gloried hem in-myddes of þy passion.

[1]6. Hij sett her toknes,[2] and ne knewe hem nouȝt as in his passyng⸍ vp sweuen.

7. Hij forsoken hijs teching⸍ as þourȝ þe wickednes of her hertes in pride, and laid it vnder þourȝ mys-bileue.

8. Hij aliȝted[3] at þe fur sanctuari, and defouleden in erþe þe tabernacle of þy name.

9. Here kynreden seiden to-gidres in her hert, Make we resten in erþe alle þe solempne daies of God.

10. We ne seȝe nouȝt our toknes, þer is nomore no prophete; and hij ne shul no more knowe vs?

11. Þyng⸍ to[4] witen, God, þat þyn enemy shal reproce þe, þe aduersarie draw out þy name in-to ende.

12. Where-to turnestou þyn honde and þy ryȝt-half in-to ende in-middes of þy bosome.[5]

13. For-soþe our kyng hys to-fore þe werldes; he has[6] wroȝt helþe amiddes þerþe.

[7]14. Þou confermed þyn halwen in þy uertu, and croused þe myȝt of fendes in peynes.

15. Þou to-brake þe pouste of þe fende, and ȝaf hym mete to þe folk⸍ of Ethiope.[8]

16. Þou brake þe welles and þe brokes, and þou dried þe flodes of Echan.

17. Þe day ys þyn, and þe nyȝt ys þyn; þou forgedest þe dawyng⸍ and þe sunne.

---

[1] fol. 68.   [2] *toknes* repeated in MS.   [3] *iȝ* corrected from *u*.   [4] Here *me* follows, but has been expuncted.   [5] MS. *be some*.   [6] *has* is preceded by an *a*, which is however expuncted.   [7] fol. 68*b*.   [8] *t* corrected from *c*.

---

5. —*And* : glorified : þy] þe.
6. —*ne* : dreme.
7. þurȝt : þurȝh + w*i*ckydnes & þurȝh.
8. fure + þe : defoiled.
9. kynrede.
10. —*ne* : —*ne*.
*11. Godd, how longe schall þine

e. reproue þe? þe adu. makeþ þin
n. in vayne into þe e.
12. riȝt honde into + þe : amiddes —*of* : bosum.
14. *conf. þ. h.*] confirmyd þe world : of þe fende.
15. þou brake : pouer.
16. *b.*] reueres : Ethan.
17. made þe mornyng.

* fol. 28*b*.

18. Þou madest alle þe cuntres of þerþe, somer and veir; þou formedest þo þynges.

19. Be þo þenchend on þys¹ þynge; þe enemy reproued þe, our Lord, and þe folk⹀ vnwyse en-engred þy name.

20. Ne ȝyf nouȝt to þe fendes þe soules shryuand to þe, and ne for-ȝete² þou nouȝt into ende þe soules of þy pouer.

21. Loke to þy testament, for þat hij þat ben cuuaytyse in erþe ben³ fulfild of werkes of wickednes.

22. Þe made mylde ne ben nouȝt turned confus; þe pouer and þe misais shul herien þy name.

⁴23. Arise, God, iuge my cause; be þou þenchand of þyn repruces of hem þat ben alday of þe vnwys.

24. Ne for-ȝete nouȝt þe werkes of þyn enemys; þe pride of hem þat hateþ þe, mounteþ euermore.

⁵PSALM 74 (75).

1. Ha God, we shal shriue to þe; we shul shriue and clepe þy name.

2. We shul tellen þy wondres; whan y shal take tyme, y shal iugen ryȝtfulnesses.

3. Þe erþe his made melting, and al þat wonen in it; ⌊y⌋ confermed my stablenes.

4. Ich seide to þe wicked, Ne willeþ nouȝt do wicked-lich; and ich seid to þe trespassand, Ne willeþ an-heȝe ȝour heuedes.⁶

5. Ne willeþ an-heȝe ȝour heued on heȝe, ne willeþ nouȝt speke wickednes oȝains God.

---

¹ Here *sy* follows, but has been struck out. (expuncted).   ⁴ fol. 69.   ⁵ Ps. 72, MS.   ² MS. *fort ȝete*.   ³ Here follows *tm*   ⁶ The first *e* is corrected from *o*.

---

18. made : vere : *f. þo þ.*] made þese.
19. Be *þou þencher of* : *en engred*] engredyd.
20. —*Ne* : fendes — *þe* : know-legyng : —*ne* : forȝete — *þou* : *into* +*þe* : *þe pouer*+men.
21. for—*þat* : couatise : fullyd —*of werkes*.
22. þe meke man† confused be noȝt t.

23. *iuge*] & deme : *be þ. þ.*] be-þenche : reproues.
24. —*Ne* : *mounteþ*] ascendit (!).

74. 1. —*Ha* : clepe+in.
2. deme riȝtfulnes.
3. dwellyþ þer-in & ich coufirmyd.
4. *Ne willeþ*] wyłł ȝe : þe] men : —*ne* : wyłł ȝe noȝt enhiȝe ȝour heued.
5. —*Ne* : Wyl ȝe noȝt enhiȝe : *ne w. n. sp.*] & spekeþ noȝt.

† MS. ma*n*d, d *being dotted out.*

6. For þat noiþer of þe est, ne out of þe west, ne of þe wilde mounteins; for God ys iuge.

7. He mekeþ[1] hym, and heʒeþ hym, for þat grace [2]ys in þe honde of our Lord ful of sharpenes medeled[3] wyþ lyþenes.

8. And he bewed[4] fram þys to þys; his iugement forsoþe nys nouʒt made littel; alle þe synʒers of þerþe shul han þer-of.

9. Y shal tellen for-soþe þe ryʒtfulnes of our Lord in þe world, and y shal syngen to þe God of Iacob.

10. Y shal breken alle þe heuedes of sinʒers; and þe heued of þe ryʒtful shul ben anheʒed.

[5]PSALM 75 (76).

1. God ys knowen in þe Iude, hys grete name is in Israel.

2. And his stede is made in pees, and hys wonyyng' ys in heuen.

3. Þere he brake myʒtes; bowe, swerde, shelde, and bataile.

4. Þou art aliʒtand wonderfullich of mounteines euer lastand; and alle þe vnwise of hert ben trubled.

5. Alle þe vnwys men perissed þurʒ her pynes, and hij ne founde nouʒt of her godenes in her hondes.

6. Ha þou God of Jakob, [6]hij. þat diden sinʒes[7] of pride perissed for þy blamyng'.

7. Þou art dredeful; and who shal stonden oʒains þe fram þan in þy vengeaunce?

8. Þou madest iugement herd fram heuen; and mannes kynde trembled, and held hem stylle.

9. Whan God ros in iugement, so þat he shuld make sauf al þe milde of mankynde.

10. For cosinage of man shal shriue to þe, and þe holinesses of þoʒtes shal don grete honur to þe.

---

[1] MS. *makeþ*. [2] fol. 69*b*. [3] The last *e* is added over the line. [4] The first *e* is corrected from *o*. [5] Ps. 73, MS. [6] fol. 70. [7] *inʒ* corrected from *un*.

---

6. —þat: noþer: no—out: no.
7. mekeþ: ful medeled with scharpnes of swetnes.
8. bowed: dome: is.
9. F. s. y.

*75. 1. Ieurye h. n. is g.
2. wonyng.

4. *al.*] liʒtyng: sturbled.
5. paynes: —*ne*: of—*her*.
6. —*Ha*.
7. with-stonde þe.
8. dome.
9. dome: *milde*] meke.
10. *c.*] þouʒt: holines of þouʒte.

* fol. 29.

11. Voweþ[1] and ȝeldeþ to þe Lord, your God, ȝe alle þat bringe ȝiftes in his cumpas,

12. To þe dredeful and to hym þat doþ oway þe gost of princes; to þe dredeful at alle þe kynges of erþe.

[2]PSALM 76 (77).

1. Ich cried wyþ my[3] voice vn-to our Lord, wyþ my voice to God; and he vnderstode me.

2. Ich by-souȝt God in þe daye of tribulacion wyþ myn hondes, and by nyȝt oȝains hym, and nam nouȝt deceiued.

[4] 3. My soule for-sake to be conforted; ich was bi-þenchand on God, and ich delited; and ich was adrad, & my gost failed.

4. Myn eȝen toke wakeinges, ich was trubled, and y ne spake nouȝt.

5. Ich þouȝt elde daies, and ich had in mynde ȝeres euerlasting'.

6. And ich biþouȝt by nyȝt in myn hert, and ich traualed and clensud my gost.

7. Þynge to witen, ȝif God shal put owai my gost wiþ-outen ende, oþer he ne sett nouȝt þat he[5] ȝit be more pleisant?

8. Oþer he shal kerue oway on ende his mercy fram kinde vn-to kynde?

9. Oþer God shal {forȝeten to haue mercy, oþer he shal holde his mercyes in his wraþþe?

10. And ich seid, Ich by-gan nov; þis is þe chaungeinge of þe heȝe ryȝthalf.

11. Ich was bi-þenchand of þe workes of our Lord; for-þy y shal be bi-þenchand fram þe bi-gynnyng of þi meruailes.

12. And y shal þenchen in alle þyne werkes, and y shal rse in alle þy fundynges.

[6] 13. Ha God, þy way his in holy; who is grete God as on God is? artou God þat doþ wonders?

---

[1] MS. *Boweþ*.   [2] Ps. 74, MS.   [3] A *g* follows but is expuncted.   [4] fol. 70*b*.
[5] MS. adds *be* after *he*.   [6] fol. 71.

---

11. Voweþ : ȝeld.
12. of þe erþe.

76. 1. *vnto*] to : *me*] to me.
2. *and nam*] y am : desayued.
3. for-soke.
4. wakynges+& : st*ur*-bled : — ne.
6. *biþouȝt*] þouȝt.

7. þynge . . . ȝif] weþer : put] noȝt cast : or he schal noȝt sett : — ȝit be : plesyng.
8. ket away into þe e. : into.
10. heȝe r.] riȝthalfe of þe hyȝe Godd.
12. vsie : fyndyngis.
13. —*Ha* : holynes : *on*] grete oure : *artou G.*] þou Godd art.

14. þou made þy uertu knowen to folkes; and þou bouȝtest in þy myȝt þy folke, þe childer of Jacob and of Joseph, þe whiche loued þe.

15. Ha God, men seȝen þe, and dreden; and þe wicked ben trubled, dredand wheþer þou be God oþer non.

16. Þe gretnes of þe soune of men ȝaf voice to þe, and þe derked in þy lawe ȝaf voice to þe.

17. For þy[1] wreches passen þe voice of þy manaces in cumpase.

18. Þy shi[n]-inges[2] liȝteþ þe world,[3] and mankynde is stired, and his trubled.

19. Þy techinge and þy amonestinge ben in þe world in many men; and þyn dedes ne shul nouȝt ben knowen.

20. [*English omitted.*]

[4] PSALM 77 (78).

1. Ha ȝe mi folk', vnderstondeþ my lawe, boweþ[5] ȝour eren to [6] þe wordes of myn mouþe.

2. Ich opened mouþe in parables, and y shal speke proposes fram þe bygynnyng'.

3. Hou many þynges we knewen and herden, & our faders told os [7] hem.

4. Hij ne ben nouȝt hid fram her sones in an oþer kynde,

5. Telland þe herieing' of our Lord and his vertu and his wondres, þat he did.

6. And he stired witnes in Iacob, and sett lawe in Israel.

7. [*Translation omitted, as also the Latin of the next verse.*]

8. Þe childer, þat shul be born and arisen, shul[8] tellen to her childer,

---

[1] Here *werkes* follows, but is expuncted.   [2] The final *s* is written on erasure.
[3] MS. *worled*, but *e* is expuncted.   [4] Ps. 75, MS.   [5] þ on erasure of *n*; then an *o* follows, which is expuncted.   [6] fol. 71*b*.   [7] MS. *toldos*.   [8] MS. *soul*.

---

14. folk: *f.*] pepiH : &—*of.*
15. —*Ha*: *dreden...non*] douted wheþer þou wer Godd or noȝt and þe w. beþ sturbled.
*16. *derked*] derk men : þy] þe.
17. *wr.*] werkes : manace.
18. þe schynynges liȝted : —*his.*
19. amoneschyng : —þe : —*ne.*
20. þou lede oute þi folk as schepe in þe kepyng of Moyses & Aaron.

77. 1. —*Ha*: law+& : *e.*] here.
2. Y schal openye my m.: purposes.
3. herde & knewe : teld vs.
4. —*ne* : be.
5. vertus.
6. *st.*] arerid.
7. How many þinges he sent to our faders to make knowyng to her childer.
8. [*Latin and English omitted.*]

* fol. 29*b*.

9. Þat hij sett her hope in God, and ne for-ȝete nouȝt þe werkes of God, & seche is comaundementȝ;

10. Þat hij ne be nouȝt made as her faders wicked kynde[1] away mode[2] of hert.

11. Kynde þat ne dresced noȝt his hert, and his gost nis nouȝt trowed wyþ God.

12. Mennes sones of Effrem,[3] bendand bowe and sendand, ben turned oȝain in daie of bataile.

13. Hij ne kept nouȝt þe testament of God, and hij ne wold nouȝt gon in his [4]lawe.

14. And hij for-ȝaten his gode dedes & hijs wondres,[5] which he shewed to hem.

15. He dede wondres in þe londe of Egipt to-fore her fadres, in þe felde of Thaneos.

16. He brake þe see, & lad hem out, and sett þe wateres as in a gourde.

17. And lad hem out in a cloude of daie, and alle þe niȝt in lyȝtyng' of fur.

18. He brake þe stone in desert, and watered hem as in michel depenes.

19. And he broȝt out þe water of þe ston, and broȝt waters as flodes.

20. And ȝete hij laiden her force to synnen to hym, and stired in ire þe heȝe in dride stede.

21. & hij tempteden God in her hertes, and hij asked me[te] to her willes.

22. And hij spak iuel of God, and seiden, Ne myȝt nouȝt God diȝten bord in wildernes.

23. For he smot þe ston; and waters ran out, and welles token[6] waters.

24. Þyng' to wyten, ȝyf he myȝt ȝyf brede oþer dyȝt borde to hys folk'.

[7]25. For-þy God herd þes wordes, and for-bare þe forsaid þynges; and fur is aliȝt in þe childer of Jakob, & ire aros in þe childer of Israel.

---

[1] MS. kymde.   [2] Read and wemode?   [3] MS. Effremm, the latter m being expuncted.   [4] fol. 72.   [5] Here follows weche, which is dotted out.   [6] MS. to hem.   [7] fol. 72b.

---

9. —ne.
10. —ne : kynde : aw. m.] & scharp.
11. —ne : nis] as : trowyng.
12. bendyng+her.
13. —ne: —ne.
14. þat.
17. cl. of+þe.

20. hyȝ+Godd : drye.
21. mete.
22. —And: —ne: ordeyne+a.
23. to hem] toke.
24. þyng . . . ȝyf] weþer : myȝt +noȝt: o. d. b.] or ordeyne mete : pepiH.
25. þer-for : forb.] toke away.

EARLY ENGLISH PSALTER. PSALM 77 (78). 95

26. For þat hij ne bileued nouȝt in God, ne hoped nouȝt in his helþe.
27. And he comanded to þe cloudes abouen, and opened þe ȝates of heuen.
28. And he rained to hem manna for to ete, and ȝaf hem brede of heuen.
29. Man ete brede of aungels, and God sent hem mete and drynke to wille.
30. He bare ouer þe wynde of þe souþe fram þe heuen, & brouȝt in þe winde of Affryk' in his vertu.
31. & he rained vp hem pudre, flesshes, and volatils feþered as grauel of þe se.
32. And hij fellen amiddes her castels and abouten her tabernacles.¹
33. And hij eten, and ben fild greteliche; and he ȝaf hem her desire, and hij ne were nouȝt deceiued of her desire.
34. And ȝete was her mete in ²her mouþe; and þe ire of God steȝe vp hem.
35. And he sloȝe her fatt, and destourbed þe chosen of Israel fram vengeaunce.
36. And ȝit hij sinned in alle þes þynges, and ne trowed noȝt in his wonders.
37. And her daies faileden in vanite,³ and her ȝeres wyþ hastyng'.
38. And as he sloȝt hem, hij soȝten hym, and turned oȝain, and com to him in þe daweing'.
39. And hij bi-þouȝten hem þat God is her help, and þe heȝe God his her oȝain-bigger.
40. And hij loued him in her mouþe, and liȝed to him in her tunges.
41. And her hert [nas nouȝt riȝt wyþ hym, & hij ne ben nouȝt] holden trewe in his testament.
42. He is forsoþe merciable, and he shal be made helpe to her sinȝes, and he shal nouȝt for-don hem.
43. And he wex so þat he did owai his ire, and he ne aliȝt nouȝt al his ire;

---

¹ Here and in other places where the word occurs, er is abbreviated by a stroke through the upper part of the b.   ² fol. 73.   ³ MS. vainte.

---

*26. —ne: ne] &.
27. com.] hote.   28. —for.
30. fram—þe.
31. v.] wyld foule.
32. castelles—and.
33. —ne: dessayuyd.
34. ascendid.
35. fatt+bestes: desturbled.
36. —ne.
37. vanite.
38. sloȝe.
41. hert+was noȝt riȝt with hym & þai be noȝt.
43. —ne.

* fol. 30.

44. And bi-þou3t hym þat hij ben flesshe, gost going and nou3t turneing o3ain.

45. Hou oft hij greued hym in wildernes[2]; hij somond him in ire in dryhede.

46. And hij ben conuerted, and temptedd God, and grueden þe holi of Israel.

47. Hij ne byþo3t hem nou3t of his help in þe daie þat he[3] bou3t hem fram þe honde of þe trubland hem;

48. As he sett in Egipt his toknes, and his wondres in þe felde of Thaneos.

49. And he turned her flodes in-to blode, and her raines þat hij ne shul nou3t drynk.

50. He sende in-to hem hounde-fle3es, and ete hem; and þe frosche, and he sprad hem abrode.

51. And he 3af her frute to þe lef-worme, and her trauails to þe grashope.

52. And he slo3e her uines wyþ hail and her mulbery-trews wyþ rim-frost.

53. He 3af her meres to hail and her habbeinges to fur.

54. He sent in-to hem þe ire of his indignacioun, indignacioun and ire, & tribulacioun in his sendeinges[4] bi wicked aungels.

55. He made waie to þe issu of his ire, and ne[6] spared nou3t her soules fram þe deþ, and he shette her meres[7] in deþ.

56. And he smote alle þe firstborn in þe londe of þe Egipt, þe first frutes of alle her trauails in þe tabernacles of Cham.

57. And he did owai his folk as shepe, and smote hem as a folk in desert.

58. And he lad hem in hope, and hij ne drad nou3t; and þo see couered her enemys.

---

[1] The London MS. begins this verse with a large ornamental initial letter, and a later hand has accordingly added the number 76 in the margin. [2] MS. *wildelnes*. [3] MS. *hem*, but the *m* is dotted out. [4] MS. *seideinges*. [5] fol. 74. [6] MS. *ne ne*. [7] MS. *medes*.

---

44. And+he.
45. wyldernes: sett: drynes.
47. *ne byþ. hem*] be-þou3t: disturblyng.
49. —*ne*: schuld.
50. sent: *spr. h. abr.*] disparpild hem.
51. fruyte: *l.w.*] ruste or lefeworme: trauayles.

52. mulbury tres: horefroste.
53. *He*] & he: bestes: possessions to þe fure.
54. hem—þe: ind. ind.—*and*: sendynges.
55. vschseu: *ne ne*] he: *medes*] bestes.
*58. —*ne*: þe.

* fol. 30b.

59. And he lad hem in-to þe mounteines of his halweinge, in-to þe mounteine þat is ryȝthalf purchased.

60. And he[1] kest oway folk' fram her face; and in lott he parted to hem þe londe in a corde of distribucioun.

61. And he did wonen in her tabernacles þe kindes of Israel.

62. And hij tempteden and greueden þe heȝe God, and ne kept nouȝt his witnisses.

63. And hii[2] turned hem, and hij ne kept noȝt þe couenaunt, as her faders ben turned into iuel maner.

64. And hij somened him in-to ire in her folies, and to en-vie hij cleped hym in þynges made wiþ fingirs.

65. God herd her folies, and refused hem, and brouȝt Israel greteliche to nouȝt.

66. And he putt oway þe tabernacle of Silo, þe tabernacle þer he woned in me[n].

67. And he ȝaf her vertu into wreched-hede, and here fairhede in þe hondes of þe enemy.

68. And he shett his folk' in a swerde, and despised his[3] heritage.

69. Fur brent her ȝongelinges, and her maidens ne ben nouȝt sorweand.

70. Her prestes fel in swerde, and her widowes ne were nouȝt wept þer-fore.

71. And our Lord is stired as slepand & as drynkand, drunken of wyn.

72. And he smote his enemys in þe hynder ende, and ȝaf to hem repruces wyþ-outen ende.

73. And he refuled þe tabernacle of Ioseph, and he ne ches nouȝt þe kynde of Effren.[4]

74. Ac he ches þe kynde of Iuda, þe mount Sion, which he loued.

---

[1] h on erasure. [2] hii corrected from he. [3] MS. hif. [4] MS. offren.

---

59. holynes: hys riȝthonde won.
60. departyd.
61. made: kynde.
62. temped (!): —ne: wytnes.
63. and—hij ne.
64. sett: with þynges made in careuyngges (ges begins a fresh line).
65. foly.
66. in me] among men.
67. wrechydnes: fairehode into.
68. in] to-geder with: his.
69. —ne.
70. —ne.
72. reproues.
73. refusid: —ne: effrem.
74. Bot: wh.] þat.

75. And he bigged his holines in vnicor*n*s in þe stede, þat he made in heue*n*s.

76. He ches Dauid his seruau*n*t, and toke hym vp out of þe flok of shepe; and holi chirche toke hym,

77. To fede Iacob, his seruant, and Isr*a*el, his heritage;

78. And he fed hem in þe in-nocence[1] of her hertes, and lad hem in þe vnderstondynges of her hondes.

[2]PSALM 78 (79).

1. Ha God, folk wyþ-outen lawe com fram þe londe of Vs into þyn heritage, into Iude; and hij filden þyn holy temple, and sett Ier*us*alem in þe kepei*n*g[4] of a man*er* of folk[4] þat was cleped Pomos.

2. Hij laiden þe dede bodis of þi[3] seruau*n*tʒ mete to þe foules of heue*n*, þe flesshe of þyn halwe*n* to bestes of þe erþe.

3. Hij [s]hadden her blode as wat*er* a-bouten Ier*us*alem; and þer nas no*n* 'þat biried hem.

4. We ben made in repr*o*ceing[4] to our neʒburʒs, scornynge and desceit to hem þat ben in our c*u*mpasse.

5. Vn-to wham, Lord, artov wroþe on onde? þi luf shal be alyʒt as fur.

6. Helde þyn ire into þe folk[4] þat ne knewe nouʒt þe, and in-to kyngdomes þat ne cleped nouʒt þy name.

7. For hij slowen Iacobes childer, and descou*n*forted his stede.

8. Ne þenche þou nouʒt on our old wickednes; sone take þy mercyes vs, for we ben made michel pouer.

9. Ha God, our helþe, helpe vs; and deliu*er* vs of iuels, Lord, for þy glorie of þy name; and for þy name, Lord, be mercyable to our synʒes.

---

[1] MS. *in nocente.*   [2] Ps. 77, MS.   [3] MS. *his.*   [4] fol. 75*b*.

---

75. *in v.*] as an vnicorne: heuen.
76. hy*m*—*vp*: *holi ch.*] fram behynde he*m* he.
78. i*n*nocence: hert.

78. 1. O: defoilyd.
2. *Hij*] þa: *his*] þi: heuen+&: holy me*n* to +þe.

3. sched: was: schuld bery.
4. reprouyng: *in our c.*] abou*t*e vs.
5. How long, Lorde, schaltow be wroþe i*n*to þe ende: loue.
*6. —*ne*: into þe k.
7. made his st. dissolate.
9. þe ioie.

* fol. 31.

10. Þat our enemys ne saien nouȝt peraunter in folkes,[1] Wher is her God? and wex it knowen in kynde to-fore our eȝen.

11. Þe wreche of þe blode of þyn seruauntes, þat his shad, þe waimentynge [of þe] fetered entre in þy syȝt.

[2] 12. Efter þe gretnes of þy myȝt þou shal welden þe sones of þe slain.

13. And ȝelde to our [3] neȝburs seven double in her bosme her lack'inge, wich, Lord, hij repruced þe.

14. For-soþe we, þy folk' and shepe of þy fold, shul shryue to þe in þe world.

15. In kynde [and kynde] we shul tellen þyn heryynge.

PSALM 79 (80).

1. Ha þou God, þat gouernest Israel, vnderstonde þat ladeþ Ioseph meke as shepe.

[4] 2. Þou þat [5] sittest up cherubyn, be þou made apert to-fore Effraim, Beniamin, and Manasse.

3. Stire,[6] Lord, þy myȝt, and cum, þat tou make us sauf.

4. Ha God conuerte vs, and shewe þy face, and we shul ben sauf.

5. Lord, God of vertu, þer-whiles þou wraþþest vp þe prayer of þy seruaunt,

6. Þou shalt confer'me vs in sharpnes of teres, and þou shalt ȝif vs waymentynge in mesure.

7. Þou sett vs in ȝain-siggeing to our neyburs, and our enemys scorned vs.

8. Ha God of vertuȝ, conuerte vs, and shew þi fac, and we shul be sauf.[8]

---

[1] Here follows an *s*, which is expuncted.   [2] fol. 76.   [3] Here follows *lord*, but it is expuncted.   [4] The English of this verse is written twice in the MS., the above text being preceded by: *þou þat sitest vp cherubyn* (the last three words are struck out by the corrector with red ink, but have no dots) *be þou made apert to-fore Effraim, Beniamyn and Masse* (!); but over the first word of this passage the corrector has written *va*, and over the last one *cat* (*vacat*).   [5] Followed by *sist*, which is expuncted.   [6] MS. *Stird*.
[7] fol. 76b.   [8] MS. *fauf*.

---

10. —*ne*: among folke: be it know among nacions.
11. w.+of men.
12. schalt haue: of men slaw.
13. seuenfolde: reproue þat þai reprouyd þe Lorde.
14. &+þe.
15. k.+& kynde: heryng.

79. 1. O: as+a.
3. Styr.
4. O: turne.
5. vertus to-whyls.
6. confirme.
7. into aȝeynesiggyng.
8. turne: safe.

EARLY ENGLISH PSALTER. PSALM 79 (80).

9. Þou broȝtest out þe .xij. kindes of Israel to Iacob sones out of Egipt, and kest hem out of þe felawship of men wiþ-outen law,[1] and settest hem in þe londe of bihest.

10. Þou was lader of wai in þe siȝt of Joseph, and sett her sones; and þerþe fulfild her childer.

11. Þe out-going of him couerd þe mounteins, and her childer þe heuens of God.

12. Þe kinde of Iacob sprad his childer vn-to þe see, and his[2] seruauntes vn-to þe flode.

13. Whi suffrestou, God, his stablenes ben destrued, and alle þat passen iuel waie de-foulen it?

14. Þe pri[3]de of hym haþ for-don hym, and þe onliche deuel of en-vie haþ bounden him.

15. Ha God of vertu, be þou turned; and loke fram heuen, and se and visite þis kynde.

16. And make hym þe which þy myȝt fourmed; and [loke] vp mennes sones which þou confermedest to þe.

17. Aliȝt þou þe fur, and dampne and for-lese þe iuel fram þe iugement of þy godhede.

18. Be þyn helpe made vp þe man of bliscing', and up mennes sones,[4] which þou fastened to þe.

19. And we depart nouȝt fram þe; and þou shalt quiken vs, and we shul klepe þy name.

20. Lord, God of vertuȝ, turne vs and conuerte vs, and[5] shewe us þy face: and we shul be sauf.

[6] PSALM 80 (81).

1. Gladeþ to God, our helper; singeþ to God of Iacob.

---

[1] MS. saw. [2] Followed by her (expuncted). [3] fol. 77. [4] Followed by a w, which is dotted out. [5] Followed by swe (expuncted). [6] Ps. 79, MS.

9. cast: cumpanye: saw] lawe.
11. goyng oute.
12. vnto — þe.
13. Godd whi sufferst þou: be: defoilid.
16. þe w.] þat: &+loke: men sonnes þat þou confourmyd.

17. þou þe] with: þi dome.
*18. men sonnes þat þ. made fast.
19. make qwyk.
20. —and conuerte vs: —us.

80. 1. h.+&.

* fol. 31b.

2. Takeþ a song, and heueþ[1] to hym liȝt[2]nes, sautre glad as wyþ ioie.

3. Gladeþ to hym in new seruise of songe, in the noble daie of ȝour solempnite.

4. For þat þis comaundement is in Israel, iugement is to God of Iacob.

5. God sett þis þynge witnes in Ioseph, as he shuld passen out of þe londe of Egipt; he herd þe tunge þat he ne knew nouȝt.

6. He turned his wille fram sinnes;[3] his hondes serued in treuþe.

7. Þou, man, clepedest me in tribulacion; and ich deliuered þe, and her þe in hid anguisses; ich proued þe atte water of oȝainsiggeinge.

8. Here þou my folk', and y shal saie þe: ȝif þou, folk' of Israel, haue herd me, fals God ne shal nouȝt be in þe, [ne þou] ne shal anoure non oþer God þen me.

9. For ich am þe Lord, þy God, þat lad þe out of þe fendes bonde; open þy mouþe, and y shal fille it wyþ wordes.

[4]10. And my folk' ne herd nouȝt my uoice, and þe folk' of Israel ne ȝaf no kepe to me.

11. And ich lete hem go efter þe desire[5] of her hertes, & so shal hij gon in her fyndynges to nouȝt.

12. Ȝif my folk' had herd me and þe folk' of Israel had gon in my waies,

13. Par auenture ich had for nouȝt lowed her enemys and sett myn honde vp þe trubland hem.[6]

14. Þe enemys of our Lord leȝe to hym, and her pine shal be in helle.

15. And he fed hem wyþ flour of whete, and wyþ hony of stoñ he fulfild hem.

---

[1] Read ȝeueþ. [2] fol. 77b. [3] MS. seruies. [4] fol. 78. [5] The first e is corrected from i. [6] MS. den.

---

2. ȝif: gl. as] gladyng.
5. —ne.
6. seruies] synnes: seruyed.
7. —and her þe: in þin anguys in priuyte+&.
8. —ne: no þou schalt honour: but.
9. fulfiH.
10. —ne: ne ȝaf] toke.
11. —And: hert.
12. &+ȝif.
13. auentour: sturblyng hem.
14. lyed: payne.
15. hony-stone: fillyd hem full.

¹PSALM 81 (82).

1. God stode in þe synagoge of þe fals goddes; for-soþe he brouȝt to nouȝt þe fals goddes amidward.
2. To whom iugen ȝe wickednes and taken þe charge of synȝes?
3. Iugeþ þe nedeful and þe moderles, ryȝteþ þe meke and þe pouer.
4. Defendeþ þe pouer and þe nedeful, and deliuereþ hem fram þe vengeaunce of þe synȝer.
5. Hii ne [wyst nouȝt] ne vnderstode nowit, and hii ne gon in vnconandnes; alle þe foundementȝ of þe erþe shul ben stired oȝainnes hym.
6. Y seyd, ȝe ben Goddes, and ȝe alle childer of þe heȝest.
7. Ȝe shul dye² for-soþe as men, and ȝe shul falle as on of þe princes.
8. Arise þou, God, and iuge þerþe, and þou shalt en-heretien in alle folkes.

³PSALM 82 (83).

1. Ha God, who shal be liche to þe? ne stille þou nouȝt, ne [be] þou, God, nouȝt destourbed.
2. For þin enemys saiden yuel, and hij þat hated þe, aheȝed her heuedes.
3. Hii maden wicked conseil vp þy folk⁴, and þouten iuel to þin halwen.
4. Hii seiden, Comeþ, and depart we hem fram men, and ne be nouȝt þe name of Israel in minde.
5. For hij þouȝt to-gidres onlich oȝains me, and hij ordeined testament in þe tabernacles of þe Ydumens and of Ysmaelites.
6. Moᵃab & Agareni, Gebal, Amon, & Amalech, cum-linges wyþ þe woniand in Tyre.
7. For Assur com wyþ hym, and hij ben made helpers to Lothes childer.

---

¹ Ps. 80, MS.   ² y corrected from e.   ³ Ps. 81, MS.   ⁴ fol. 79.

---

81. 1. of — þe: goddes+&: —þe.
2. How long deme: takeþ.
3. Demeþ: iustifieþ.
4. veniaunce.
5. Þai wyst noȝt, no vnderstode noȝt witt, & þai go in vncunnyngnes all — þe: mouyd.
6. all+beþ.
*8. deme: enherite among all folke.

82. 1. O: ne stille...dest.] be þou noȝt still no be desturbyd.
2. enhyed.
4. —ne: Isr.+more.
5. of Ydumenes & of þe Ysmaeletes.
6. cum-linges] alienes: wonnyng.
7. ben] were.

* fol. 82.

8. Do to[1] hem as to Madian and Cisare, and as to Iabin in þe broke of Syon.

9. Hij perissiden in Endor, and hij ben made as dunge of þe erþe.

10. Sett her princes as Oreb and ȝeb and ȝe-bee and Salamana,

11. Alle her princes þat seiden, Welde we in heritage þe scunari of God.

12. Ha þou my God, sett hem as a whele and as stuble to-fore þe face of þy wynde.

13. As[2] fur þat brenneþ þe wode, and as lowe brennand þe mounteins,

14. Þou shalt pursuen hem in þyn vengeaunce, and þou shalt trublen hem in þyn ire.

15. Fulfil her face wiþ wicked los[3]; and sechen hij, Lord, þy name.

16. Ben hij asshamed and trubled in þe world of world; and ben hij confounded, and perissen hij,

17. [4]'Þat hij know þat Lord ys þy name; þou alon art heȝest in al erþe.

[5]PSALM 83 (84).

1. Ha Lord of vertu, ful luuesum ben þyn tabernacles; my soule coueiteþ, and failed in þe halles of our Lord.

2. Myn hert and my flesshe ioiden in God liueand.

3. For þe sparow fonde hym an hous, and þe turtel nest, þer she liggeþ her briddes.

4. Þyn auters, Lord, beþ of vertuȝ, þou art my kyng and my God.

5. And hij ben blisced þat wonen in þyn hous, hij shul herien þe in heuen.

6. Blisced be þe man of whom þe help is of þe; he ordeined steiȝenge in his hert, in þe valei of teres, in þe stede þat he sett.

---

[1] MS. co.   [2] ? MS. al.   [3] MS. wicked des.   [4] fol. 79b.   [5] Ps. 82, MS.

---

8. co] to : & to C.
9. hij ben] were.
11. her] þer : w.] haue.
12. O : þy] þe.
13. As : liet.
15. des] los : seche.
16. sturbled : þe w. of w.] heuen : hij] hey (!).

83. 1. O : vertus how louyd beþ.
2. lyfyng Godd.
3. founde : turtil + his : leggeþ.
5. be : hous+&.
6. ascension.

7. For þe berar of þe lawe shal ȝeue blisceinge to God; hij shul go fram vertu to vertu, and þe God of goddes shal be sen in þe heuen.

8. Lord, God of vertuȝ, here myn orison; ha God of sones of Iacob, take it wyþ þyn eren.

¹9. Ha God, our defendour, se and loke in-to þe face of þy preste anoint wyþ creme.

10. For o day is better in þy ioies vp a þousand ioies of þe wicked.

11. Y ches to be cast out o þe hous of my God more þan to wonen in þe tabernacles of synȝers.

12. For God loueþ mercy and soþenes, our Lord shal ȝyf grace and glorie to þe gode.

13. He ne shal nouȝt depriue hem of goddes, þat gon in innocente; ha Lord of vertuȝ, blisced be þe man þat hopeþ in þe.

²PSALM 84 (85).

1. Lord, þou blisced þyn erþe, þou turnedest oway þe chaityfs of þe childer of Iacob.

2. Þou for-ȝaf þe wikednes of þy folkꞌ, and hilled alle her synȝes.

3. Þou litteled al þin ire, and turned hem fram þe ire of þyn iudignacioun.

4. Conuerte vs, Lord, our helþe, and turne oway þyn ire fram vs.

5. Þyngꞌ to witen ȝyf þou shalt be wraþed to vs wyþ-outen ende, oþer þou shal put þyn honde ³fram kinde to kind?

6. Þou, God, turned shalt quiken vs, and þy folkꞌ shal gladen in þe.

7. Shew to vs, Lord, þy mercy, and ȝiue us þyn helþe.

8. Y shal here what þyng our Lord spekeþ in me; for he shal speke pes in his folkꞌ,

9. And vp his halwen and hem þat ben turned to hert.

---

¹ fol. 80.   ² Ps. 83, MS.   ³ fol. 80b.

---

7. þe b.] þe þe berer: seȝe: —þe.
8. vertu: of þe sonnes: eres.
9. O: anoite.
10. þan.
11. o] of.
*13. —ne: clennes o.

84. 1. erþe+and: wrechidnes.

2. þy] þe: hylid.
4. Conuerte .. helþe] Godd our h. turne vs.
5. þyng .. ȝyf] waþer: 1. schalt +noȝt.
6. qu. vs] make vs qwyk.
7. ȝif+to.

* fol. 32b.

EARLY ENGLISH PSALTER. PSALM 85 (86).

10. For-soþe his helþe is nere honde to hem [1] þat douten him, þat glorie won in our erþe.

11. Mercy and soþnes mett wyþ hym; ryʒtfulnes and pes ben kist.

12. Soþenes ys born of þerþe, and ryʒtfulnes loked fram þe heuen.

13. For our Lord shal ʒiue bliscednes, and our erþe shal ʒeuen his frut.

14. Ryʒtfulnes shal go to-fore hym, and shal sett his go-inges in his waie.

[2] PSALM 85 (86).

1. Lord, bowe þyn ere, and here me; [for ich am wrecched & pouer].

2. [Kepe my soule,] for ich am holi; ha mi God, make sauf þy seruant hopand in þe.

3. Haue mercy on me, Lord, for ich cried to þe al dai; glade, Lord, þo soule of þy seruant, for ich lifted to þe, Lorde, [3] my soule.

4. For þou, Lord, art soft and de-boner, and of mychel merci to alle þo þat clepen þe.

5. Take, Louerd, myn orison in þyn eren, and vnder-stonde þe voice of [4] my praier.

6. Y cried to þe in þe daie of my tribulacioun, for þou herdest me.

7. Lord, non is lich to þe in goddes, and non is efter þyn werkes.

8. Lord, al folk[1] þat tou madest shul comen and anour to-fore þe and glorifie þy name.

9. For þou art grete, and þou art [5] on God doand wonders.

10. Lade me, Lord, in þy waie, and y shal entre in þy soþnes; glade min hert, þat it drede þy name.

11. Lord, my God, y shal shryue to þe in alle my hert, & glorifien þy name wyþ-outen ende.

12. For þy mercy is grete vp me, and þou defended my soule fram þe deppest helle.

---

[1] MS. ben. [2] Ps. 84, MS. [3] fol. 81. [4] Followed by *mercy* (expuncted).
[5] MS. *nart*, but the *n* is dotted out.

---

10. *nere . . . gl.*] neʒ to hem þat douteþ h. þat his ioie.
12. fram — þe.

85. 1. me+for ich am wreched & pouer.
2. *For*] Kepe my soule for: o: my.

3. lift+vp.
4. *d.*] meke: all men clepyng þe.
5. Lord: *with*: eres.
8. *anour*] honour.
9. grete+& makeyng wonderful þinges: onlich Godd — *d.w.*

13. Ha Lord, þe wicked aros vp me, and þe sinagoge of myȝtful soȝten my soule; and hij ne sett nout þe in her syȝt.

[1]14. For þou, Lord God, art pityful and merciable, suffrand and of michel mercy and soþefast.

15. Loke to me, and haue mercy on me; ȝif comauntdement to þy child, and make sauf þe sone of þyn hondemaiden.

16. Make wyþ me tokne in gode, þat hii þat haten me se and be confounded; for þou Lord halp me, and conforted me.

[2]PSALM 86 (87).

1. Our Lord loueþ þe soules of his cosen vp al þe heȝest kinde of Iacob; þe foundementes of hym ben in þe holy heuens.

2. Ha þou holi soule, cite of God, glorious þynges ben said of þe.

3. Y, God, shal þenchen of Raab and Babilon, witan me and nouȝt trowand in me.

4. Se, straunge and Tyre and þe folk[4] of Ethiope, hii weren þer, and destrued hem.

5. Þynge to wyten þat man shal saie of þe [3] holi soule, and man shal gladen in þat, and þe he[4]ȝest founded[5] it?

6. Our Lord shal tellen in scriptures of folk[4] and of princes and of þe honours þat weren in hym.

7. Wonynge, Lord, ys in þe as of [6] alle gladeand.

[7]PSALM 87 (88).

1. Lord God of myn helpe, ich cried to þe in þe daie and in þe nyȝt to-fore þe.

2. My orison com into þy siȝt; bow þyn ere to my praier.

---

[1] fol. 81b. [2] Ps. 85, MS. [3] MS. þe so, but so is expuncted. [4] fol. 82.
[5] MS. foundest. [6] MS. os with a round s. [7] Ps. 86, MS.

---

13. —ne.
14. merc.+&.
*15. — and: hondemayde.
16. tokyng: helpid.

86. 1. chosyn: kyndes: in—þe.
2. vp þe.
3. witan ... trow.] knowyng me & leuyng noȝt.

4. Lo.
5. þynge ... þat] For: schal+ noȝt: man ... it] whþer (!) þe hiest Godd haue made it.
7. os] of.

87. 1. in day & nyȝt.
2. Cum myn orysun: syȝt+&.

* fol. 33.

3. For my soule is fulfild of iuels, and my lyf drow to helle.

4. Ich am vnderstonden wyþ þe fallan*d* in-to helle, and ich made as a man ded wyþoute*n* helpe, fre amonge þe ded.

5. As þe de-fouled wyþ syn̉es beand in her beriels, of whiche þou art nouȝt þenchand no more, and ben put fram þyn helpe.

6. Hij deden me in þe lowest [helle], in derknes, and in þe shadow of deþ.

7. Þi[1] wraþþe ys conferred up me, and[2] [þou] broȝtest vp me alle þyne assautes.

8. Þou madest my knowe*n* fer fram me, and hij sett me to hem in wlatei*n*ge.

9. Ich am ȝeue*n* in langour, and y ne went nouȝt out fram hym; min cȝe*n* la*n*guissed for me-sais.[3]

10. Lord, ich cried to þe al dai; ich bred out mi*n* hondes to þe bisechand mercy.

11. Þyn[g] to wyten ȝyf þou shal do wondres to þe ded, oþer leches shul arere*n*[4] hym, and sh*u*l shryue*n* to þe?

12. Þyng to wite*n* ȝyf anny shal tellen þy mercy in byriels and þy soþenes in forlesei*n*g?

13. Þynge to wyten ȝyf þy wo*n*ders shul ben knowe*n* in derkenes and þy ryȝtf*u*lnes in helle?

14. And ich, Lord, cried to þe, and my*n*[5] oreison shal erleche cum to-fore þe.

15. Why, Lord, puttestou oway myn oreison, & tu*r*nest fram me þy face?

16. Ich am pou*er* and i*n* trauails fram my ȝyngþe; ich a*m* heȝed for-soþe, am lowed and trubled.

[6]17. Þyn ires passeden in me, and þy dredefulnisses trubleden me.

---

[1] MS. þe.   [2] fol. 82*b*.   [3] MS. *me saif*.   [4] MS. *cirere*n.   [5] Last word of the line. The *y*'s are always dotted, but here the *y* decidedly has a long stroke over it instead of the dot.   [6] fol. 83.

---

3. *fulf.*] fild : *drow*] come neȝ.
4. þe] men : *a man ded*] mon.
5. defoiled : þou ... *more*] þer is no more þouȝt.
6. put : lowest+heII : in — þe.
7. þe] þi : fast : & +þou.
8. *my kn.*] me knowen men : into abho*m*inacion.
9. into sorow : —*ne* : angwyssed

(g *added over line*) for mysays.
10. *b.*] spred : praying+þi.
11. þyn ... ȝyf] Wheþer : schalt +noȝt : arere hem.
12. þyng ... ȝyf] Wheþer noȝt.
13. þynge ... ȝyf] Wheþer noȝt.
15. putestow.
16. ȝougeþe : soþe — am.
17. wraþes : gastnes.

18. And hij compassed me ich dai, as þe water goþ aboute þerþe; hij enuironed me togidres.

19. Þou drowe fram me frend and[1] neȝbur, and my knowen fram mysais.

[2]PSALM 88 (89).

1. Y shal synge wyþ-outen ende þe mercyes of our Lord.

2. Y shal tellen þy soþenesses in my mouþe fro kynde to kynde.

3. For þou seidest, mercies shulden oway[3] ben edefied in heuens wyþ-outen ende; þy soþenes shalt ben diȝt in hem.

4. Ich ordeined my testament to myn chosen; and y swore to Dauid, my seruant, Y shal diȝten þi sede vnto wiþ-outen ende.

5. Y shal edefien þi sede in kyndes to kindes.

6. Lord, þe heuens, shul hy graunten þyn wondres & þy soþnesses in þe chirche of halwen?[4]

7. For who shal be euenned to our Lord in cloudes? he shal ben liche to God in Goddes chosen.

[5]8. God, þat his glorified in þe conseil of holi, he is grete and dredful vp alle þat ben in[6] his cumpas.

9. Lord God of vertuȝ, who ys lich to þe? Lord, þou art myȝtful, and þy soþnesse ys in þy cumpas.

10. Þou lord-shippest þe pouste of þe seo, þou for-soþe pesest þe stiryng of hys flodes.

11. Þou lowedest þe proud as þe wounded, and þou departedest þyn enemys in þe pouste of þy vertu.

12. Þe heuens ben þyn, and þe [erþe] is þyne; þou founded þe world and his plente, þe norþ and þe see þou four-modest.

---

[1] Here follows ȝe, which is expuncted.   [2] Ps. 87, MS.   [3] Instead of alway.
[4] MS. lawe.   [5] fol. 83b.   [6] in is added over the line.

---

18. cumpast: as—þe: enclosed.
*88. 2. soþnes.
3. mercye schal be edified withoute e. in h.
4. —vnto.
5. sete fram k. into k.
6. þe] þi: hy gr.] knowlege: soþnes: lawe] halowen.

7. euenned] made euen: amonge þe chosen of Godd.
8. halowen.
10. þou hast lordschip to þe power: see—þou: slakest: mouyng of þe f. þer-of.
11. made low: power.
12. þe+erþe: wrold: made.

* fol. 33b.

EARLY ENGLISH PSALTER. PSALM 88 (89).

13. Thabor & Hermon shal gladen in þy name; þy pouste ys wyþ myʒt.

14. Be þi[1] strengþe fastened, and be þyn helpe[2] an heʒed;[3] ryʒtfulnes and iugement ben þe diʒteyng' of þe sege of God.

15. Mercy and soþenes shul go to-fore þy face; blisced be þe folk' þat conen gladyng'.

16. [4]Þe ryʒtful, Lord, shul gon in þe lyʒt of þy face, and shul gladen aldai in þy name; and hij shul ben anheʒed in þy ryʒtfulnes.

17. For þou art þe glorie of her vertu; and our ioie shal be heryed in þy wele-quemand,

18. For-þy þat our vp-steiʒeing ys of our Lord and of our kyng', þe holy of Israel.

19. Þan spake þou in syʒt to þy holy, and saidest, Y sett help in þe myʒtful, and heʒed[5] myn chosen in[6] my folk'.

20. Ich fonde Dauid, my seruant, and y stablyst hym in myn holy mercy.

21. For my strengþe shal helpen hym, and my pouerte shal conferme hym.

22. Ne þe enemy ne shal nouʒt profiʒt in hym, ne þe fende ne shal nouʒt sett strengþe[7] forto anoien hym.

23. And y shal departent hys enemys fram his face, and y shal turne in fleinge alle þat haten[8] hym.

24. And my soþenes and my mercy is wyþ hym, and hys ioie shal ben heʒed in[9] my name.

[10]25. And y shal sett hys strengþe in Gode, and [in] hys conabletes his helpe.

26. He cleped me, þou art my fader, mi God, and taker of myn helþe.

27. And y shal sett hym frest biʒeten, heʒe to-fore þe kynges of erþe.

---

[1] MS. þe. [2] MS. *be þou helped*, of which the *d* is dotted out. [3] MS. *and heʒed*.
[4] fol. 84. [5] MS. *heʒest*. [6] MS. *and*. [7] MS. *arengþe*. [8] *hate in*, MS.
[9] MS. *and*. [10] fol. 84*b*.

---

13. þe power.
14. þi: made faste & be þin help enhied: beþ ordenaunce of his sete.
15. cunne.
16. L. þe r.
17. ioie: enhyed: *w.q.*] plesyng.
18. *For ... vpst.*] For *our* takyng: *kyng þe h.*] holy k.
19. & þou sayde: hyed: *and*] in.

20. sett.
21. *pouerte*] power: confirme.
22. —1. *Ne*: —2. *ne*: —4. *ne*: strengþ to noie.
23. depart: *hate in*] hateþ.
24. soþnes: *heʒed and*] enhied in.
25. & in hys couenabletes.
27. first beʒetyn†: *of*+þe.

† After *beʒetyn* a *g* is erased.

28. Y shal kepe to him wyþ-outen ende ; my mercy and my testament shal be leal to hym.

29. And y shal setten his kinde in þe heuen, and his trone as þe daie of heuen.

30. ȝyf his childer for-soþe haue for-saken my lawe, and ne haue nouȝt gon in my iugement,

31. ȝyf hij haue de-fouled my ryȝtfulnesses, and haue nouȝt kept my comandementȝ :

32. Y shal uisite in chasteing¹ her wickednesses, and her synȝes in vengeaunce.

33. Y shalt nouȝt departen fram hym my mercy, ne y ne shal nouȝt anoien hym in my soþenes.

34. And y shal ¹nouȝt file my testament, and þe wordes þat gon out of my lippes y shal nouȝt maken vain.

35. Y swor ones in my holi, ȝif y liȝe to Dauid, his kinde shal last wyþ-outen ende ;

36. And his trone as þe sunne in my siȝt, and as þe mone parfit wyþ-outen ende ; and his witnes shal be trewe in heuen.

37. For-soþe þou putted oway and despised þe gode, and putted owai fram þe þi Crist.

38. Þou dest owai þe testament fram þy seruant, and filed in erþe his sanctuari.

39. Þou destrued alle his soþenes, and laid dredand his stedfastnes.

40. Alle þe passand her way rauist hym, and so he hys made reproce to his neȝburs.

41. Þou heȝed his helpe of þe wrekand hym, and made ioiful al his enemys.

42. Þou dest oway þe helpe of his defens, and þou ne halp hym nouȝt in bataille.

---

¹ fol. 85.

*28. trew.
30. F. s. ȝif h. ch.: — ne : domes.
31. defoiled.
32. wykkydnes.
33. schal : y—ne.
34. foule.

38. dest] turnyd : filed—in erþe.
39. his] þe : laid dr.] settest drede.
40. þe] men : reproue.
41. þe wr.] men castyng doune : glade.
42. dyd : —ne : halp] help.

* fol. 34.

43. þou destrued hym fram clennes, ¹and þou hurteled his sege in erþe.

44. þou made littel þe daies of his tyme, and turnedest hym in confusion.

45. To wham, þou Lord, þou turneste on ende? þy wraþe shal bren as fur.

46. By-þenche þe, wat is my substaunce; þyngᵢ to wyten ʒif þou setted in uaine alle mennesones?

47. Which man ys yt þat shal lyuen and nouʒt se þe deþ, and shal defende his soule fram þe strengþe of helle?

48. Where ben, Lord, þyn old mercies,² as tov swore to Dauid in þy soþenes?

49. Lord, be þou bi-þenchand of þe repruce of þy seruauntʒ, which repruceing ich held in my bosom of many men;

50. þe which þyn enemys, Lord, reproced, þat reproued þe chaungeing of þy prest a-noint wyþ creme.

51. Blisced be our Lord wyþ-outen ende; be it don, be it don.

³PSALM 89 (90).

1. Lord, þou art made socour to ous fram kynde to kinde.

2. To-fore þat þe mounteins were made, oþer þerþe were ⁴fourmed and þe werld, þou art God fram þe world vnto þe world wyþ-outen ende.

3. Ne turne þou nouʒt into mildnes; and þou seidest, ʒe childer of men, turneþ ʒou.

4. For a þousand ʒeres ben to-fore þyn eʒen as ʒisterdai, þat is passed.

5. And þe kepyngᵢ o nyʒt, þat for nouʒt ben had, shul be her ʒeres.

6. Passe he as gresse in þe mornyngᵢ; florische he in þe mornyngᵢ, and passe; falle he at heuen, and harden and wax he drie.

---

¹ fol. 85b.   ² es on erasure.   ³ Ps. 88, MS.   ⁴ fol. 86.

---

43. sete.
45. How longe: turnest þou þe into e.
46. þyngᵢ ... ʒif] wheþer: sett+noʒt: —in: men sonnes.
47. Who is þat man þat schal lif and+schal.
48. Lorde where beþ.
49. reproue: þat—repruceing.

50. L. þe wh. þ. e.: reprouyd: anoite.

89. 2. þe erþe+or þe world: — and þe w.
3. —ne: mekenes.
5. o] of.
*6. foloresch: atte euen: harde.

* fol. 34b.

7. For we failed in þyn ire, and we ben desturbed in þyn vengeaunce.

8. Þou laidest our[1] wickednesse in þy siȝt; our[2] world ys in liȝtyng of þy chere.

9. For alle our daies faileden, and we failed in þyn yre.

10. Our ȝeres shal þenchen as þe lob, þe daies of our ȝeres in þe seuenti ȝere.

11. For-soþe ȝyf eȝti ȝere ben in myȝtes, þe more ouer hem shal be[3] trauail and sorowe.

12. For mildnes com þer-on; and we shul be wiþnumen.

13. [4] Who knew þe myȝt of þyn ire, and to tellen þy wraþe for þy drede?

14. Make so þyn helpe knowen, and þe lered of hert in wisdome.

15. Lord, be þou turned vnto nov, and be þou bidlich vp þy seruantes.

16. We ben fulfild erlich of þy mercy, we shul gladen and deliten in alle our daies.

17. We gladed in þe daies, in which þou[5] lowed us for þe ȝeres in which we seiȝen iuels.

18. Loke to þy seruauntes and to þyn werkes, and dresce her sones.

19. And þe shynyng of our Lord God be vp vs, and dresce vp us þe werkes of our hondes, [and dresce þe werkes of our hondes.]

[6] PSALM 90 (91).

1. He þat whoneþ in þe helpe of þe heȝest, he shal dwelle in þe defens of God of heuen.

2. He shal saie to our Lord, þou art my taker and my refut; mi God, y shal hopen in hym.

3. For he deliuerd me fram þe trappes of þe fendes and fram asper word of men.

---

[1] c corrected from v. [2] Here follows lord, which is expuncted. [3] MS. ben, but n is expuncted. [4] fol. 86b. [5] Here lord followed, but is expuncted. [6] Ps. 89, MS.

---

10. þe lob] grauel: in þe] in hem schal be.
11. be: þe] þer.
12. mekenes come aboue: withnym.
13. knoweþ: þe wraþe of.
15. v.n.] hidertoward: prayable.

16. gladen] galde (!).
17. dayes in+þe.
19. hondes+& dress þe warkes of our hondes.

90. 3. gryn: scharp.

EARLY ENGLISH PSALTER. PSALM 91 (92).

[1]4. And he shal shadow þe wyþ hys shulderis, and þou shalt hope vnder hys feþers.

5. Þe soþenes of hym shal cumpas þe wyþ shelde, and þou ne shalt nouȝt doute of þe drede of nyȝt,

6. Of temptacioun waxand in daie, fram nede goand in derkenes, fram þe curs of þe fende[2] bryȝt shynyng.

7. A þousand temptaciouns shul fallen fram þi[3] syde, and ten þousandes fram þy ryȝthalf; þe deuel for-soþe ne shal noȝt comen to þe.

8. Þou shalt se for-soþe wyþ þyn eȝen, þou shalt se þe ȝeldyng of synȝers.

9. For þou, Lord, art myn hope, and þou setted þy refut alderheȝest.

10. Yuel ne shal nouȝt com to þe, and turment ne shal nouȝt com nere þy tabernacle.

11. For he sent to his aungels of þe, þat hij kepe þe in alle þyn waies.

12. Hij shul bere þe in hondes, þat tou ne hirt nouȝt [4]perauenture þy gost wyþ vices.

13. Þou shalt gon vp queintis[5] and godenes, and þou shalt de-foule þe fende and helle.

14. For he hoped in me, and y shal deliuer hym; y shal defenden hym, for he knew my name.

15. He cried to me, and y shal here hym; ich am wyþ hym in tribulacioun, y shal defend him and glorifien hym.

16. Y shal fulfillen hym wyþ lengþe of daies, and y shal shewe hym min helþe.

[6]PSALM 91 (92).

1. Gode it is to shryue to our Lord, and heȝestlich[7] singe to þy name;
2. For to tellen erliche þy mercy and þy soþenes by nyȝt;
3. In þy .x. comaundementȝ, wyþ songe and harpe.

---

[1] fol. 87.   [2] Here follows biȝt, dotted out as well as scored through.   [3] MS þe.
[4] fol. 87b.   [5] MS. quenitis.   [6] Ps. 90, MS.   [7] ȝ (expuncted) heȝefflich.

---

4. truste : feders.
5. —ne.
7. þi sydes : þouȝand : —ne.
8. eȝen+and : reward.
9. a.] hiest.
10. —ne : —ne : —com.
12. tou ... vices] per auentur þou

hurte noȝt þy goste or fote with vice or atte stone.
13. qu.] wysdome : defoile.
14. —and.

*91. 1. It is gode : hilich.

* fol. 35.

4. For þou, Lord, delited vp me in þy makeing; and y shal gladen in þe werkes of þyn hondes.

5. Hou michel, Lord, þin werkes ben heried; her þoutes ben ful michel deped.

6. ¹Þe man vnwys ne shal nouȝt knowen, and þe fole ne shal nouȝt vnderstonde þes þynges.

7. Whan synȝers ben born as hay multipliand, and alle þat wirchen wickednisse apered,

8. þat hij dyen in þe world of worldes, þou for-soþe, Lord, art heȝest wyþ-outen ende.

9. For se, Lord, þyn enemys shul perischen, and alle þat wirchen wickednes shul ben sprade abrode.

10. And my voice shal be anheȝed as horne of þe vnycorne, and myn elde and mercy plentifous.

11. And myn eȝe despised min enemys, and min ere shal here þe wordes of hem þat arysen oȝains me, and of wicked.

12. Þe ryȝtful shal floris as palme, and shal be multiplied as cedres of Libani.

13. Þe plaunted² in þe hous of our Lord shul flurissen in þe halles of þe hous of our Lord.

14. Hij shul be ȝete multiplied in elde plentifous, and hij shul ben wele likand, þat hij tellen þe gode.

15. For þe Lord, our God, is ryȝtful, ³and wickednes nys nouȝt in hym.

⁴PSALM 92 (93).

1. Our Lord regned,⁵ and cloþed hym wyþ fairenes; our Lord is cloþed in strengþe, and þer-wyþ he girt hym.

2. For he fastened þe world, þat ne shal nouȝt be stired.

---

¹ fol. 88. ² *te* on erasure. ³ fol. 88*b*. ⁴ Ps. 91, MS. ⁵ MS. *regneþ*.

---

5. Lorde, so much þi w. beþ made grete, her þouȝtes beþ to much depe.
6. þe vnwys man—*ne* : —*ne*.
8. for s. þou.
9. on brode.
10. as+þe : age.
12. ceder of þe Libane.

13. þe *pl.*] & schal be sett: 1. Lorde+&.
14. age of plente. 15. *nys*] is.

92. 1. regnyd & is cloþyd (!) fairenes : cloþd—*in*.
2. *f.*] made : —*ne* : mouyd.

3. Ha God, fram þan ys þy sete made redy; þou art honourd of þe world.

4. Þe flodes, Lord, heȝed þe, þe flodes an-heȝed her voice.

5. Þe flodes an-heȝed her flowynges fram þe voices of mani waters.

6. Þe shewe-inges of þe se ben wondurful, our Lord ys wonderful on heȝt.

7. Þy wytnes ben made ful wele to louen; holines, Lord, bisemeþ þyn hous into lengþe of daies.

[1]PSALM 93 (94).

1. God ys Lord of vengeaunces; God of vengeaunce did frelich.

2. Þou þat iugest þerþe, be þou an-heȝed, and ȝelde ȝeldeinge to þe proude.

3. Unto wham, Lord, þe synȝers, vnto whan [2]þe synȝers shul gladen?

4. Hij shul saie and speken wickednes, alle shul speken þat wirchen vnryȝtfulnes.

5. Hij loweden, Lord, þy folk, and trauailed þyn heritage.

6. Hij slowen wydowes and straunge, and slowen þe moderles.

7. And hij seiden, Our Lord ne shal nouȝt sen it, ne þe God Iacob ne shal nouȝt vnderstonde it.

8. Ha ȝe nouȝt wyse in þe folk, vnderstondeþ, and ȝe foles, by-comeþ sumtyme wyse.

9. He þat sett ere, ne shal nouȝt here; oþer he þat feined hys eȝe, ne seþ nouȝt?

10. He þat chastieþ men, ne shal nouȝt reprucen; þe which techeþ mani coninge?

11. Our Lord wote þe þoȝtes of men, for hii ben ydel.

---

[1] Ps. 92, MS.   [2] fol. 89.

3. *sete*] sett.
4. *h. þe*] arered hem : arered.
5. arered.
6. *se*] waters : in heȝt.
7. *w. to l.*] trouable : *bis.*]semeþ : into+þe.

93. 1. *vengeaunce*] vengances.
2. demest : *ȝeldeinge*] reward.
3. Hou longe, Lorde, schal þe synnars glade, & iterum.
5. Lorde þai lowed.
6. straungers : m.+chylder.
7. —*ne shal nouȝt* : —*ne* : Godd +of : —*ne*.
8. —*Ha* : ȝe vnwys amonge.
9. *sett e.*] his ere setteþ : —*ne* : or : —*ne*.
10. —*ne* : man cunnyng.

12. Lord, blisced be þe man þat tou hast lered, and hast tauȝt hym þy lawe.

13. Þatou asswage hym fram iuel daies, þer-whiles þat dicheþ[1] be doluen to þe synȝer.

14. For our Lord ne shal nouȝt put owai his folk¹, and he ne shal nouȝt for-sake hys heritage.

15. [2] Þat whiles þat ryȝtfulnes be turned into iugement, and alle þo[3] by hym, þat ben of ryȝtful hert.

16. Who shal arisen wyþ me oȝains þe wicked? oþer who shal stonde wyþ me oȝains þe wirchand wickednes?

17. Bot ȝyf our Lord for-þi had holpen me, my soule nere honde had woned in helle.

18. Ȝyf ich seid, My fote is stired, Lord, þy mercy halp me.

19. Efter þe michelnes of my sorowes in myn hert, þy confortes gladeden my soule.

20. Þyng¹ to wyten ȝyf sege of wickednes draweþ to þe, þat feineþ sorowe in comaundement?

21. Þe wicked couayted dampnacioun in þe soule of þe ryȝtful, and condempned þe blode of þe innocent.

22. And our Lord is made to me in refut, and my God into helpe of myn hope.

23. And he shal ȝelde hem her wickednes and spradden hem in her malice, and Gode, our Lord, shal departem hem.

[4]PSALM 94 (95).

1. Comeþ, glade we to our Lord, singe we to God, our helþe.
2. Take we forþe his face in shryȝt, and singe we to hym in songes.
3. For God ys a grete Lord and grete kyng¹ vp alle goddes.

---

[1] Read diches or diche. [2] fol. 89b. [3] Corrected from þe. [4] Ps. 93, MS.

---

*12. Lor: þe] þat.
13. slake: dicheþ] þe diche.
14. —ne: —ne.
15. þ. w.] Vnto þe tyme: dome.
17. helpid: nere] neȝ.
18. mouyd: helpid.
20. þyng ... ȝyf] weþer: dr.+ noȝt: commaundementes.

21. couayt d. aȝen þe: dempned.
23. spradden] he schal sparpiłł: & Godd+& Godd.

94. 1. Commeþ+&.
2. Ocupie we his f. in schryft: psalmes.

* fol. 35b.

4. For in his hondes ben alle[1] þe cuntreis of þerþe, and al þe heȝnes of þe mounteins ben of hym.

5. For þe se is his; and he made hit, and his hondes founded þe drihede.

6. Comeþ, anore we, and synge and [wepe] we to-fore our Lord, þat made us; for [he] hys þe Lord our God,

7. & we þe folk of his pasture and þe shepe of his honde.

8. Ȝyf he[2] han herd to-daie his voice, ne willeþ ȝe nouȝt harden ȝour hertes,

9. As in taryinge efter þe dai of temptacioun in desert.

10. Þer [ȝ]our fadres tempteden me, hii proueden and seiȝen my werkes.

11. And y whas wroþe to þat kynde by fourty ȝere, and seide alwai, Hij [3]erren in hert.

12. & þes ne knew nouȝt myn waies, as ich swore in myn ire, ȝyf hij shul entren in-to my rest.

[4]PSALM 95 (96).

1. Syngeþ to our Lord a new songe; ha alle erþe, syngeþ to our Lord.

2. Syngeþ to our Lord, & blisceþ hys name, and telleþ his helþe fram dai to daie.

3. Telleþ amonge men his glorie, and his wondres to alle folkes.

4. For our Lord ys michel and worþshipful and dredeful vp alle godes.

5. For alle þe goddes of men ben fendes, our Lord for-soþe made þe heuenes.

6. Shrift & fairnes ben in hijs siȝt, holines and heriyng ben in his halwing.

7. Þe cuntreis of men, bryngeþ to our Lord, bringeþ to our Lord glorie and honour, bringeþ glorie to our Lord and to his name.

---

[1] MS. be ualle. [2] i.e. ȝe. [3] fol. 90b. [4] Ps. 94, MS.

4. beþ all: —al.
5. hondes f. þe d.] made drynes.
6. Cum ȝe, & honour we, & fall we doune, & wepe we to-for: hys] he is.
8. ȝe: ne ... harden] will noȝt hard.
9. tar.] voidyng.
10. our] ȝoure.

12. —ne.

95. 1. —ha alle] all þe.
3. ioie: folk.
4. aboue all goddes.
5. f. s. our L.
*6. halowen.
7. Ȝe cuntres: ioie: ioie.

* fol. 36.

8. Bryngeþ offryndes, and en¹treþ into his halles, and anoureþ our Lord in his holines.

9. Alle þerþe be stired fram his face; say ȝe, men, to folkes þat our Lord regned.

10. For he amended þe world, þe wich ne shal nouȝt be styred; he shal iuge þe folk*es* in euen*n*esse.

11. Gladeþ ȝe heue*n*s, and ioie þerþe, and be þe see and hys plente stired; þe feldes shul gladen, and alle þynges þat ben in hem.

12. Þan shul alle þe trews of þe wodes gladen of þe face of our Lord, for he comeþ; for he comeþ to iugen þerþe.

13. He shal iuge þe world in euenesse, and þe folkᵗ in soþenesse.

²PSALM 96 (97).

1. Our Lord regneþ; glade þerþe, and ioien many yldes.

2. Cloudes and derknes ben in his cumpasse, ryȝtfulnes and iugement ben þe amendement of his sege.

3. Fur shal gon to-forn hym, and brenen³ hys enemys abouten hym.

4. ⁴Hys liȝtyngens aliȝted þe world; he seiȝe, and þe erþe ys styred.

5. Þe mou*n*teins melted as wax fram þe face of our Lord, al þe erþe fram þe⁵ face of our Lord.

6. Þe heuens telden his ryȝtfulnes, and al þe folkes seȝen his gl*orie*.

7. Ben hij alle confou*n*ded þat anoure*n* y-magerie & þat gladen in her maumetes.

8. Alle ȝe hys aungels, anoure*n* hym; þe folkᵗ of Syon herd God and ioied.

9. And þe doȝters of Iude gladed, Lord, for þy iugement.

10. For þou, Lord, art heȝest up alle þe erþe; mychel þou art heȝed vp alle þe godes.

---

¹ fol. 91. ² Ps. 95, MS. ³ r on erasure. ⁴ fol. 91*b*. ⁵ *fram* þe twice in MS.

---

8. offery*n*ges : hono*u*reþ.
9. mouyd.
10. þe w. ne] þat: mouyd: deme.
11. Glade þe h. : *and h. pl. st.*] in his plente mouyd.
12. trows : ioie : deme.
13. deme : in his soþnes.

96. 1. haþ regned : yles.

2. dome.
4. liȝtynges a.+to : seȝt : mouyd.
5. *al*] & aH.
6. schewed : folk seȝ : ioie.
7. *anouren*...&]honoureþ grauen ymagerye & þai : maumemetries(!).
8. honou*r*et.
9. domes.
10. aH goddes.

11. ʒe þat loue our Lord, hateþ iuel; our Lord kepeþ þe soules of his halwen; and he shal liuer hem fram þe pouste of þe synʒer.

12. Lyʒt hijs sprongen to þe ryʒtful, and ioie to þe ryʒtful of hert.

13. Gladeþ, þe ryʒtful in our Lord, and shryueþ to þe mynde of hys halwyngʻ.

¹PSALM 97 ² (98).

1. ʒe men, syngeþ to our Lord a newe songe, for he haþ don wonderful þynges.

2. He saued to hym þe helpe of hys chosen and hys holi pouste.

3. Our Lord made hys helþe knowen, and shewed hys ryʒtfulnes in syʒt of men.

4. He þouʒt on hys merey and on hys soþenes³ to þe hous of Israel.

5. Alle þe contre-hys⁴ of þe erþe seʒen þe helþe of our Lord God; he⁵ alle þerþe, ioieþ to God, and syngeþ and gladeþ and ver-saileþ.

6. Syngeþ to our Lord in harp and in voice of psalme, in trumpes beten and voice of trumpes of horne.

7. Gladeþ in þe syʒt of þe kyng, our Lord; be þe se stired and hys plente, þe world, and hij þat wonen þer-inne.

8. Þe flodes shul ioien togidres wyþ honde, and mounteins shul gladen of þe syʒt of our Lord; for he ⁶comeþ to iuge þerþe.

9. He shal iuge þe world in ryʒtfulnes, and þe folkes in euennes.

⁷PSALM 98 (99).

1. For þat our Lord regned, wraþ-þen þe folkes; þou þat sittest up cherubyn, by þe erþe styred.

2. Our Lord ys grete in heuen and he⁸ vp alle folkes.

3. Shryuen hij to þy grete name, for it ys⁹ dredeful and holi; and þe honour of þe kyngʻ loueþ iugement.

---

¹ fol. 92. ² Ps. 96, MS. ³ e added over line. ⁴ Read contreis. ⁵ i.e. ʒe.
⁶ fol. 92b. ⁷ Ps. 97, MS. ⁸ I.e. heʒe, hiʒe. ⁹ After ys, MS. has dede deleted.

---

11. deliuer: p.] honde.
12. spr.] ryse.   13. halowen.

97. 2. pouer.
5. contre hys] cuntres: — Lord: —he: ioie: singeþ—and: vers.] psalmeþ.
6. harpe+in harpe: * of tr.] of trumpe.

7. in — þe: mouyd: þere world.
8. and] þe: deme.
9. deme.

98. 1. þe folkes wraþed: by] be: mouyd.
2. he] hyʒ.
3. Be þai chryf.

* fol. 36b.

4. Þou dittest dresceinges, and þou madest iugement & ryȝtfulnes in Iacob sones.

5. And heȝeþ þe Lord, our Lord, and anoureþ þe shamel of hys fete, for hit is holy.

6. Moyses and Aaron wyþ her prestes, and Samuel amonges hem þat clepen hys name.

7. Hij clepeden our Lord, and he herd hem; he spake to hem in a piler of a cloude.

8. Hij keptten hys[1] witnesses and þe comaundement þat he ȝaf to hem.

9. [2]Ha Lord, our God, þou herd hem; þou, God, was mercyful to hem and byginnand to wreke in alle her fyndeynges.

10. And heȝeþ þe Lord, our God, and anoureþ hym in hys holy heuen; for þe Lord, our God, ys holy.

PSALM 99 (100).

1. Ha alle erþe, gladeþ to God, serueþ our Lord in gladnes.
2. Entreþ in his syȝt in ioie.
3. Weteþ þat our Lord he is God; he made us, and nouȝt we us seluen.
4. We ben hys folk‘ and þe shepe of hys pasture; entre hys ȝates in shrift, and schryueþ to hym in hys temple in songes.
5. Herieþ hys name; for our Lord ys milde, hys mercy ys wyþ-outen ende, and hys soþnesse ys in kende and kinde.

PSALM 100 (101).

1. Lord, y shal synge mercy and iugement to þe; y shal versail and vnderstonde in wai unfiled, whan þou shal come to me.
2. [3]Y ȝede in þe innocens of myn hert, amiddes þe wylle of myn hert, in-middes myn hous.[4]

---

[1] MS. *hyȝt.*   [2] fol. 93.   [3] fol. 93b.   [4] *Notabile* in margin, written by a later hand.

---

4. diȝtest: iugement: Iacobes.
5. *A. h.*]Enhieþ: honoureþ: stole.
8. kept his wyttnes: commaundementis.
9. O our Lorde Godd: hard: *b. to wr.*] auengyng.
10. *A. h.*] Enhieþ: honoureþ.

99. 1. *Ha alle*] Aħ þe: Godd+&: *o.L.*] Godd.
3. *Weteþ*] Wyt ȝe.
4. entreþ: *songes*] ympnes.
5. meke.

100. 1. *versail*] psalme: vnfulyd.
2. *inn.*] clennes: *amiddes*] amyd.

3. Y ne sett nouȝt to-fore myn eȝen þyng vnryȝtful, and ich hated þe trespassynges.

4. Wicked hert ne come nouȝt to me; y ne knew nouȝt þe wicked bowand fram me.

5. Y ne pursued hym þat bacbiteþ priuelich hys neȝbur.

6. Y ne ete nouȝt wyþ þe prude eȝe, and wiþ hert þat ne may nouȝt be fulfild.

7. Myn eȝen ben to þe trew of þerþe, þat hij sit wyþ me; þe goand in vnfiled wai, he serued me.

8. He þat [doþ] pride ne shal nouȝt wonen amiddes myn houus; he þat spekeþ yuel, y ne dresced hym nouȝt in þe syȝt of myn eȝen.

9. Ich sloȝe in þe mornyng' alle þe synȝers of erþe, þat y shuld departent out of our Lordes cite alle þe wirchand wickednes.

[1]PSALM 101 (102).

1. Here, Lord, my praiere, and my crye come to þe.

2. Ne turne þou nouȝt þy face fram [2] me; in wich daie þat ich be trubled, bow to me þyn ere.

3. In which daie þat ich had cleped to þe, here þou me hastilich.

4. For my daies failed as smoke, and my bones dried as craukes.

5. Ich am smyten as hay, and myn hert dryed; for ich for-ȝate to ete my brede.

6. Of þe voice of my waymentynge [3] my bon droȝ to my flesshe.

7. Ich am made lich to þe pellican of ones, and ich am made as þe nyȝtrauin in þe euesynges.

8. Y woke, and made as þe sparowe wonand on in [4] þe hous.

9. Myn enemys vp-braided me aldai, and hij þat praised me swore oȝains me.

---

[1] fol. 94. [2] Followed by þe, which is dotted out. [3] The final e is corrected from the loop of g'. [4] in added above the line.

---

3. —ne: vnr. þyng: þe tr.] men trespassyng.
4. —ne: —ne.
5. —ne: bakbyted.
6. —ne: and] no: with+þe: —ne.
8. þat+doþ: —ne: amyd: —ne.
9. of+þe: * departe.

101. 1. Lord here.
2. —Ne: am sturbled.
3. haue: hastelich.
4. smeche.
5. cleued.
7. ones] wyldernes: ouesyng.
8. wonand on in] wylde in þe helyengt of.
9. vpbrade.

* fol. 37. † Second e corrected from i.

10. For ich ete my brede as asken, and medeled my drynkⁱ wyþ wepyngⁱ.

11. Fram þe ¹face of þe ire of þi indignacioun; for þou liftand me norissed me.

12. My daies boweden as shadow, & hij² d[r]eied as hai.

13. Þou, Lord, forsoþe dwellest wyþ-outen ende, and þi mynde is in kinde and in-to kynde.³

14. Þou, Lord, arisand shalt haue pite of þe folke of Syon ; for þe time of hijs mercynge, for þe time comeþ.

15. For hijs fastnes pleised to þi seruantes, and hij shul haue pite of his erþe.

16. And þe folke, Lord, shul douten þy name, and alle þe kynges of þe erþe þi glorie.

17. For our Lord edefied þe heuen, and shal be sen in hijs glorie.

18. He loked in-to þe oreison of þe meke, and he ne despised nouȝt her praier.

19. Be þes þynges wryten in þat oþer kinde; and þe folkⁱ þat shal be fourmed shal heryen our Lord.

20. For he loked fram hys eȝe heuen ; our Lord loked fram heuen into erþe ;

⁴21. Þat he herd þe waie-mentynges of þe fettered and vnbinde þe soþenes of þe slain.

22. Þat hij telle in Syon þe name of our Lord and hys hereinge in Ierusalem.

23. In acordand þe folkes in on, and þe kynges, þat hii serue to our Lord.

24. He answerd hym in voice of his vertou, Telle to me þe fewenes of my daies.

---

¹ fol. 94b. ² I.e., y (ego). ³ MS. *in toknynge to kynde,* of which *toknyngs* is dotted and struck out. ⁴ fol. 95.

---

11. þine ire : arered me norischyng me.
12. *b.*] auanesched : as+a : dried.
13. F. s. þ. L.
14. *of þe*] of þi : þe+þe : *m.*] hauyng m*er*cye.
15. s*er*uant.
16. ioie.

17. *Omitted, as it ended with the same word as the preceding verse.*
18. —*ne.*
20. hie.
21. waylynges : vnbyde (!) þe sonnes of þe men slawe.
22. herying.
23. s*er*uy.

25. Ne clepe þou me nouȝt oȝayn in þe half dele of mi daies, in kynde and in-to kynde of þe ȝere.

26. Lord, þou founded þerþe atte gynnyng', and þe heuens ben þe werkes of þyn hondes.

27. Hij shul perissen, þou for-soþe dwellest; and alle shul by-gynne at elden as cloþyng'.

28. And þou shalt chaungen hem as couertour,[1] and hij shul be chaunged; þou for-soþe art þat ich, and þy ȝeres ne shul nouȝt failen.

29. Þe sones of þy seruauntes shul wonen, and here sede shalt be dresced in þe world.

[2] PSALM 102 (103).

1. Ha þou my soule, blisce our Lord; and alle þynges þat ben wyþ-innen me, blisce hys holi name.

2. Ha þou my soule, blisce our Lord; and ne wille þou nouȝt for-ȝete alle his ȝelde-inges;

3. Þe which is merciful to alle þin wickednesses; þe which helþe alle þy sekenisses;

4. Þe which ransoun-neþ þy lif fram deþ; þe which crouneþ þe wyþ mercy and pites;

5. Þe which fulfilleþ þy[4] desire in goddes; þy ȝengþe shal be made new as of an erne.

6. Our Lord is doand[3] mercies and iugement to alle þe suffrand wronge.

7. He made hys waies knowen to Moyses, he did to þe childer of Israel her willes.

8. Our Lord is ryȝtful and merciable and of longe wille and michel merciable.

9. He ne shal nouȝt wraþþe him wyþ-outen ende, [ne he ne shal nouȝt manacen wyþ-outen ende.]

---

[1] MS. to uertour.   [2] fol. 95b.   [3] Corrected from deand.   [4] MS. þe.

―26. ―Ỹà in þe begynnyng.
27. perisch+&: byg. at e.] wex elde.
28. couertour: þou . . . ich] f. s. þou art he: —ne.
29. shalt] schal.

102. 1. O.

*2. O: —ne: —his: ȝeldyng.
3. sekenes.
4. corouneþ: petes.
5. þi: godes: ȝengeþ: egil.
6. dome: —þe.
8. r.] redeful.
9. —ne: ende+& he schal noȝt manace with-oute ende.

* fol. 37b.

10. He ne did nouȝt to us efter our synȝes, ne he ne[1] ȝeldeþ nouȝt to vs efter[2] our wickednes.

11. [3]For efter þe heȝt of heuen fram erþe he streinþed[4] hys mercy vp hem þat dreden hym.

12. He made fer fram us our wickednes, as þe este departeþ fram þe west.

13. As þe fader has mercy on his childer, our Lord is merciable of hem þat dreden hym ; for he knowe[5] [our] faintes.

14. He recorded þat we ben pouder[6] ; man ys as hai, hys daies ben as floure[7] of þe feld, so he shal florissen.

15. For gost shal passen in hym ; and he ne shal nouȝt dwelle, and he ne shal no more knowen his stede.

16. Þe mercy of our Lord is forsoþe fram wyþ-outen [ende vnto wyþ-outen ende] up hem þat dreden hym.

17. And his riȝtfulnes is into child of childer to hem þa[t] kepen his testament.

18. And hij ben remembraunt of his comaundementȝ to don hem.

19. Our Lord shal diȝten his sete in heuen, and his kyng'dome shal lord-ship alle.

[8]20. Ha alle his angeles, miȝtful of uertu, doand his worde, to here þe uoice of hys wordes, blisceþ our Lord.

21. Ha alle his uertu, blisceþ our Lord ; ȝe his ministris, þat don hys wille, blisced our Lord.

22. Ȝe alle werke of our Lord, blisceþ our Lord in alle stedes of his lordship ; ha þou my soule, blische our Lord.

---

[1] *did nouȝt* follows next, but is expuncted and struck out. [2] *ef* on erasure. [3] fol. 96. [4] MS. *streined* with a *y* or the abbreviation for *ur* over the interval between *n* and *e*. [5] Here an erasure of several letters follows. [6] MS. *prude*. [7] MS. *floures*, but *s* is dotted for deletion. [8] fol. 96*b*.

---

10. —*ne* : *ne he ne*] & he.
11. strengþid : vp men dredyng hym.
12. made+as.
13. *of*] to : knew our fayntenes.
14. were pouder : as a flour : felde +&.
15. —*ne* : —*ne*.
16. with-oute +ende vnto with-oute ende.
17. *child*] childer : þat.
18. remembryng.
20. O : angels : blisseþ our Lorde doyng h. w. to his voice to be herd of h. w.
21. O : vertus : *blisced*] blysseþ.
22. werkes : o : blyss+to.

PSALM 103 (104).

1. Ha þou my soule, blisce our Lord; ha Lord, mi God, þou art greteliche heried.

2. Þou clad schryft and fairnes, hiled wyþ lyʒt as wyþ cloþyng',

3. Spredand out þe heuen as a skyn; þe which couered þe alderheʒestnes¹ wyþ waters;

4. Þat settest þe cloude þy wendyng up; þat gost vp þe swiftnes of þe wynde;

5. Þat makest þyn angeles gostes, and þy ministres sengeand [fur];

6. Þat foundest þerþe ² vp his stablenes; it ne shal nouʒt be bowed in þe worled of þe worldes.

7. Depenes ys hys couertour as cloþyng'; waters shul stonde vp mounteines.

8. Hij shul fle fram þe lackeinge, & hij shul douten of þe voice of þy þonder.

9. Þe mounteyns steyʒen up, and þe feldes fallen in-to þe stede þat-ou founded to hem.

10. Þou setted þe terme, þe which hij ne shul nouʒt passe ouer; ne hij ne shul nouʒt be turned oʒain to hilen þerþe.

11. Þou þat sendest welles in valeis; þe waters shul passen amiddes þe mounteines.

12. Alle bestes of þe felde shul drynken, þe wilde asses shul abiden in her þrest.

13. Þe foules of heuen shulle ³ whonen vp þat erþe, þe waters shul ʒeuen voice of þe middel of þe stones.

14. Dewand þe mounteines of þyn ouermor, þerþe shal be fulfild of þe frut of þy werkes.

---

¹ MS. *alder ʒe* (ʒe is expuncted) *heʒestnes.* ² fol. 97. ³ *le* begins a new line.

---

103. 1. O : o.
2. cloþd.
3. *þe w.*] þat: *alderheʒestnes*] hiest þinges.
4. *w. up*] ascencyon.
5. brennyng+fure.
6. —*ne.*

*8. *l.*] blame.
9. feH : foundeþ.
10. sett: *þe w.*] þat : —*ne* : — *ne* : —*ne* : hely.
12. —*þe wilde* : *ab.*] haue byde : fryste.
14. Wateryng : ouermast+þinges.

* fol. 38.

15. þou art bryngand forþe hay to meres[1] and grasse to seruice of men;

16. þat tou brynge forþ brede of þerþe, and wyn glade [2]mannes hert.

17. Þe tres of þerþe shul be fulfild, and þe cedres of Lyban, which he sette; sparowes shul make þer her nestes.

18. Þe hous of faucouns is her lader, þe heȝe mounteins to hertes, þe ston is refut to heyrouns.

19. He made þe mone in-to times, þe sonne knewe hys goingdoun.

20. Þou settest derkenes, and nyȝt ys made; al þe bestes of þerþe shul passen þer-ynne.

21. Þe whelpes of þe liouns rumyand, þat hij rauissen and aske metes to hem of God.

22. Þe sonne ys rysen, and hij ben gadered, and shul be laid in her couches.[3]

23. Man shal go forþ to his werke, and to his wircheing vn-to þe euenynge.

24. Hou michel þyn werkes ben heried, Lord! þou madest alle þynges in wisdome; þerþe is fulfild of þyn habbyng.

25. Þis see hys michel and large to hondes; þer-inne ben crepand þynges, of which nis no noumbre:

[4]26. Bestes litel wyþ michel; þer shul shippes passen:

27. Þys dragon þatou fourmedest to by-gylen him: alle abyden, þatou ȝif to hem mete in tyme.

28. Þe ȝeuand to hem, hij shul gaderen; þe openand þyn honde, alle þynges shul be fulfild of godenes.

29. Þe for-soþe turnand owai þy face, hij shul be trubled; þou shal take fram hem þy gost, and hij shul failen, and shul be turned into her poudre.

30. Sende for þy[5] gost, and hij shul be fourmed; and þou shalt make newe þe face of þerþe.

---

[1] MS. *mere ci*.   [2] fol. 97b.   [3] MS. *couthes*.   [4] fol. 98.   [5] i.e. *forþ þy*

---

15. *mere ci*] bestes: *gr.*] herbe.
17. of þe L.] þat.
18. yrchounes.
21. *and*] þat þai.
22. arys.
24. possession.

25. *þis*] þe: is.
26. muche.
27. made: ha-bydeþ.
28. — *hij*: hondes.
29. For-soþe þe.
30. *for*] forþe.

EARLY ENGLISH PSALTER. PSALM 104 (105).

31. Be þe glorie of our Lord in þe world; our Lord shul gladen in his werkes;

32. Þe which lokeþ to þerþe and makeþ it to tremblen; þe which toucheþ þe mounteyns, and hij shul smoken.

33. Y shal syngen to our Lord in[1] my liif, and synge to my God as longe as ich am.

34. Be my word to hym ioiful; ich for-sothe shal gladen in our Lord.

35. [2]Defailen þe synȝers of þerþe,[3] and þe wicked so þat hij ne be nouȝt; ha, þou my soule, blisce our Lord.

PSALM 104 (105).

1. Shriueþ to our Lord, and clepeþ[4] his name; telleþ amonges folke hys werkes.

2. Syngeþ to hym, and psalmeþ to hym; telleþ alle his wondres; be ȝe heried in hys holi name.

3. Glade þe hert of þe secheand our Lord; secheþ[5] our Lord, and beþ confermed; secheþ alway hys face.

4. By-þencheþ ȝou of his wondres þat he did; & his toknes ben þe iugementȝ of his mouþe.

5. Ha þou sede of Abraham, his seruauntȝ; ha ȝe Iacob sones, his chosen,[6] biþencheþ of God.

6. He his þe Lord, our God; his iuge[me]ntȝ ben in alle erþe.

7. He was by-þenchand in þe world of his testament, and of his world þat he sent into a þousand kyndes.

8. Which worde he ordeined to Abraham and his oþe to Ysaac.

[7]9. And he stablist þat to Iacob in comaundement, and to þe sones of Israel in testament wyþ-outen ende,

10. Saiand, Y shal ȝeue þe þe londe of Chanaan in a corde of [ȝ]our herytage.

---

[1] MS. and. [2] fol. 98b. [3] MS. þe þerþe. [4] MS. clepleþ. [5] MS. adds and here. [6] MS. repeats his chosen. [7] fol. 99.

---

31. ioie.
32. tougeþ: *smeke.
33. and my] in my.
34. f. s. y.
35. Defayle: þe þerþe] þe erþe: —ne: ha] o: —soule.

104. 1. clepeþ.

3. s.—and: confirmede.
4. —þe: domes.
5. O: seruant: o.
6. domes.
7. in] of.
8. 1. to] & (!).
9. sett.
10. londe] bonde(!): ȝoure.

* fol. 38b.

11. As ȝ[1] were in lytel noumbre and her tyliers[2] alderfewest:

12. And hij passeden fram folk⸺ to folk⸺, and fram kyngdom to anoþer folk⸺;

13. He ne suffred nouȝt man greuen hem, and he repruued[3] kynges fram hem,

14. Saiand, Ne wil ȝe nouȝt touchen my prestes anoint wyþ creyme, and ne wylle ȝe nouȝt weryen in my prophetes.

15. And he cleped hunger vp þe londe of Chanaan, and de-fouled al þe fastnes of brede.

16. Jacob sent þe man Joseph oȝayn his breþer, Joseph was solde to þral þurth hem.

17. Hij loweden þe fete of Ioseph in fetteres, yren passed þourȝ þe soule of Iacob to þat þe word of Ioseph come to hym.

18. Þe word of our Lord brent Ioseph; þe kyng Pharaon sent for hym [4]to þe prison, and vnbonde hym of bondes; þe prince of folk⸺ did hym of pyne.

19. He stablist hym lord of hys[5] hous and prince of alle hys habbynge,

20. Þat he lered hys prynces as hym self and tauȝt hys elde quaintyse.

21. And þe fende anoied greteliche hys folk⸺, and fastened it up hys enemys,

22. [*Latin and English omitted.*]

23. Þe fende turned þe hertes of þe Egipciens, þat hij hated hys folk⸺ and dede trecherie oȝain Goddes seruauntes.

24. Our Lord sent Moyses, [hys] seruaunt, and þat Aaron þat he ches.

25. He[6] sett in hym wordes of his toknes and of his wondres in þe londe of Cham.

---

[1] I.e., *hy* or *hij* (ei).   [2] MS. *tyriels.*   [3] MS. *repruuded.*   [4] fol. 99*b.*
[5] *lord* follows, but is dotted out.   [6] MS. *Be.*

---

11. *y*] þei: tiliers.
13. —*ne*: reproued k. for.
14. —*ne*: anoittyd: creme:— *ne*: curs.
15. defoiled.
16. aȝens: þraldom þurȝ.
17. made lowe: yse: come—*to.*
19. *st.*] made: possession.

20. schuld lere: schuld teche: olde men wysdome.
21. *it*] him.
22. & Israel entred in Egipt, & Jacob was tylier in þe londe of Cham.
23. of—þe: gyle aȝenes.
24. Moises+his.
25. He.

26. He sent derknisses,[1] and made derke þe Egipciens, and ne enegred nouȝt þe wordes of Moyses,

27. He turned her waters into blode, and sloȝe her fisshes.

28. And her erþe ȝaf frosches in þynges of her kynges gode to parte.

29. Moyses [2]seide to our Lord of þe hardnes of Egipciens, and hounde-fleȝes and gnattes comeþ in alle her londes.

30. He sett[3] her raynes hail and fur brynand in her londe;

31. And smote her vynes and her fygers,[4] and defouled þe wode of her londe.

32. Moyses seid to our Lord of þe hardnes of Pharaon in þe sones of Iacob, and grashoppes come and breses, of which no noumbre was of.

33. And he ete alle þe hai in her londe, and ete al þe fruit[5] of her londe.

34. And he smote alle þe first biȝetynge of her londe and þe first byȝetyng¹ of alle her trauaile.

35. And he lad out Iacob sones wyþ gold and syluer, and syke man nas nouȝt founden in alle her kyn-redenis.

36. Egipt was glad in þe forþgoing of Iacobes childer, for þe drede of hem touched vp hem.

37. And he shewed cloude in-to her proteccioun and fur, þat it shuld alyȝt to hem by nyȝt.

38. [6] Hij askeden flesches; and curlu come to hem, and fulfild hem of brede of heuen.

39. God brake þe stone, and waters ran out, and flodes ȝede þurȝ drienes.

40. For he was byþenchand of his holy worde, þe which he had to Abraham, hys childe.

41. And God lad forþ hys folk¹ wyþ gladnes and hys chosen wyþ ioie.

---

[1] n is corrected from e. [2] fol. 100. [3] MS. seit. [4] MS. fyngers.
[5] Or frutt. [6] fol. 100b.

---

*26. —ne : agreued.
28. irogges.   29. gnattet† com.
30. sett : rayne : brennyng.
31. —vynes a. her : figares : defoiled.

32. breres : was—of.
35. was : kyndes.
36. forgoyng : touchyng.
38. of] with.

* fol. 39.   † Second t added over line.

130   EARLY ENGLISH PSALTER.   PSALM 105 (106).

42. And he ȝaf[1] hem kyngdomes of men, and hij hadden þe trauailes of folkes,

43. Þat hij kepten riȝtfulnesses and soȝten his lawe.

PSALM 105 (106).

1. Shryueþ to our Lord, for he his God, for in þe world is his mercy.

2. Who shal speke þe myȝtes of our Lord? he shal make alle hys heryynges herd.

3. Blisced ben hij þat kepen iugement and don ryȝtfulnes in alle time.

4. Þenche, Lord, on vs in þe wele-likand of þy folk', and visit vs in þyne helþe,

5. For to se in þe godenes of þyn chosen, to gladen in þe gladnisse of þy folke, þatou be heried in þyne herytage.

6. We han synȝed wyþ our fadres, we han wroȝt vnryȝtfullich, and we han don wickednisse.

7. Our fadres in Egipt ne vnderstode noȝt þyn wondres, and hij were nouȝt þenchand on þe multitude of þyn mercy.

8. And hij tariden þe Egipciens wendand vp in[2] þe see, [þe Reed See;] and he saued hem for his name, þat he made his myȝt knowen.

9. And he wyþ-droȝe þe Reed See, and it ys dried; and lad þe Egipciens in depenes as in þe desert.

10. And he saued þe .xii. kindes of Iacob fram þe honde of þe enemy.

11. And þe water couerd þe trybuland hem, and þer ne laft nouȝt on of hem.

12. And þe .xij. kindes byleueden his worde and heried his heryyng.

13. Sone hij faileden, and forȝaten hys werkes, and[3] [4]ne susteined nouȝt hys conseil.

14. And hij couaited couaitise in desert, & tempteden God in driehede.

15. And he ȝaf hem her askyng, & sent fulnes in-to her soules.

16. And hij tariden Moyses in castels & Aaron, þe holy of our Lord.

---

[1] Before ȝaf a letter is erased.   [2] in added over the line.   [3] fol. 101b.   [4] Here follows suffre, which is dotted out.

---

43. kepe riȝtfulnes.

105. 1. his m.] m.
4. þi wel plesyng.
5. þi godenes.   7. —ne.
8. se+þe Rede See.

*9. in—þe.
11. couerde trublyng (men expuncted) hem: —ne.
13. —ne.
14. couayte couatise: drynes.
16. wraþed: holy+man.

* fol. 39b.

17. Þe erthe ys opened, & swolwed Datham, & couered vp þe gaderyng of Abyron.

18. And fur brent in her sinagoge, & lait brent þe sinȝers.

19. And hij maden[1] a chalf in Oreb, & anoured þyng made wyþ fingers.

20. And hij chaungeden her glorie in-to þe likenes of chalf etand haye.

21. Hij for-haten[2] God þat saued hem, þat grete þynges did in Egipt, in þe londe of Cham, dredeful þynges in þe Reed Se.

22. God seid þat he shuld for-done hem, ȝyf Moyses, his chosen, ne had nouȝt stonden in brekeyng in his syȝt;

23. Þat he turned hys wraþþe, [3]þat he ne fordid hem nouȝt; and hij had for nouȝt þe londe desiderable.

24. And hij ne leued nouȝt his worde & gruched in her tabernacles, and hij ne herd nouȝt þe voice of our Lord.

25. And he lifted his vengeaunce vp hem, þat he feld hem doun in wildernesse.

26. And þat he out-kest her sede in þerþes[4] and departed hem in kyngdomes.

27. And hij ben sacrified to Belphegor, & eten þe pines of þe dampned.

28. And hij taried hym in her fyndynges, and fallyng doun is multiplied in hem.

29. And Finees stode and plesed, & crossyng cessed.

30. And it is told to hym in-to ryȝtfulnes in kynde to kynde vn-to euere lastend.

31. And hij tariden Moyses atte water of ȝainsygeinge, and he ys trauayled for hem þat greued hys gost.

---

[1] *hym* follows, but is expuncted. [2] Blunder for *forȝaten*. [3] fol. 102. [4] MS. *inberþes* (?), the *b* being obliterated.

---

17. Dathan.
18. lyet.
19. honoured.
20. ioie : —þe : of+a.
21. forȝate : Cham+&.
22. —ne.
23. schuld turne : —ne : desirable londe.
24. —ne : beleuyd : —ne.
25. lif(!).

26. he schuld cast oute : þerþes] nacions : desparple—hem.
27. sacred : peynes.
28. —doun : in hem *before* is.
29. *pl.*] plantyd : crossyng] þe schakyng.
30. putt : in k.]framk. : vnto e. l.] with-oute ende.
31. And taried at þe water of contradiccion.

32. And he distincted in his lippes; & hij ne spracł nouȝt men which our Lord seid to hem.

33. ¹And hij ben meined among folk¹ wyþ-outen lawe, and lerned her werkes, and serueden to her fals ym[a]ges, and þat ys made to hem in sclaunder.

34. And hij sacrifiden her sones and her douters to debleries,²

35. And shadde blode nouȝt filed, and blode of her sones and her douȝters, which hij sacrified to þe fals ymages of Chanaam.

36. And þer[þe] is slaine for synȝes & filed in her werkes, & dede horedome in her fyndeinges.

37. And our Lord wraþed hym in hys vengeaunce oȝains his folk¹, and loþed hys heritage.

38. And he ȝaf hem in-to þe hondes of folkes wyþ-outen lawe, and hij þat hated hem lord-shipped hem.

39. And her enemys trubled hem, and hij ben meked vnder her hondes; often our Lord deliuerd hem of iuel.

40. Hij for-soþe greueden him in her conseils, and hij ben lowed in her wickednisses.

41. And he seȝe whan hij were trubled, & herd her praier.

42. And he was by-þen-chand on hys testament, & it hym for-þouȝt efter þe multitude of hys mercy.

43. And he ȝaf hem in his mercies in syȝt of alle þat hadde taken hem.

44. Ha Lord God, make us sauf, & gader us to-gider of straunge kynredens,

45. þat we shryue to þyn holy name, & þat we gladen in þy heryynge.

46. Be our Lord, God of Israel, blisced of þys world, here and vnto þe world þat euer shal last; & alle þe puple shal saie, Be it don, be it don.

---

¹ fol. 102b.   ² Or *dobleries*.

---

32. depardid — *in: ne spr.*] sparpeled.
33. mengyd: ymages — *and.*
34. doȝters to fendes.
35. *bl. n. f. and bl.*] vngilty bl.: *which*] þat.
36. þer] þe erþe: slawe: foiled: fornicacion.
*38. *lordsh.*] had lordschip of.
39. maked: oft: deliuereþ.
40. F. s. þai: wykkydnes.
44. to-gader fram str. nacions.
46. folke.

* fol. 40.

PSALM 106 (107).

1. Shryueþ to our Lord, for he ys gode, for in þe world ys hys mercy.
2. Siggen hij nov þat ben bouȝt of our Lord, which he bouȝt[1] fram þe honde of þe enemy, of straunge kyngdomes he gadered hem.
3. Fram þe rysyng of þe sunne[2] vnto þe goynge adoune, fram þe norþe & þe see.
4. Þe childer of Israel erreden in onhede & in dryhede, and hij ne fonde nouȝt [3]þe waie of ioye euer lastand.
5. Hungerand & þrestand,[4] her soule faileden in hem.
6. And hij criden to our Lord, as hij were trubled, & hij deliuered hem of alle her nedefulnes.[5]
7. And he lad hem in þe ryȝt waie, þat hij heden[6] into ioie[7] euerlastand
8. Shryue to our Lord hys mercies, & hys wonders to mennes sones.
9. For he fulfild idel soule, and fulfild hungri[8] soules of godes,
10. Sittand in derknes & in shadue of deþ, bonden in wrechedhede [&] in iren.
11. For hij anegreden þe wordes of our Lord, & maden vain þe conseil of þe heȝest.
12. And her hert ys lowed in her trauailes, and hij ben syke ; & þer nas non þat halpe hem.
13. And hij crieden to our Lord, as hij weren trubled, & he deliuered hem of alle her nedefulnisses.
14. And he lad hem fram derknesses & shadowe [of deþ], & brake her bondes.
15. Shryue to our Lord hys merci[9]es & hys wonders to mennes sones.
16. For he de[fouled] þe ȝates of brasse, & brake þe lockes of iren.

---

[1] MS. brouȝt. [2] MS. synȝes. [3] fol. 103b. [4] Or þrostand. [5] MS. herne de fulnes, the u being corrected from another letter. [6] Miswritten for ȝeden. [7] MS. ieie. [8] MS. hunger. [9] fol. 104.

---

106. 2. brouȝt] bouȝt.
3. sunne : ad.] doune.
4. wyldernes : —ne.
5. affrystyng.
7. ȝode : euerlastyng ioie.
8. Be our Lordes mercies know to our Lorde : men.
9. hungry soule with.
10. schade : wrechidnes & in yse.
11. wreþid.
12. was : helpid.
13. as] wen : nedefulnes.
14. derknes : schade+of deþ.
15. Sh.] Be know : men.
16. de] defoyled : yse.

17. He toke hem fram þe waie of wickednes, for hij ben lowed for her vnryȝtfulnes.

18. Her soule wlated al techyng¹ of helþe, & aproched to þe ȝates of deþ.

19. And hij criden to our Lord, as hij weren trubled; and he deliuered hem of alle her nedefulnisses.

20. Shryue to our Lord hys mercies, & hys wondres to mennes sones,

21. Þat hij [sacrifien] sacrifice of heryynge and telle his werkes in ioie.

22. Þe which comen in-to þe see in shippes, makand wercheinge¹ in mani waters,

23. Hij seȝen þe werkes of our Lord, & his wonders in þe depenes.

24. God seid, & þe gost of tempest stode, & his flodes ben anheȝed.

25. Hij steȝen vp vnto þe heuens, & fallen a-doun into depnes; her soule quoke in yuels.

26. Hij ben trubled, ² and hij ben stired as drunken, and alle her wisdomes is deuoured.

27. And hij criden to our Lord, as hij were trubled; and he lad hem out of her nedefulnisses.

28. And he stablist his tempest in þe wynde, & alle his flodes were stille.

29. And hij ioiden, for þe flodes were stille; and God lad hem to þe hauen of her wille.

30. Shryue to our Lord is mercies, & his wondres to mennes sones.

31. And heȝen hij hym in þe chirches of folkes, & heri hym in þe chaier of olde.

32. He³ sett her flodes in desert & þe goinges of waters in þrust,

33. Erþe berand frut in saltmerche for þe wickednesse of þe wonand þer-inne.

---

¹ MS. *wrecheinge*.   ² fol. 104b.   ³ *Her* MS.

---

18. *wl.*] had abhominacion : *ap. to*] com nere.
19. sturbled : nedefulnes.
20. knoulegeþ : *men.
21. þai+sacrifie.†
22. wyrchyng.
25. styed : —þe : fell : schakid.
26. sturbled : mouyd : wysdome.
27. when : sturbled : nedefulnes.
28. stabled.
30. Be know : *is*] his : men.
31. olde+men.
32. He : vschus : þurst.
33. saltmersche : of men wonnyng.

* fol. 40b.   † *e* on erasure of two letters.

34. He sett þe desert in pondes of waters, & þerþe wyþ-outen water at out-goynge of waters.

35. And he sett þerþe hungri, & hij stablist cite of wonyng.

36. And hij sewen feldes, and sett vines, & maden frut of birþe.

37. [1]And he blisced hem, and hij ben michel multiplied; & he ne litteled nouȝt her meres.

38. And hij ben made fewe, & ben trauailed fro þe tribulacion of wicked & fro sorow.

39. Strif is hald[2] vp þe princes, & þe fende made hem to erren in wilde stede, & nouȝt in þe waie.

40. And he halpe þe pouer of his mesais, & set þe menȝes as shepe.

41. Þe ryȝtful shul sen & gladen, & alle wicked shal stoppe her mouþe.

42. Which wise shal kepe þes þynges & vnderstonde þe merci[3] of our Lord?

PSALM 107 (108).

1. Ha God, myn hert hys made redi; myn hert his made redy, & y shal syngen, & y shal psalmen in my glorie.

2. Aryse sautrie & harpe, and y shal arysen in þe morwenyng'.

3. Y shal shryue to þe, Lord, for þe folkes; and y shal syngen to þe for þe kyndes.

4. For þy mercy ys grete vp þe heuens, & þy soþenes is vn-to þe cloudes.

5. Be þou an-heȝed [4]vp þe heuenes; & þy glorie is vp alle þerþe, þat þyn frendes ben deliuered.

6. Make me sauf, & here me for þy myȝt; God spak' in hys holy.

7. Y shal gladen & departen þe dryhede, & y shal mete þe ualeye of tabernacles.

8. Galaad ys myn, & Manasses is myn, Effraym ys þe takeyng' of myn heued.

---

[1] fol. 105. [2] MS. *hard*. [3] MS. *merþi* (struck out) *merci*. [4] fol. 105*b*.

---

34. atte þe vschus.
35. stabled+þe.
36. sowed: beryng.
37. blessed: —*ne*: bestes.
39. *hard*] schad: in way.
40. heped(!): myssays: menȝe.
42. What w.+man.

107. 1. syng &—*y shal*: ioie.
2. sauter: harp—*and*: mornyng.
3. —*Lord*.
4. vp—*þe*.
5. ioie.
7. dryhode.

9. Juda ys my kynge, Moab is þe caudron of myn hope.

10. Y shal shewe myn hoseing in Ydume; strange ben made my frendes.

11. Who shal lede me in-to a cite warnist? who shal lede me in-to Ydume?

12. Noȝt þou, God, þat put vs oway; & þou ne shal nouȝt, God, gon out in our vertuȝ.

13. ȝyf vs helpe of tribulacioun, for helþe of man ys ydel.

14. We shal do vertu in God, and he shal bringe to nouȝt our enemis.

PSALM 108 (109).

1. Ha God, ne haue þou nouȝt stilled myn heryynge; for þe mouþe of þe synȝer & þe mouþe[1] of þe treche[2]rous is open up me.

2. And hij spaken to me wyþ trecherous tunge, and encumpassed [me] wyþ wordes of hating, & faȝten wyþ me[3] wyþ wille.

3. For þat þe gode loued me, þe wicked bacbiten me; & ich praied for hem.

4. And hij sett to me iuels for godes & hate for my loue.

5. Stables þe synȝer vp þe wicked; & þe fende stonde at hys ryȝthalf.

6. As he ys iuged, go he out condempned, & be hys prayer made into synȝe.

7. Ben his dayes made fewe, & anoþer tak' his bischopriche.[4]

8. Ben hys childer made faderles, & wif widowe.

9. Be hys sones made stumbland, & biggen hij; and ben hij outcusten of her woninges.

10. Secheþ þe usurer alle hys substaunce, & þe straunge rauis[5] her trauales.

11. Ne be nouȝt to hym helper, ne þer ne be non þat haue pite of his moderles.

---

[1] MS. repeats & þe mouþe.   [2] fol. 106.   [3] Followed by wylle, which is dotted out.
[4] MS. bischop bride.   [5] raines MS.

---

*10. made] mde(!).
11. warnischt.
12. puttest: —ne.

108. 1. O Godd, þou schalt noȝt still myn herying: gileful is opned.
2. gyleful: enclosed+me.
3. þe g.] Godd: bakbytyd.

4. gode.
5. Sett: stonde þe f.: r. syde.
6. When: demyd.
7. take ane oþer: byschopriche.
8. &+his.
9. sturblyng: begg: outecaste.
10. Seche: rauische: trauailes.
11. —Ne: ne þer ne be] & be þer.

* fol. 41.

12. Be his childer made in-to deþ, & be hys name don oway in o kynde.

13. ¹Turne þe wickednes of hys fadres in-to mynde in þe siȝt of our Lord, and þe synȝe of his moder be nouȝt don oway.

14. Hij ben made al-way oȝains our Lord, & peris [her] mynde fram þerþe, for þat he ne had nouȝt in mynde to do mercy,

15. And pursued þe gode man, þe mesays and þe biggeand, & to sle man prikked in hert.

16. And he loued waryynge, & it shal come to hym; and he nold nouȝt blisceing, & it shal be don fer fram hym.

17. And he cloþed wareing as cloþyng, & it entred as water in-to his in-nermast þinges & as oile in his bones.

18. Be made to hym as cloyþng, wyþ which he is [couered, & as a girdel, wyþ which he is] euermore girt.

19. Þis is þe werk¹ of hem þat bacbiten me to our Lord, & hij þat speken iuel þynges oȝain my soule.

20. & þou, Lord, do mercy wyþ me for þy name; for þy mercy is mylde.

21. Deliuer me of iuel; for ich am nedeful ²& pouer, and myn hert is trubled wyþ-innen me.

22. Ich am don oway as shadowe, whan it boweþ doun, & ich am shaken out as grashoppes.

23. Myn knowes ben sike led³ of fastyng, & my flesshe is chaunged for oile.

24. And ich am made to hem vpbraidynge; & hij seiȝen me, & styreden her heuedes.

25. Ha Lord, my God, helpe me; make me sauf efter þy mercy.

26. And hij shul wyten þat þys his þyn helpe, and þou, Lord, made it.

---

¹ fol. 106b.   ² fol. 107.   ³ Thus MS., for *sikelech, siklich*?

---

12. into o k.
14. Be þai: perisch+her: —ne.
15. And+he: mysays: beggar.
16. curssyng: wolde.
17. warying: *innermast þ.*] entrailes.
18. *Be*] He: *euerm. girt*] couerd

& as a girdel with which he is euer gyrd.
20. meke.   21. sturbled.
22. *shaken*] smyte.
23. beþ vnfast for fastyng.
24. reproue: moued.
25. O.

27. Hij shul waryen, and þou shalt bliscen; be hii confounded þat arisen oʒains me, & þy seruant shal gladen.

28. Ben hij cloþed wyþ shame þat bacbiten me, ben hij couered wyþ confusion as wyþ double cloþyngᵗ.

29. Y shal shryue michel to our Lord in my mouþe, & y shal herien hym amiddes mani,

30. Þe wich[1] stode at þe ryʒt-half of þe pouer in gost, þat he made me sauf fram þe pursuand my soule.

[2]PSALM 109 (110).

1. Þe Lord, fader of heuen, seid to his sone, my Lord, Sitt þou at my ryʒthalf,

2. Þer-whiles þat y sett þyn enemys shamel of þy fete.[3]

3. Our Lord shal sende fram Syon Marie, þe ʒerde of þy vertu; lordship þou in-middes þin enemys.

4. Þe bi-ginynge is wyþ þe in þe daie of þy uertu in shinynges of holy, ymade wyþ me of my pouste to-fore Lucifer.

5. Our Lord swore, and it ne shal nouʒt forþenchen hym; þou art prest wyþouten ende efter þe order of Melchisedech.

6. Our Lord is at þy ryʒthalf, & he shal for-don kynges in þe daie of his ire.

7. He shal iuge in kyndes & fulfillen[4] fallinges; he shal crouse in erþe þe wicked dedes of mani.

8. He drankᵗ in þe way of þe wille of grace, for-þy he heʒed his heued.

PSALM 110 (111).

[5]1. Lord, y shal shryue to þe in al myn hert in þe conseil & in þe gaderyngᵗ of ryʒtful.

---

[1] MS. *wicked*.   [2] fol. 107*b*.   [3] Corrected from *fote*.   [4] MS. *fulfild*.
[5] fol. 108.

---

27. *cu*rsse :*blise.
29. muche.
30. *w.*] whych: r. side: fram men p*ur*suyng.

109. 1. r. side.
2. —þat : *sh.*] þe stole.

3. *lordsh. . . . inm.*] forto haue lordschipe amyddes.
4. holy+men : power.
5. —*ne.*
6. r. side.
7. deme : fulfil : schake.
8. *wille . . . þy*] weH of þe weH of gr. þ*er*-fore.

* fol. 41*b*.

EARLY ENGLISH PSALTER. PSALM 111 (112). 139

2. Þe werkes of our Lord be grete, soȝt in-to alle his willes.

3. His werk[1] ys shryf and hereing, &[2] his ryȝtfulnes woneþ in þe heuen.

4. Our Lord piteful & merciful made minde of his wondres; he ȝaf mete to þe doutand hym.

5. He shal be biþenchand in þe world of his testament; he shal tellen to his folkᶦ þe vertu of his werkes.

6. Þat he ȝaf hem heritage of men, þe werkes of his hondes ben soþenisse & iugement.

7. Alle hys comaundementȝ ben trew, confermed[3] in þe worled of world, made in soþenes & euenhede.

8. Our Lord sent raunsoun to his folkᶦ, & comaunded hys testament wyþ-outen ende.

9. His name is holy & dredeful, þe biginnyngᶦ of wisdome is dredyngᶦ of our Lord.

10. Gode vnderstondynge ys to alle doand [hym]; his hereingᶦ woneþ in þe heuens.

[4]PSALM 111 (112).

1. Blisced be þe man þat douteþ our Lord; he shal wil greteliche in his comaundementȝ.

2. His sede shal be ryȝtful in erþe; þe kynde of þe ryȝtful shal be blisced.

3. Glorie & riches ben in his hous, & his ryȝtfulnes woneþ in heuens.

4. Lyȝt hys sprungen in derkenes to þe ryȝtful; merciful & reuful & riȝtful.

5. Þat man shal be ioieful þat haþ pite and laneþ & ordeineþ his wordes in iugement, for he ne shal nouȝt be stired wyþ-outen ende.

6. Þe ryȝtful shal be in mynde euerlastand, & he ne shal nouȝt douten of iuel hereing.[5]

---

[1] MS. werkes, but es is dotted out.   [2] MS. in.   [3] The second e corrected from o.
[4] fol. 108b.   [5] MS. herieing.

---

110. 3. werkes(!) is schryft: herying & : —woneþ.
4. to men dredyng.
5. beþencher of his t. into þe w.
6. ȝif : soþnes & dome.
7. euenhode.
9. dredyng] drede.
10. doyng+him (added over line) :
herying : in — þe.

111. 1. dredeþ.
2. be r.] be miȝtful : be+be.
3. Ioie.
4. sprong : reuf.] peteful.
5. dome : —ne : mouyd.
*6. —ne : heryng.

* fol. 42.

7. His hert is diȝt to hope in our Lord, & his hert is conformed; & ho shal nouȝt be stired to þat he despise his enemis.

8. He de-parted, & ȝaf to pouer; is ryȝtfulnes wones in þe heuens, his heued shal be an-heȝed in glorie.

9. Þe synȝer shal sen is iuel and be wroþe, and he shal gnaist wyþ his teþ for py¹nes, and he shal failen of holines; þe desire of þe synȝers shal peris.

PSALM 112 (113).

1. Ha ȝe childer, herieþ our Lord, herieþ þe name of our Lord.
2. Be þe² name of our Lord blisced, nou of þis & vnto heuen.
3. Þe name of our Lord ys worþshipful fram þe birþe of þe sunne³ vnto þe going-doun.
4. Our Lord is heȝe vp alle men, & his glorie his vp heuens.
5. Who is as God, our Lord, þat woneþ on heȝt & loked to þe meke þinges in heuen & in erþe?
6. Liftand þe mysays fram þerþe & dressand up þe pouer out of dung,
7. Þat he sett him wyþ princes, wyþ princes of his folk¹;
8. Þat doþ þe barain moder of childer to wonen in þe hous ioyand.

PSALM 113 (114).

1. In þe out-going of þe childer of Israel of Egipt, of þe men of Iacob hous [fram] þe strange folk¹,
2. Iude is made his halwyng, Israel is made his pouste.
3. Þe see saȝe hem, & fled hem; and so his þe flum Iordan [turned] oȝain[ward].
⁴4. Hij heden⁵ þe mounteyns as weþeres, & þe littel hilles as lambren of shepe.

---

¹ fol. 109.   ² MS. he.   ³ MS. sinȝe.   ⁴ fol. 109b.   ⁵ i e. heiden, heȝeden.

---

7. confirmed: mouyd.
8. woneþ in—þe: ioie.
9. grynte: paynes: of—þe.

112. 1. O.
2. he] þe: nou ... heuen] fram þis tyme wiþoute ende.
3. worschipful: rysyng: sune.
4. aboue heuen.
5. lokeþ: &—in.

6. Areryng.
7. wiþ þe princes of h. popiH.

113. 1. out-g.] passyng oute: hous+fram.
2. power.
3. oȝain] turned aȝenward.
4. Hij ... m.] þe mountaynes ioed (!): lambren] bombe (!).

5. Ha þou see, what þyng is to þe, þat tou fleddest, & þou flum Iordan, for þou art turned oȝainward?

6. Ha ȝe[1] childer of Israel, ȝe anheȝed þe mounteyns [as weþeres] and þe littel hulles as lambren of shepe.

7. Þe erþe is stired fram þe face of our Lord, fram þe face of God of Iacob;

8. Þe which turned þe stone to flodes of waters and þe roche to welles of waters.

(PSALM 115.) 1. Nouȝt to us, Lord, nouȝt to us; bot ȝif glorie to þy name.

2. Be we vp þy mercy and vp þy soþenes, þat þe folk ne say nouȝt, Wher is her God?

3. For-soþe our God is [in] heuen; he made al þyng' þat he wolde.

4. Þe ymagerie of men wyþ-outen lawe ben gold and seluer, werkes of mennes hondes.

5. Hij han mouþe, & hij ne shal nouȝt speken; hij han eȝen, & hij ne shal nouȝt se.

6. Hij han eren, and hij ne shul nouȝt[2] [heren; hij] han noses, and hij ne shul nouȝt smullen.

7. Hij han hondes, & hij ne shul nouȝt fele; hij han fete, & hij ne [3]shul nouȝt gon; hij ne shul nouȝt crien in her þrote.

8. Hij þat maken hem be liche to hem, & hij þat affien in hem.

9. Þe folk· of þe hous of Israel hoped in our Lord; he is her helper & her defendour.

10. Þe hous of Aaron hoped in our Lord; he his her helpe[r] & her defendour.

11. Hij þat dreden our Lord hoped in our Lord, he his her helper & her defendour.

---

[1] ȝe added over line. [2] The words *and hij ne shul nouȝt* are erroneously dotted out.
[3] fol. 110.

---

5. O: —þyng.
6. O: m.+as weþers: lombe.
7. mouɤd: Lorde+&.
8. þe wh.t.] He þat turneþ: flode.

(115) 2. —ne. 3. is+in.
4. maumetrie.
5. —ne: —ne.

6. —ne: 1. noȝt+here þai: — ne: smell.
7. —ne: —ne: —ne: crie with.
8. be] be þai made: *hij þ. aff.*] all þat beleueþ.
9. —of þe hous.
10. h.] folke: helper.
11. in+hym.

12. Our Lord was þenchand on vs, and blesced us.
13. He blisced þe folk¹ of Israel, he blesced þe folk¹ of Aaron.
14. He blisced alle þat douten our Lord, þe littel wyþ þe mechel.
15. Cast our ¹ Lord grace vp ȝou, vp ȝou & up ȝour sones.²
16. Blisced be he ³ god of our Lord, þat made heuen and erþe.
17. Þe heuens ȝauen heuen to our Lord, & he ȝaf þerþe to mennes sones.
18. Þe dampned, Lord, ne shul nouȝt herien þe, ne alle þo þat descenden in-to helle.
19. Bot we þat lyuen, blisce our Lord nou and þanne vnto þe worled.

PSALM 114 (116).

1. Ich loued ⁴our Lord; for our Lord shal here þe voice of my praier.
2. For he bowed his ere to me, & y shal clepe him in mi daies.
3. Sorowes of deþ ȝede a-bouȝt me, & þe perils of helle fonde me.
4. Y funde tribulacion & sorowe, & cleped þe name of our Lord.
5. Ha þou Lord, ryȝtful & merciable, deliuer my soule; and our Lord haþ mercy.
6. Our Lord is kepand þe littel; ich am made buxum, & he deliuered me of iuels.
7. Turne my soule in-to þy reste, for our Lord haþ don wele to me.
8. For he defended my soule fram deþ, myn eȝen fram teres, myn fete fram slideinge.
9. Y shal pleise to our Lord in þe kyngdom of þe leueand.

PSALM 115 (116 continued).

1. Y byleued þat y spake; ich am for-soþe michel lowed.
2. Y said in my passing, Ich man is liȝer.

---

¹ r on erasure.   ² MS. fones.   ³ Read ȝe.   ⁴ fol. 110b.

---

*13. blessed: Israel+& : blessed +to.
14. dredeþ.
15. childer.
16. ȝe gode.
18. Lorde þe d.—ne : ne] no.
19. nou...] fram now vnto þe w.

3. þe sorows: ȝede ab.] aclosed (d is corrected from þ) : fonde] haþ founde.
4. fonde: cl. our Lordis n.
5. O.
8. teres+&.
9. plese : leuyng.

114. 2. & in my d. y sch. c. h.   115. 1. muche.

* fol. 42b.

3. What þyng shal y ȝeue to our Lord for alle þyng þat he haþ ȝeuen to me?

4. Y shal take þe chalice of helpe & clepe þe name of our Lord.

5. Y shal ȝelde to our Lord myn vowes[1] to-fore alle his folk'; þe deþ of his holy is precious in þe siȝt of our Lord.

6. Ha Lord, for þat ich am þy seruaunt[2] & þe sone of þyn honde-mayden,

7. Þou to-brak' myn bondes; y shal sacrefie to þe offrand of hereing', & y shal clepen þe name of our Lord.

8. Y shal ȝelde vowes to our Lord in þe siȝt of alle his folke, in þe halles of þe hous of our Lord amiddes of Ierusalem.

PSALM 116 (117).

1. Ȝe alle folkes, herieþ our Lord; ȝe alle folkes, herieþ hym.

2. For his mercy is conferned vp us, and þe soþenes of our Lord woneþ wyþ-outen ende.

PSALM 117 (118).

1. Þe folkes, shriueþ to our Lord, for he his God; for his mercy is in þe worled.

2. Saie nov þe folk' of Israel, for he his god, for in þe world is his mercy.

3. Saie nov þe hous of þe folk of Aaron, for his mercy ys in þe world.

4. Saien hij nov þat dreden our Lord, for in þe wor[l]d is his mercy.

[3]5. Ich cleped our Lord in my tribulacioun, and our Lord herd me in brede.

6. Be our Lord myn helper, & y shal despisen myn enemys.

7. Gode is to affien in our Lord þan to affien in man.

8. Gode is to hopen in our Lord þan to hopen in princes.

---

[1] MS. bowes.   [2] MS. seruanut.   [3] fol. 111b.

---

3. —þyng: ȝelde: þinges—þat.
4. &+y schal.
5. vowes: holy+men: in . . . Lord] in his siȝt.
6. O Lorde fo (!) y am þi s.+y am þi seruant: honde-mayde.
7. þou brake: offryng.
8. of þe Jerusalem.

116. 2. c.] fest.

117. 1. ȝe: in þe w.] with-oute ende.
2. for our Lord is gode, for his mercye is with-oute ende.
3. folk of þe hous of Aa.: i. þ. w.] with-oute ende.
4. for his mercy is withoute ende.
5. brodnes.
7. Better is to leue: *leue.
8. Better.

* fol. 43.

9. Alle folkes wyþ-outen lawe bisett me wyþ iuels, and in þe name of our Lord; for ich am venged in hem.

10. Þe encumpassand iuels encumpassed me wyþ iuels, and in þe name of our Lord; for ich am venged in hem.

11. Hij encumpassed me as [1] ben, & brenden as fur in þornes, & in þe name of our Lord; for ich [am] venged in hem.

12. Ich am putt oȝain & turned oȝain, þat y shuld fallen, & our Lord toke me vp.

13. Our Lord ys my strengþe & myn hereing, & he is made to me in-to helþe.

14. He is voice of ioie & of helþe in þe tabernacles of ryȝtful.

15. Þe help of our Lord did vertu, þe helpe of our Lord anheȝed me, þe helpe [of] our Lord did vertu.

16. Y ne shal noȝt dien, bot y[2] shal liuen & telle þe werkes of our Lord.

17. Our Lord chastiand chastied [me], & ne ȝaf me nouȝt to deþ.

18. Openeþ to me þe ȝates of riȝtfulnes; ich, entred in-to hem, shal shriue to our Lord; þat is þe ȝate of our Lord, þe ryȝtful shul entren þer-inne.

19. Y shal shryue to þe, for[3] þou herd me; & þou art made to me in-to helþe.

20. Þe stone which þe biggand reproued, and it is made oȝain þe heued[4] of þe corner.

21. Þis þynge is made of our Lord, and it is wonder-ful in our eȝen.

22. Þis ys þe daie þat our Lord made; ioie we, glade we in yt.

23. Ha Lord, make me sauf; ha Lord, be þou wele enprospered; blisced be he þat comeþ in þe name of our Lord.

24. We haue blisced ȝou of þe hous of our Lord; God is our Lord, and he shone vnto vs.

---

[1] Here *of* follows, but is expuncted. [2] fol. 112. [3] MS. repeats *þe for*. [4] MS. *heried*.

10. *Omitted*.
11. closed: bene &+þay: y+ am.
12. —2. oȝain.
13. heryiug.
15. *help*] riȝt honde: *did*] haþ made: *h.*] riȝt honde: haþ enhied: *h.*] riȝt honde of: *did*] haþ made.
16. —*ne*: but—*y schal*: &+ schal.

17. chastesyng chasted+me: —*ne*.
18. *þeriȝtful*] r. men: *inne*] þurgȝ.
19. *Y*] Lorde, y.
20. *wh.*] þat: þe *b.*] þai: *and it*] þat: oȝ. þ. *h.*] into þe heuyd.
22. *in yt*] þer-in.
23. *w. enpr.* þou in wel-fare.
24. *God...vs*] & Godd *our* Lorde liȝtyd to vs.

25. Stablis þe solempne daie in þikkenesses vnto corner of þe auter.

26. Þou art my God, & y shal shryue to þe; [þou art my God, & y shal an-heȝe þe].

27. Y shal shryue to þe, for þou herd me; and þou art made to me into helþe.

[1]28. Shriueþ to our Lord, for he his God; for his mercy is in þe world.

PSALM 118 (119).

Aleph.[2]

1. Þe vnfiled in her waie ben blisced, þat gon in þe lawe of our Lord.

2. Ben hi blesced þat sechen his witnes & sechen hem in alle his hert.

3. For hij þat wirchen wickednes, ne ȝede nouȝt in his waies.

4. Þou comaunded þy comaundement to ben greteliche kept.

5. God ȝyf þat min waies ben dresced for to kepe þy ryȝtfulnes.

6. Þanne shal y nouȝt be confounded, whan ichaue loked in alle þyn comaundementȝ.

7. Y shal shryue to þe in drescynge of hert, in þat ichaue lerned þe iugementȝ of þy ryȝtfulnes.

8. Y shal kepe þy ryȝtfulnes; ne forsake me nouȝt in no manere.

Beth.

9. In what þynge amendeþ þe ȝenge man his waie in keping þy wordes?

10. Ichaue bi-soȝt þe in alle myn hert, ne putt me nouȝt owaie fram þyne comaundementȝ.

11. Ich hidde þy spekynges in [3]myn hert, þat y ne synȝe[4] nouȝt to þe.

12. Ha Lord, þou art blisced; teche me þy ryȝtfulnisses.

---

[1] fol. 112b.   [2] *Aleph* is omitted in MS.   [3] fol. 113.   [4] *synȝe* on erasure.

---

25. *St. þe*] Ych ordeyned te a: vnto+þe.
26. þe+þou art my God, & ych schal enhye þe.
28. *i. þ. w.*] with-oute ende.

118. Alla.—1. Þe ... bl.] Blyssid be þe vnfilde: *lawe*] way.
2. Blissyd be þai: her hert.
3. —ne.

4. sent þi commaundmentes.
5. Godd wold: —*ben*.
6. y schal loke.
7. þat+þat: domes.
8. riȝtfulnesses—*ne*.

Beth.—9. ȝonge—*man*.
10. —*ne*.
11. speches: —*ne*.
12. ryȝtfulnes.

13. Ichaue shewed for-þe in myn lippes alle[1] þe iugementȝ of þy mouþe.
14. Ich delithed me in þe waie of þy witnisses as[2] in alle riches.
15. Y shal be haunted in þy comaundement, & y shal sen þyn waies.
16. Y shal be þenchand in þyn ryȝtfulnesses, & y ne shal nouȝt for-ȝete þyn wordes.

Gymel.

17. Ha God, ȝif grace to þy seruaunt, & quike me; & y shal kepe þyn wordes.
18. Shewe myn eȝen, and y shal kepe þe wondres of þy lawe.
19. Ich am tilier in erþe, ne hide þou noȝt fram me þyn comaundement.
20. My soule haþ couaited for to desiren þy ryȝtfulnesses in alle time.
21. Þou blamed þe proude; hij ben weried þat bowen fram þyn comaundement.
22. Do fro me vpbradeing & despite, for ich haue soȝt þyn witnisses.
[3]23. For princes seten and spoken oȝains me; þin seruaunt for-soþe was haunted in þy riȝtynnges.
24. For my[4] þouȝt is þy witnisses, & þy ryȝtfulnisses ben m[i] conseil.

Beleth.

25. My soule drow to stablenes; quike me efter þy worde.
26. Ich told myn waies, and þou herdest me; teche me þy ryȝtfulnisses.
27. Teche me þe[5] way of þy ryȝtfulnes, and y shal be haunted in þy wondres.

---

[1] MS. *atte*. [2] MS. twice *as*. [3] fol. 113b. [4] Here þoute follows first, but it is dotted out. [5] e on erasure.

---

*13. all þe domes.
14. delityd: richesses.
15. vsed: commaundmentes.
16. be vsyd in þi riȝtwysnesses: —ne.

Gymel.—17. make me qwyk.
19. —ne: commaundmentes.
20. c.] couayte: ryȝtfulnes.
21. curssed: declineþ: commandmentis.

22. reproue—& *despite*.
23. For+soþe: —*for-soþe*: vsed in riȝtwysnesses.
24. mynde: & my conseyle is þi riȝtwysneses(!).

Beleth.—25. *drow*] cleuyd: make me quyk.
26. schewyd.
27. ryȝtfulnesses: vsyd.

* fol. 43b.

28. My soule trembleþ for anguisse ; conferme me in þy wordes.
29. Do fro me þe way of wickednes, & haue mercy on me for þy lawe.
30. Y chese þe way of þe soþenes, and y ne for-ȝate nouȝt þyn iugementȝ.
31. Lord, y droȝ to þyn wittenisses, ne wil þou nouȝt confounde me.
32. Ichaue vrnen þe wai of þy comaundementȝ, as tou enlarged mi hert in godnisse.

He.

33. Sett, Lord, lawe to me, way of þyn ryȝtynges, & y shal euer seche it.
34. Ȝif me vnderstondyng ; and y shal [1]seche þy lawe & kepe it in alle myn hert.
35. Lade me in þe bi-stiȝe of þy comaundement, for ich wold it.
36. Bowe myn hert into þy witnisses, & nouȝt in-to auarice.
37. Turne owai myn eȝen, þat y[2] ne se no uanites ; quik me in þy[3] waie.
38. Stablisce to þy seruant þy worde in þy drede.
39. Schre[d] owai my reproce, þat ich haue in suspeccioun ; for þyn iugementȝ ben ioiful.
40. Se, ich couaited þy comaundementȝ ; quike me in þin euennisse.

Vau.[4]

41. & cum þy mercy, Lord, vp me, þyn helþe efter þy spekynge.
42. And y shal answere to þe reprouaund to me word, for ich hoped in þy wordes.
43. And ne do þou noȝt out of my mouþe worde of soþenes in non maner, for ich hoped in þin iugement.
44. And y shal kepe þy lawe euer more in þe world and in þe heuen.
45. And ich ȝede in brede, for ichaue souȝt þyn comaundementȝ.

---

[1] fol. 114. [2] i.e. hy = Latin ei. [3] Here name follows, but is expuncted and struck out. [4] MS. Paau.

28. trembled : confirme.
29. & of þi l. haue mercye on me.
30. —ne : domes.
31. droȝ] haue cleuyd : —ne.
32. ȝorne : sprad.

Hee.—33. way] þe lawe : riȝtwysnesses.
34. kepe] y schal kepe.

35. paþe : commaundmentȝ.
37. y ne] þai : make me qwyk.
38. Sett.
39. Cutt away my reproue : suspecyon : domes.
40. Lo : couayte : make me qwyk.

Vau.—42. wordes] worders.
43. —ne : domes.
44. into þe w. & iu h.

46. And y spake of þin witnes in ¹syȝt of kynges, & y ne was nouȝt confounded.

47. And y shal þenchen in þin comaundementȝ, which y loued.

48. Y ne lefted myn hondes to þy comaundementȝ, þat y loued; and y shal be haunted in þy riȝtinges.

Zai.

49. Be þo biþenchand on þy worde to þy seruaunt, in which þou ȝaf me hope.

50. Þis hope conforted me in my meknes, for þi spekyng quikened me.

51. Þe proude deden iuel on ich a side; y for-soþe ne bowed nouȝt fram þy lawe.

52. Ich was, Lord, biþenchand on þy iugementȝ of þe world, & ich [am] conforted.

53. Defaut held me for þe synȝers for-sakand þi lawe.

54. Þy riȝtinges were songelich to me instede of my pilgrimage.

55. Ich was, Lord, bi-þenchand of þy name in þe niȝt, & ich kept þy lawe.

56. Þy[s] lawe is made to me, for þat y soȝt þyn riȝtinges.

Beth.

57. Ha Lord, myn porcioun, y seid to kepen þy lawe.

²58. Ich bi-þouȝt þy face in alle min hert; haue mercy on me efter þy worde.

59. Ich bi-þouȝt myn waies, and turned my fet into þy witnesses.

60. Ich am made redy; & y nam nouȝt ytroubled, þat y kepe þy comandementȝ.

---

¹ fol. 114b. ² fol. 115.

---

*46. witnesses: —*ne.*
47. *wh.*] þat.
48. & y lift+vp: vsed: riȝtful-nesses.

Zai.—49. þou: in+þe: *me h.*] hope to me.
50. speche made me qwyk.
51. *iuel ... side*] wickydlych on ech syde & : —*ne.*

52. Lorde y was: domes: y am conforde.
54. riȝtfulnesses were praysable: in þe st.
55. Lord y was.
56. þy] þis: riȝtfulnesses.

Beth (!)—57. *Ha ... seid*] Lorde y sayde is (!).
60. am noȝt made sturbled (*u* added over the line).

* fol. 44.

61. Þe wickednisses of sinȝers enbraceden me, & y ne for-ȝate nouȝt þy law.
62. Ich ros vp at midniȝt to shriue to þe vp þe iugement of þy riȝtinge.
63. Ich am partener of alle þe dredand þe & kepand þy comaundementȝ.
64. Þerþe, Lord, is ful of þy mercy; teche me þin ryȝtinges.

Teth.

65. Lord, þou didest godenes wiþ þy seruaunt efter þy worde.
66. Teche me godenes, discipline, and cuninge [1]; for ich bileued in þy comaundement.
67. Y trespassed to-forn þat y was lowed; for-þy y kept þy worde.
68. Þou art gode; & teche in þy godenes þyn ryȝtynges.
69. Þe wicked[nes] of pride[2] is multiplied up me; y shal seche for-soþe in alle myn [3] hert þyn comaundementȝ.
70. Her hert is runnen to-gideres as milk, ich for-soþe soȝt þy lawe.
71. Gode þing it is to me, þat þou lowedest me, þat ich lerne þy riȝtinges.
72. Gode þyng ys to me þe lawe of þy mouþe vp a þousand talens of seluer & gold.

Loth.

73. Þyn hondes made me, & fourmed me; ȝeue me vnderstondynge, þat ich lern þyn comaundementȝ.
74. Hij þat dreden þe shul sen me & gladen, for ich vp hoped in þy wordes.
75. Ich knew, Lord, þat þyn iugement ben euenhede, & þou lowedest me in þy soþnes.

---

[1] MS. *tuninge.*   [2] Should be *prude, proude.*   [3] fol. 115b.

---

61. *enbr.*] haþ enclosed: —*ne.*
62. domes: riȝtwysnes.
63. partyner: all men dredyng.
64. Lorde þe erþe: riȝtwysnesses.

Theth.—65. *efter*] ef (!).
66. *d.*] lore: cunnyng: commaundmentȝ.
67. þer-for.
68. & þi g. teche me þi riȝtwysnes.
69. wickydnes of proude+men: for-soþe y schal seche.

70. ȝorne to-gider: for-soþe y had in mynde þi l.
71. —*it*: made me meke: riȝtwysnesses.
72. talentes: &+of.

Loth.—74. drede me(!): se þe: —*vp.*
*75. domes: euennes: in þi s. þou made me meke.

* fol. 44b.

76. Be þy mercy made þat it conforted me; be it made to þy seruaunt efter þy worde.

77. Cum to me þyn mercies, & y shal liue; for þy lawe is my þenching.

78. Ben þe[1] proude confounded, for hij diden wickednes in me wyþ wrong; y for soþe shal be haunted in þy comaundementʒ.

79. Be þe dredand þe turned to me, & hij þat knowen þy witnes.

[2]80. Be myn hert made vnfiled in[3] þy riʒtinges, þat ich ne be nouʒt confounded.

Chap.

81. My soule failed in þin helþe, & ich hoped in þi worde.

82. Min eʒen faileden in þy worde, saiand, Whan shal tou conforten me?

83. For ich am made as way in rimfrost; y ne haue nouʒt forʒeten þy riʒtinges.

84. Hou mani ben þe daies of þi seruaunt? whan shalt tou make iugement of þe pursuand me?

85. Þe wicked telden me tales, ac nouʒt as þi law.

86. Alle þyn comaundementʒ ben soþnes; þe wicked pursued me, helpe þou me.

87. Hij hadden nere honde casten me in erþe, for-soþe y ne for-soke nouʒt þin comaundement.

88. Quike me efter þy mercy, & y shal kepe þe wittnisses of þi mouþe.

Lameth.

89. Lord, þi worde dwelleþ wyþ-outen ende in heuen.

90. Þy soþnes is in kinde & kinde; þou founded þerþe, & it dwelleþ.

91. Þe daie lasteþ þurʒ þin ordinaunce, for alle þinges seruen to þe.

---

[1] MS. þy. [2] fol. 116. [3] MS. *in in.*

---

76. conforte.
77. þi m. to me: mynde.
78. þy pr.] proude men: haue do w. wrongfulich aʒens me, f. s. y was vsyd.
79. þe dr.] men dredyng: knew.
80. riʒtfulnesses: —ne.

Cahap.—83. as + a: horefrost: —ne: riʒtfulnesses.

85. told: bot.
86. —þou.
87. nere .. me] neʒ hendyd me by a lytil: —ne: commaundmentʒ.
88. Make me qwyk.

Lameth.—89. woncþ.
90. made.

[1]92. Bot þat þy lawe is mi þouȝt, þan peraunter ich had perissed in my lowenisse.

93. Y ne shal nouȝt for-ȝete þin riȝttinges wyþ-outen ende, for þou quiked me in hem.

94. Ich am þy; make me sauf, for ichaue soȝt þi ryȝtinges.

95. Sinȝers abiden me, þat hij shuld destruen me; ichaue vnderstonden þy witnesses.

96. Ich seiȝe þe endeing of alle fulfilling, [þi comaundement is much large].

Mem.[2]

97. Hou, Lord, loued ich þy lawe? al dai it is my þouȝt.

98. þou madest me quainte vp myn enemis to þi comaundement, for it is to me wiþ-outen ende.

99. Ich vnderstode vp alle techand me; for ich þouȝt þin witnisses ben[3] mi þouȝt.

100. Ich vnderstode vp þe olde, for ich soȝt þin comaundement.

101. Ich defended mi[4] fete fram ich iuel way, þat ich kepe þin wordes.

102. Y ne bowed nouȝt fram þin iugement, for þou sett lawe to me.

103. Ful swete ben þi wordes [5]to mi cheke, more þan huni[6] to my mouþe.

104. Ich vnderstode witt of þy comaundement, for-þi ich hated ich way of wickednes.

Nun.

105. Þy worde is lanterne to mi fete & liȝt to my bisties.

106. Ich swore & stablist to kepe þe iugementȝ of þy riȝtfulnes.

107. Ich am lowed on ich half; quicke me efter þyn worde.

---

[1] fol. 116b. [2] MS. Oren. [3] e corrected from o. [4] MS. ni. [5] fol. 117. [6] MS. hi mi.

---

92. þat] if : is] be : mynde : mekenes.
93. —ne : riȝtfulnesses—w. o. ende: in hem þou hast made me qwyk.
94. riȝtwysnes.
95. ab.] haue byde : witnes.
96. ende : fulf.+þi commaundment is much large.

[Mem].—97. Lorde how.
98. qu.] wys.

99. all+men: witnes is: mynde.
100. vp olde men : commaundmentȝ.
101. my.
102. —ne : domes.
103. chekes : hony.
104. commaundmentes.

Nun.—105. paþes.
106. sett: domes.
107. syde, make (—me) qwyk.

108. Make, Lord, þe wilful þinges of mi mouþe in gode plesaunce, & teche me þin iugement.

109. My soule is alway in myn hondes, & y ne haue nouȝt for-ȝeten þi lawe.

110. Sinȝers laiden gnare to me, and y ne erred nouȝt for þy comaundementȝ.

111. Ichaue purchased wyþ-outen ende þin witnesses in heritage, for hij ben þe ioie of min hert.

112. Ich bowed min hert to do þy riȝtinges wyþ-outen ende for mede.

Samec.

113. Ich hade þe wicked in hateing, & ich loued þi lawe.

114. Þou art min helper & mi taker, & ich hoped in þi worde.

115. Ha ȝe wicked, boweþ[1] fram me, and y shal se[2]chen þe comaundement of my God.

116. Take me efter þy worde, and y shal leuen; & ne confounde me nouȝt fram myn abidyng.

117. Helpe me, & y shal be sauf; & y shal euermore þenchen in þy riȝtinges.

118. Þou despised alle þe descendand fram þin iugementȝ; for her þouȝt is wrongful.

119. Ich told alle þe sinȝers of erþe for-fetand; for-þy loued ich þy wittnesses.

120. Feche my flesshes in þi drede, for y was agaist of þy iugementȝ.

Aym.

121. Ich did iugement & riȝt, ne ȝif me nouȝt to þe chalangand me.

122. Take vp þi seruaunt in gode, þat þe proude ne chalenge me nouȝt.

---

[1] MS. *loweþ*.   [2] fol. 117*b*.

---

*108. domes.
109. —*ne.*
110. *gn.*] þe grynne : —*ne* : *for*] of.
111. Haue y gete: witnes — *in h.*: ioying.
112. riȝ*t*wysnesses (*t* added over line.

Sameth.—113. hate.
115. *l.*] goþ : hestes.

116. —*ne.*
117. riȝtwysnesses.
118. all men departyng : domes.
119. *t.*] held : of+þe : trespassyng þer-for y loue.
120. Styk : agaste : domes.

Aym.—121. dome : —*ne* : þe] men.
122. —*ne.*

* fol. 45.

EARLY ENGLISH PSALTER. PSALM 118 (119). 153

123. Min eȝen faileden in þin helþe & in þe worde of þi riȝt.
124. Do wyþ þy seruaunt efter þy mercy, & teche me þi riȝtinges.
125. Ich am þi seruaunt; ȝif to me vnderstondynge, þat ich cunne þi witnesses.
126. Lord, it is time to do wreche, þe wicked han wasted þi lawe.
127. For-þi loue ich þi [1]comaundement vp gold & topaz.
128. For-þi was ich dresced to þi comaundement, & ichad alle iuel way iu hatynge.

Phe.

129. Ha Lord, wonderful ben þin witnesses; for-þi my soule soȝt hem.
130. Þe shewynge of þin wordes aliȝteþ me, & ȝeueþ vnderstondyng to litel.
131. Ich opened my mouþe, & droȝe þe gost, for þat ich desired þi comaundementȝ.
132. Loke in me, & haue mercy on me efter þe iugementȝ of him þat louen þi name.
133. Dresce min goinges efter þi worde, & al vnriȝt-fulnes ne lord-ship me nouȝt.
134. Raunsoun me fram þe chalanges of men, þat ich kepe þin comaundementȝ.
135. Liȝt þi face vp þi seruant, & teche me þy riȝtinges.
136. Myn eȝen ladden outgoinges of waters, for þat hij kepten þi lawe.

Sade.[2]

137. Lord, þou art riȝtful, & þi iugementȝ is riȝtful.
138. Þou sendest riȝtfulnesses þin wittnesses & þi soþenes greteliche.
139. Mi loue made me to quaken, for þyn enemis forȝaten þin wordes.

---

[1] fol. 118. [2] No heading and no paragraph in the MS.

124. riȝtfulnesses.
126. Lor.
127. þer-for y louyd þi hestes aboue.
128. to+all : commaundmentȝ : y had : hate.

Phe.—130. liȝteþ : ȝif.
131. —þat.

132. in] to : dome.
133. ne ... nouȝt] haue noȝt lord-ship on me.
135. me+vp : riȝtwysnesses.
136. ladd oute vschus.

[Sade] (No heading and no paragraph in MS.).—137. dome.
138. sentest : ryȝtfulnes.

140. ¹Þy worde is michel aliȝted, and þin seruaunt loued it.

141. Ich am honge² & despised, and y ne haue nouȝt for-ȝeten þin riȝtinges.

142. Þy riȝt, Lord, is riȝt wyþ-outen ende, & þi lawe is soþenes.

143. Tribulacioun and anguis founden me; my þouȝt is þi comaundement.

144. Þi witnesses ben euenhede wyþ-outen ende; ȝif me vnderstondynge, and y shal lyuen.

Ceph.

145. Ich cried in alle myn hert; Lord, her me, y shal sechen þy riȝtinges.

146. Ich cried to þe; make me sauf, þat ich kepe þin comaundement.

147. Ich com for-þe in melshede & cried, & ich hoped in þyn worde.

148. Min eȝen com to-fore to þe in þe morwening, þat ich þouȝt þin wordes.

149. Here my voice, Lord, efter þy mercy, and quick¹ me after þy iugement.

150. Þe persuand me drowen to wickednesse; hij for soþe ben made fer fram þy lawe.

151. Lord, þou art neȝe, & alle þin waies ben soþenes.

152. ³Ich knew fram þe bigynnyng¹ of þi wittnesses, for þou fonded hem wyþ-outen ende.

Res.

153. Se my mekenisse, & defende me fram iuel; for y ne for-ȝate nouȝt þy lawe.⁴

154. Iuge my iugement, & bigge me oȝain, & quike me for þi worde.

155. Helþe his fer fram sinȝers, for hij ne souȝt nouȝt þy riȝtfulnesses.

156. Lord, þy mercius ben mani; quike⁵ me efter þy iugement.

---

¹ fol. 118b.   ² Read ȝonge.   ³ fol. 119.   ⁴ MS. sawe, with a round s.
⁵ MS. quiken, but n is expuncted.

---

140. muche.
*141. ȝong: —ne: riȝtwysnesses.
143. commaundentȝ.
144. euenhode.

Seph.—145. riȝtwysnesses.
146. commaundmentȝ.
147. melschhode.
148. mornyng: þoȝt+in.

149. make me qwyk: dome.
150. pursuing: f. s. þai.
152. foundid.

Res.—153. —ne: sawe] lawe.
154. Deme my dome: make me qwyke.
155. —ne: ryȝtfulnes.
156. make me qwyk: dome.

* fol. 45b.

157. Mani þer ben þat pursuen me; y ne bowe[d] nouȝt fram þy witnes.
158. Ich seiȝe þe forfetours, & ich quaked, for þat hij ne kep nouȝt þy wordes.
159. Se, Lord, for ich loued þin comaundementȝ; quike me in þy mercy.
160. Þe by-ginnyng of þy wordes is soþ; so ben wiþ-outen ende alle þe iugementȝ of þy riȝtfulnisse.

Syn.

161. Princes pursued me wyþ wille, & myn hert dradde of þin wordes.
162. Y shal glade vp þi wordes, as he þat findeþ many spolinges.
163. [1]Ichade wickednisse in hateinge, and ich loþed it, & loued þy lawe.
164. Ich seid hereinge[2] to þe seuen siþes on þe daie vp þe iugement of þi riȝt.
165. Muchel pes is to þe louand þy lawe, & sclaunder nis nouȝt to hem.
166. Ich abode, Lord, þin helþe, and ich loued þin comaundementȝ.
167. My soule kept þi witnesses, & ich loued hem greteliche.
168. Ich kept þy comaundementȝ & þi witnisses, for alle my waies ben in þy siȝt.

Thau.

169. Cum, Lord, my praier in þy siȝt; ȝif me vnder-stondynge efter þy worde.
170. *Latin and English omitted.*
171. My lippes shul shewe songe, whan þou hast tauȝt me þy riȝtinges.
172. My tunge shal putt forþe þy worde, for al þy comaundementȝ ben euenhede.[3]
173. Ben þin honde made þat it saue me, for þat ich loued þy comaundementȝ.
174. Lord, ich loued þin helþe, & þy lawe is my þouȝt.
175. My soule shal lyuen & herien þe, & þi iugementȝ shal [4]helpe me.

---

[1] fol. 119b.   [2] The second e is corrected from i.   [3] Preceded by euende, which is dotted out.   [4] fol. 120.

157. —ne: bowed: witnesses.
158. se men trespassyng: —ne: kepide.
159. make me qwyk.
160. soþ ... ende] soþnes withoute ende so beþ: domes: ryȝtfulnesses.

Syn.—161. w.w.] wilfullych: dred.
162. spoiles.
163. Y had: hate.

164. herying: on þe d.] a day: dome.
165. Much: þe] men: is.
166. ab.] ha bode.

Thau.—169. Lorde cum; in] nere.
170. Entre my askyng in þi siȝt, & deliuer me efter þi worde.
171. riȝtwysnesses.
172. 2. þy] þ (!): euennes.
*175. sh. l.] leuyþ: & it schal hery: domes.

* fol. 46.

176. Ich erred[1] as a shepe þat perissed; seche, Lord, þy seruant, for y ne forȝate noȝt þy comaundement.

PSALM 119 (120).

1. Ich cried to our Lord, as ich was trubled, & he herd me.
2. Lord, deliuer my soule fram þe wicked lippes & fram þe trecherous tunge.
3. What þinge be ȝeuen to þe? oþer what be sett to þe trecherous tunge?
4. Sharpe arwen of þe miȝtful wyþ coles dis-confortables.
5. Alas to me; for my dwellynge is proloyngned; ich[2] woned wiþ þe woniand of Cedar, my soule was tilier michel.
6. Ich whas peisible wyþ hem þat hateden pes; as y spak' to hem, hij smiten me wyþ wille.

PSALM 120 (121).

1. Ich lifted myn eȝen to þe heuens, whennes helpe com to me.
2. Myn helpe is of our Lord, þat made heuen and erþe.
3. Ha þou gode man, þat God þat kepeþ þe ne ȝif nouȝt þy fote in stirynge, ne he ne shal nouȝt refusen hem.
4. [3]Our Lord kepeþ þe, & our Lord is þy fendour vp þi riȝt honde.
5. Brynynge of vice ne shal nouȝt brulen þe bi daie, ne enticement bi niȝt.
6. Our Lord kepeþ þe fram alle iuels; our Lord kepe þi soule.
7. Our Lord kepe þin entre and þin yssu fram þis nov vnto þe world.

---

[1] MS. *Icherred*.   [2] *ich* is added over the line.   [3] fol. 120*b*.

---

176. —*ne*: commaundmentȝ.

119. 1. when: sturbled.
2. þe *tr.*] trichourus.
3. or what þing is sett to þe to a trichorours tung.
4. myȝty: disconfortable.
5. proloyned: withmen wonnyng atte Cedar+&.
6. pesable: when: smote.

120. 1. lift+vp: fram whens: schal cum.
3. O: —*ne*: *in st. ne*] or strengþ into mouyng & he: —*ne*: *hem*] þe.
4. *f.*] defendyng
5. Brennyng: vices: —*ne*: bren: *ne*] no.
6. euyH.
7. oute-goyng fram þis tyme now +&.

PSALM 121 (122).

1. Ich am gladed in þe þynges þat ben yseid to me; we shul go into þe hous of our Lord.
2. Ha þou heuen, our fete wer stondand in þin halles, whan we do wele.
3. Þe heuen þat is edefied as cite, of wham takyng part is in þat ich þing.
4. For þider mounted þe kyndes[1] of kindes of our Lord, þe witnesse of þe childer of Israel, to shriue to þe name of our Lord.
5. For þat satten þe chosen in iugement, þe chosen vp þe folk⋅ of þe hous of Dauid.
6. Ha ȝe heuens, askeþ þinges þat ben in pes, & wexing be to þe louand[2] þe.
7. Be pes made in þy vertu & wexing in þy miȝtes.
8. *Translation omitted.*
9. For þe houus of God, our Lord, y soȝt godes to þe.

PSALM 122 (123).

1. Þou þat wonest in þe heuens, ich lifte myn eȝen to þe.
2. Se, as þe eȝen of þe seruauntes ben in þe hondes of her lordes;
3. As þe eȝen of þe hondemaiden ben in [3] þe hondes[3] of þe ladi, so ben our eȝen to God, þer-whiles þat he haue merci on vs.
4. Ha mercy on vs, Lord, haue merci [on] us, for we ben michel fulfild of despite.
5. For þat our soule is greteliche fulfild wyþ synȝes, reprucynge be to þe wexyng & despite to þe proude.

---

[1] Corrected from *kynges* by another scribe. [2] MS. *louauand*. [3] The MS. has þeȝen instead of þe hondes.

---

121. glade : þe] þi.
2. O : dyd gode.
3. as+a.
4. come : kyndes of þe kynde : knowlege.
5. þat] þer : dome : vp] of.
6. O : in] to : encresyng : to men louyng þe.
7. encresyng : toures or miȝtes.

8. For my breþer & my neȝpurs y spake pees of þe.
9. of our Lorde Godd y gate.

122. 1. in—þe : eȝe.
3. & as : þeȝen] þe hondes : þe]
her : þ. w. þ.] to tyme.
4. *Ha*] Haue : +on : much.
5 —þat : much : of syn : encresyng.

PSALM 123 (124).

1. Bot ȝif our Lord were in vs, sai nou þe folkˈ of Israel, bot ȝif God were in us:
2. As men arisen oȝains vs, peraunter hij hadden deuoured vs al quike.
3. As her wodeship was wroþe oȝains us, water peraunter hade swolwed vs.
4. Our soule passed trauail; perchaunce our soule had passed peine þat maie nouȝt be suffred.
5. Blisced be our Lord, þat [1] [2] ne ȝaf vs nauȝt in takyng to her teþe.
6. Our soule is defended as þe sparowe fram þe gnare of þe fouler.
7. Þe trappe of þe fend is to-broke wyþ þe deþ of Crist, & we ben deliuered fro dampnacioun.
8. Our helpe is in þe name of our Lord, þat made heuen and erþe.

PSALM 124 (125).

1. Hij þat affien hem in our Lord, as þe folkˈ of Syon, ben gode; ne he þat woneþ in heuen ne shalt nouȝt be stired wiþ-outen ende.
2. Þe ioies ben in his cumpas, & our Lord is in þe cumpas of his folkˈ fram nou & into heuen.
3. For our Lord ne shal nouȝt for-sake þe penaunce of þe sinȝer[s] vp þe lot of þe riȝtful, þat þe riȝtful ne shewe nouȝt her hondes to wickednes.
4. Do wele, Lord, to þe gode & riȝtful of hert.
5. Our Lord shal laden þe bowand fram gode in-to bindeing wyþ þe wircheand wickednes; pes be vp þe folkˈ of Israel.

---

[1] MS. þat þat.   [2] fol. 121b.

---

*123. 2. As] Whem (!): ros.
3. When: peraunter water: deuourd.
4. peraunter.
5. þat—þat ne.
6. deliuerd as a sp.: gryn.
7. gryn: fendeȝ: wyþ] by.

124. 1. ne he] & he: —ne: schal: mouyd.
2. —1. þe: & i. h.] with-oute ende.
3. —ne: of synners: ne sh.] sprede.
5. Our] For-soþe our: þe b.] men declynyng.

* fol. 46b.

PSALM 125 (126).

1. We ben made as conforted, our Lord turnand chaitifs of [1]þe folk· of Syon.
2. þan is our mouþe fulfild of ioie, & our tunge in gladenes.
3. þan shul hij saien a-monge men : Our Lord heried to do wyþ hem mercy.
4. Our Lord heried to do wyþ us, so be we made ioiand.
5. Lord, wil þou turne our chaitifnes, as þi grace is in heuen.
6. Hij þat repenten her sinȝes in teres, hij shul liuen in heuen wiþ ioie.
7. Þe dyand ȝede out of þe world & wept, sendand her dedes.
8. And hij comaund in-to heuen shul cum wyþ ioie, berand to God her honours.

PSALM 126 (127).

1. Bot ȝif ȝour Lord haue bigged þe hous in vain, hij trauaileden þat it sett.
2. Bot ȝif our Lord haue kept þe cite, he þat kepeþ it wakeþ al on idel.
3. Ydel þing it is to ȝou for to arisen to fore liȝt; ȝe þat han don dedelich sinȝe, ariseþ, sen þat ȝe han made dwelling.
[2]4. Ȝe childer, marchaundis & frut of þe wombe, seþ þe heritage of our Lord, whan he had ȝeuen reste to his loued.
5. As arwen ben in þe honde of þe miȝtful, so ben þe sones of þe smiten.
6. Blisced be þe man þat fulfild his desire of hem; he ne shal nouȝt be confounded, as he shal speken to his enemis in þe ȝate of Paradis.

---

[1] fol. 122.   [2] fol. 122b.

---

125. 1. — as: c. + to: *turnandch.*] was in *turnyng* þe wrechidnes.
4. gladyng.
5. willtow: wrechydnes.
7. wepe.
8. cumyng.

126. 1. ȝour] our: *b.*] made: *s.*] made.

2. on] in.
3. Vayne: *sen þat*] seþ : tarying.
4. Seþ he haþ ȝif rest to his louyd, lo, ȝe childer, þe h. of our Lorde is marchandys of þe frute of þe w.
6. —ne: when.

PSALM 127 (128).

1. Blisced ben hij al þat dreden our Lord, þe which þat gon in his waies.
2. Ha þou man, þou art blisced, & wele þe shal be, for þou shalt eten þe trauailes of þin hondes.
3. Þy wyf shal be as a vine wexand in þe sides of þyn hous.
4. Þy childer shul ben as braunches of oliues a-bout þy table.
5. Se, þus shal þe man be blisced þat dredeþ our Lord.
6. Þe Lord of þe folk' of Syon blisce þe, þat tou se þe godes of heuen alle þe daies of þy lif;
7. Þat tou se þe sone[s] of þi sones, pes vp þe childer of Israel.

PSALM 128 (129).

1. Þe wicked foeten oftȝ oȝains ¹me fram my ȝengþe, sai nou þe folk' of Israel.
2. Þe wicked foȝten oft oȝains me fram my ȝouþe, for hij ne miȝten nouȝt to me.
3. Þe synȝers forgeden folies vp my rigge, & hij proloined her wickednes.
4. Our Lord riȝtful shal keruen þe haterels of þe sinȝers; ben hij alle confounded & turned þat hateden þe folk'of Syon.
5. Ben hij made as hai of houses þat dried, ar þat it be drawen vp;
6. Of which he þat shal repen, ne fild nouȝt his honde, ne he his bosme þat shal gader þe honde-fouls.
7. And hij þat passeden ne saiden nouȝt, þe blisceing of our Lord be vp ȝou, [we blisced ȝou] in þe name of our Lord.

---

¹ fol. 123.

---

127. 1. þe wh.] &.
2. O — þou.
*3. wexyng vine.
5. Lo : schalt.
7. sone] sonnes.

128. faȝt oft : ȝongþ.

2. faȝt : ȝongþe : —ne.
3. wroȝt.
4. Our r. L. : hateþ.
6. Of+þe : ne fild] fil : ne he] no : — þe : hanfuls.
7. —ne : ȝou+we blys ȝou.

* fol. 47.

PSALM 129 (130).

1. Ich cried, Lord, to þe for þe depe; Lord, here my uoice.
2. Ben þin eres made vnder-stondand to þe voice of mi praier.
3. Lord, ʒif þou hast kept wickednes, Lord, who shal holde hem vp?
4. For help is to þe, & ich susteined [1]þe, Lorde, for þy lawe.
5. My soule helde vp gode in his[2] worde, my soule hoped in our Lord.
6. Hope þe folkᵗ of Israel in our Lord fram þe mornynge kepinge vn-to þe niʒt.
7. For merci is at our Lord, & at him is plentiuose raunsoun.
8. And he shal raunsoun þe folkᵗ of Israel fram alle her wickednes.

PSALM 130 (131).

1. Lord, myn hert nis nouʒt anheʒed, ne min eʒen ne ben noʒt born on heʒe.
2. Ne ich ne ʒede nouʒt in grete þinges, ne in wonderful þinges vp me.
3. ʒif y ne feld nouʒt lowelich, bot haue heʒed mi soule:
4. As þe souking is vp his moder, so is ʒeldyngᵗ in my soule.
5. Hope þe folkᵗ of Israel in our Lord, nou fram þis time and to þe heuens.

PSALM 131 (132).

1. Bi-þenche þe, Louerd, of Dauid & of alle his mildenes.
2. As he swore to our Lord, he avowed vowe[3] to þe God of Iacob.
3. ʒif ichaue entred in-to þe tabernacle of mi [4]hous, ʒif[5] ichaue went vp into þe bedde of myn apparaile;

---

[1] fol. 123b. [2] hi on erasure. [3] MS. abowed bowe. [4] fol. 124. [5] Here follows ich ʒa, but is expuncted.

---

129 1. Lord y cryd.
3. hast k.] schalt kepe.
4. to] at.
5. h. vp] susteyned.
6. m. vnto þe euen kepyng.
7. plenteous.
8. wykkydnesses.

130. 1. is: ne] no: —ne: b.o.h.] proude.

2. No ych ʒode: 1. in] in, written over amonge, which is expuncted: ne] no.
3. ne feld] fred: bot+y.
4. reward.
5. nou...h.] fram now withoute ende.

131. 1. Lord: mekenes.
2. wouyd a wou.

4. ȝif ichaue ȝeuen sleping to myn eȝen & slomeringe to myn eȝen-liddes,

5. And rest to my tymes, þer-whiles þat ich finde stede to our Lord, tabernacle to God of Iacob :

6. Se, we herd it in Effrata, we finde it in þe heuen.

7. We shul entre in-to þe tabernacle of God, & we shul anouren in þe stede, þer his fete stode.

8. Arise, Lord, in-to þi rest, þou & þe houche of [þin] halwing.

9. Þyn prestes ben cladde wiþ riȝt-fulnisses, & glade þin holi.

10. Ne turne nouȝt þe face of þi prest anoint wiþ creme for Dauid, [þi] seruant.

11. Our Lord swore to Dauid soþenes, & he ne shal nouȝt deceiue him; y shal laie vp þi sege of þe frut of þi wombe.

12. ȝif þi childer haue kept mi testament & mi[1] witnesses, þo þinges þat y shal teche hem,

13. Her childer shul siten vp þi sete vn-to þe world.

14. [2]For our Lord ches þe folk' of Syon, he ches hem in-to wonyng' to him.

15. Þis wonyng is rest to me in heuen, her shal ich wone, for iches it.

16. Ich blisceand shal blisce his widowe, y shal fulfil his pouer of loues.[3]

17. Y shal cloþen his prestes wiþ helþe, & his holi shul gladen [wyþ] ioie.

18. Þer[4] shal y bringe forþe þe power of Dauid; and y made rady þe laterne to mi preste anoint wyþ creme.

19. Y shal cloþe his enemis wiþ confusioun; myn halweing for-soþe shal florissen vp hym.

---

[1] The MS. has þi testament & þi w.   [2] fol. 124b.   [3] MS. leues.   [4] Instead of þer, the MS. has a y.

---

5. þ. w. þ.] to(!) : Lorde+& a.
6. Lo : fonde.
7. honour.
8. huche of+þi.
9. cloþd : ryȝtfulnes.
*10. —ne : anoyt : D.+þi.
11. —ne : dissayue : sett : sete.
12. kepyd my (corrected from þi) t. & my (corrected from þi) witnes & þes þinges.

13. Her] & her : vnto þe w. sch. syt vp þ. s.
15. is my rest : y schal.
16. loues.
17. glade+with.
18. Y schal—y : forþe+þeder : anoyte.
19. holynes.

* fol. 47b.

PSALM 132 (133).

1. Se, hou gode & hou ioiful þing it is, breþer to wonen in on;
2. As onement in þe heued, þat falleþ into þe berde, þe berde of Aaron;
3. Þe which fel in-to þe hemme of his cloþinge, as dew of Hermon þat fel in þe mounteine of Syon.
4. For our Lord sent þider his blisceinge, and lif vnto þe heuen.

¹PSALM 133 (134).

1. Ha ȝe alle seruantes of our Lord, seþ, blisceþ our Lord nou.
2. He² þat stonde in þe hous of our Lord, in þe halles of our Goddes hous,
3. Heȝeþ your hondes bi niȝtes in-to holi þinges, & blisceþ our Lord.
4. Our Lord blisced þe, Marie of Syon, þat made heuene & erþe.

PSALM 134 (135).

1. Ha ȝe seruauntȝ, herieþ our Lord, herieþ þe name of our Lord.
2. Ȝe þat stonde in þe hous of our Lord, in þe halles of þe hous of our Lord,
3. Herieþ our Lord, for he is gode; singeþ to his name, for it is milde.
4. For our Lord ches Iacob to him, Israel to him in possessioun.
5. For ich knew þat our Lord is gret, and our God is to-fore alle goddes.³
6. Our Lord made alle þinges þat he wolde, in heuen & in erþe, in see and in halle depenisses.⁴
7. He his ladand out cloudes of þe last ende of þerþe, & he made liȝtinges in raine.

---

¹ fol. 125. ² Read ȝe. ³ First d added over line. ⁴ MS. dennnsses, of which the first e is dotted out.

---

132. 1. Lo : ioyful — þing : breþeren.
2. vnement.
3. lappe of (of *is wrongly dotted out*) hym (*dotted out*) his cl. : falleþ into þe hiH.
4. v. þ. h.] with ende (!).

133. 1. —seþ.
2. He] ȝe : Lorde+& : of þe hous of our Godd.

134. 1. Lorde+&.
2. Lorde+&.
3. meke.
4. & Israel.
6. aH depenesses.
7. lad.] brynging : ottermast endes : into.

EARLY ENGLISH PSALTER. PSALM 134 (135).

8. Þe which þat putteþ forþe þe windes of [1]his tresour, þo which smote þe first borne of Egipt fram man vnto beste,

9. And sett his to-knes & his wondres in-middes of þe Egipt, oȝayn Pharaon his seruauntes;

10. Þe which smote mani folkes, & sloȝe stronge kynges,

11. Seon, Kyng[2] of Amorreux,

12. And Og,[3] kyng of Basan,

13. And alle þe kyngdomes of Chanaan.

14. And he ȝaf her [londe] heritage, into heritage to his folkᵗ of Israel.

15. Lord, þy name is wyþ-outen ende, þi minde is in kynde and in-to kinde.

16. For our Lord shal iuggen his folkᵗ and praie for his seruauntes.

17. Þe[4] y-magerie of men ben seluer & gold, werkes of mennes hondes.

18. Hij han mouþe, and hij ne shul nouȝt speken; hij han eȝen, and ne shul nouȝt sen.

19. Hij[5] han eren, and hij ne shul nouȝt heren; and no gost is in her mouþe.

20. Hij þat maken hem be made lich to hem, and alle þat affien[6] in hem.

21. Ha he[7] folkᵗ of Israel, blisceþ our Lord; ha ȝe folkᵗ of Aaron, blisceþ our Lord.

[8]22. Þe folke of Leui, blisceþ our Lord; ȝe þat douteþ our Lord, blisceþ our Lord.

23. Blisced be our Lord of þe folkᵗ[9] of Syon þat woneþ in heuen.

---

[1] fol. 125b. [2] Followed by an *a*, which is expuncted. [3] Followed by an *h*, which is dotted out. [4] MS. *ye*. [5] MS. *Hij hij*. [6] *ie* on erasure. [7] Read ȝe. [8] fol. 126. [9] The flourish at the *k* is different from the usual one, as, instead of forming a loop, it simply goes downward similar to a long comma.

---

8. — þat: tresours + & : þe : borne] beȝetyng.
9. & he sent : of — þe : Pharo+&.
10. folke : —kynges.
11. Amoreour.
14. her+londe.
15. fram k. into k.
16. deme.
17. þe.
*18. —ne : ne] þai.
19. —ne : and no g. is] no forsoþe þer is no goste.
20. Hij... made] Be þai þat make hem : leueþ.
21. he] ȝe : ha] and.
22. þe] ȝe : Lorde+& : drede.

* fol. 48.

PSALM 135 (136).

1. Shriueþ to our Lord, for he is god, for hys[1] merci is in þe world.
2. Shriueþ to þe God of goddes;
3. Shriueþ to þe Lord of lordes ;
4. Þe which bi him on deþ[2] grete wondres ;
5. Þe which made þe heuens in vnder-stondinge ;[3]
6. Þe which fastened þerþe vp waters ;
7. Þe which made grete liʒtes,
8. Þe sonne in-to þe miʒt of þe dai,
9. Þe mone and þe sterres in-to miʒt of þe niʒt ;
10. Þe which smote Egipt wyþ her first biʒeten.
11. Þe which lad out þe childer of Israel fram amiddes hem,
12. In myʒt-ful honde[4] and heʒe arme ;[5]
13. Þe wiche departed þe Reed See in departynges ;
[6]14. Þe wiche[7] lad þe folk[t] of Israel þurʒ-out it ;
15. Þe which smote Pharaon and his vertuʒ in þe Reed[8] See ;
16. Þe which lad his folk þourʒ desert ;
17. Þe which smote grete kinges,
18. And sloʒe stal-worþ kinges,
19. Seon, kynge of Amorreux,
20. And Og,[9] kyng' of Basan,
21. And alle þe kyngdoms of Chanaan.
22. And he ʒaf her londe heritage,
23. Heritage to Israel, his seruaunt.
24. Þe which was bi-þenchand on us in our mekenes,

---

[1] y corrected from e. [2] on deþ on erasure. [3] The English of this verse and the Latin of this as well as of the next verse is written on a long erasure. [4] MS. myʒt fulbonde. [5] Then v. 10-12 are repeated, thus : þe which smete Egipte wyþ her fir[st] biʒeten. þe which lad out (MS. ladent) þe childer of Israel fram amiddes hem. Smiʒt (!) fulhonde & heʒe arme. [6] fol. 126b. [7] wicked, MS. [8] Second e added over line. [9] MS. h og (h expuncted).

---

135. 1. i. þ. w.] with oute ende.
4. bi . . . deþ] allon doþ many.
5. into.
6. vp+þe.
8. power.
9. into þe power.
10. byʒetyngʒ.
12. honde & hie power.
13. deuysions.
14. þe whych ladd+oute : by amiddes it.
15. and] in.
18. strong.
19. S.+þe : Amoreneʒ.
20. Ogg+þe.
24. biþ.] þenchyng.

25. And rau*n*souned vs fram our enemis;
26. þe which ȝeueþ mete to ich flesshe.
27. Shriueþ to þe God of heue*n*;
28. Shriueþ to þe Lord of lordes;
29. For in¹ þe world is his mercy.

PSALM 136 (138).

1. Y shal shriue, Lord, to þe in alle myn hert, for þou herdest þe worde of my mouþe.
2. Y shal singe to þe in þe siȝt of au*n*gels, & y shal anoure þe to þin holi te*m*ple, & ich shal shriue to þi name,
3. Vp þi merci & þi soþenes; for þou heried þin holi name vp alle þi*n*ge.
4. ² In whiche daie þat ichaue cleped þe, her me; þou shalt multiplien vertu in my soule.
5. Shriue, Lord, to þe alle þe kinges of erþe; for hij harden alle þe wordes of þi mouþe;
6. þat hij singe in þe waies of our Lord, for þe glorie of our Lord is grete.
7. For our Lord is heȝe; & he lokeþ þe lowe þinges, & knoweþ þe heȝe þinges fram fer.
8. Ȝif ich haue go*n* amiddes of [my] tribulacion, þou shalt quike me; & þou sheweþ þin honde vp þe wraþe of min enemis; þi miȝt made me sauf.
9. Our Lord shal ȝelden for me; þi merci, Lord, [is] in þe world; ne despise þe werkes of þin hondes.

PSALM 137.

1. Þer-whiles þat we bi-þouȝt vs of þe heue*n*, we satt & wept þer vp þe assautes of þe fende.

---

¹ *i*n added over line.   ² fol. 127.

---

25. *A. r.*] þe which rau*n*son.
27. Schryue ȝou to—þe.
28. Schryue+ȝow.
29. Fo. h. m. is w*ith*-oute ende.

136. 1. Lorde y sch. schr.: wordes.
2. honou*r*: *name*] holy name.
3. aboue.
4. what: y schal clepe: me+&.

5. Lord, aH þe k. of þe e. schryue to þe: my.
6. way: ioie.
7. seþ.
8. of +my: mak me qwyke: *sheweþ*] spredest.
9. *in*] is i*n*: *ne desp.*] desp. noȝt.

137. 1. *heuen*] in heuen: wepe.

2. We heng our ioies in passand þinges in-middes of him.

3. Why ¹hij, deuels, þat ladden vs chaitifs, asked vs þer wordes of songes.

4. And hij þat ladden vs out of godenes, seiden to vs : Singeþ to us of þe songe of heuen.

5. Hou shul we singe þe songe² of our Lord in iuel liif ?

6. Ha ȝe folkᵗ of gode liif,³ seid our Lord, if þat ich for-ȝete ȝou, be mi miȝt ȝeuen to forȝetinge.

7. Fast drawe my tunge to my chekes, ȝif y þenche nouȝt on þe.

8. Yf y ne sett nouȝt forþe gode folkᵗ in þe biginnynge of my ioie.

9. Be þou bi-þenchand of wicked childer in þe daie of iugement of gode men ;

10. Þe which wicked sain, For-doþ þe gode, fordoþ þe gode vnto þe foundement [in it].

11. Ha þou soule, filed þurȝ þe fende, þou art chaitif ; blisced be he þat ȝeldeþ to þe þi ȝeldinge, þe which þat tou ȝelde to vs gode.

12. Blisced be he þat shal holde him in godenes & put his gode dedes to stondynge.

PSALM 138 (139).

⁴1. Lord, þou prouedest me, and þou knewe [me ; þou knewe] my sittyngᵗ and my risynge.

2. Þou vnderstonde mi þoȝutes fram fer ; þou soȝt my bisti and myn acorde.

3. And þou for-seȝest alle myn waies, for þer nis no worde in my tunge.

4. Se, Lord, þou kneu alle þe last þynges & þe old ; þou fourmed me, and sett vp me þin helpe.

---

¹ fol. 127b.   ² MS. senge.   ³ MS. his with a round s.   ⁴ fol. 128.

---

*3. þer] þe.
4. songes.
5. songe of+of.
6. O : his] life : be] by.
7. cleue.
8. —ne.
9. dome.
10. —1. þe gode : 2. þe gode] gode men : foundement+in it.

11. O þou defoilyd s. : wrechid : þi] þe : ȝeldid.
12. dedes] de (!).
138. 1. knew+me þou knew.
2. þoȝtes : trased my bystye : ac.] corde.
3. þou seȝ to-fore : is.
4. —sett.

* fol. 48b.

5. Þy conynge is made wonderful vp me; it is conforted, and y ne mai nouȝt þer-to.

6. Whider shal y go fram þy gost, and whider shal y fle fro þy face?

7. Ȝif ich steiȝe to heuen, þou art þer; ȝif ich go a-doun to helle, þou comest þider.

8. Ȝif þat y take my liȝtynges in þe morning and wonne in þe vtterest of þe see,

9. Whi hy¹ þin helpe² shal lede me þider, and þy miȝt shal holde me.

10. And y seid perchaunce, derkenesses shul defoulen me, and þe nyȝt is my liȝting in my delites.

³11. For derkenesses ne shul nouȝt be derke of þe, and þe nyȝt shal be briȝted as þe daie; as his derknesses ben, so is his liȝt.

12. For þou weldedest mie reines, and toke me fro þe wombe of my moder.

13. Y shal shriue to þe; for þou art dredefullich heried; þin werkes ben wonderful, and my soule shal knowe hem gretelich.

14. My mouþe nis nouȝt hidde fro þe, which þou made in priuete, and my substaunce is in þe neþerest of þerþe.

15. Þyn eȝen sen myn vnparfitnes, & al shul be writen in þi boke; þe daies shul be fourmed, and no man in hem.

16. Ha God, þin frendes for-soþe ben michel worþshiped to me, her principalte is mychel conforted.

17. Y shal telle hem, & hij shul ben multiplied vp grauel; ich aros, & ȝete ich am wyþ þe.

18. Ha God, ȝif þou sle þe synȝers, helpe me; ȝe men suiled wyþ sinȝe, bowe fro me.

---

¹ MS. *why þi hy*, but *þi* is expuncted.   ² The MS. has an *n* here, which is dotted out.   ³ fol. 128*b*.

---

5. —*ne*.
6. *fle*] go.
7. *st.*] go vp: *ad.*] doune: art neȝ.
8. —þ*at*: swyftnes: .vtter*mast*.
9. *Whi* (þ*i*) *hy*] And for-soþe.
10. peraun*ter* derknes.
11. derknes—*ne* : *derke*] made derk: briȝt: derknes.

12. haddest my.
14. is: *which*] þat: *neþ*.] inermast.
15. þ*i*] þe.
16. O Godd f.s. þi fr.; wyrchypt(!): *pri*ncehode: much.
17. aboue þe gr.
*18. O: fyled: *bowe*] goþ.

* fol. 49.

19. For þat ȝe say in [ȝ]our þouȝtes, Taken þe gode in[1] vaine her medes.

20. [2]Þinge to wyten ȝif ich hated þe hatend þe, Lord, and failled vp myn enemis?

21. Ich hated hem wip*ar*fite[3] hate, and hij ben made enemys to me.

22. Proue me, God, and wite myn hert; aske me, and knowe my sties.

23. And se, ȝif waye of wickednes is in me, and lade me in waie euerlastend.

PSALM 139 (140).

1. Defend me, Lord, fro þe wicked man, and defende me fro þe man vnriȝtful.

2. Þe which þoȝten wickednes in hert, hij stablist batails aldai.

3. Hij sharped her tunges as naddres, venym of aspides is vnder her lippes.

4. Kepe me, Lord, fram þe honde of þe sinn*er*, & defende me fram þe vnriȝtful me*n*.

5. Þe which þouȝten to supplau*n*ten my ganginges, þe p*r*oude hidden gnares to me.

6. Hij spradden out wickednesses into gnare, hij sett sclau*n*der to me by þe waye.

7. Y seid to our Lord, þou art my God; here, Lord, þe voice [4]of my prayere.

8. Þou Lord, Lord, uertu of myn helþe; þou shadued, Lord, vp mi*n* heuede in þe daie of bataile oȝai*n*s þe fende.

9. Ne ȝyf me nouȝt fro my desire to þe sinȝer; þe wicked þouȝten oȝai*n*s me, þat hij ne be nouȝt p*er*au*n*ter an-heȝed.

---

[1] *i* on erasure (of *o*?).   [2] fol. 129.   [3] i.e., *wiþ parfite*.   [4] fol. 129*b*.

19. *our*] ȝ*our*.
20. þ*ynge...Lord*] Lorde wheþer y hatyd noȝt he*m* þat hatyd þe.
21. *wi*] wit*h*: —*me*.
22. *wite*] know: paþes.
23. euerlastyng waie.

139. 1. *defende*] delyu*er*.
2. þ*e wh.*] þai þat: —*hij*: sett all d. batayle.

3. venu*m*.
5. þ*e wh.*] þai þat: wayes: pr. +me*n*: grynnes.
6. Þai sett wickydnes to me into a grynne, & by þe way þai put scl. to me.
8. schaduest.
9. —*Ne*: þoȝt+euyl: þat p*er*aunter þai b. n. enhyed.

170 EARLY ENGLISH PSALTER. PSALM 140 (141).

10. þe heued of her cumpassement & þe trauail of her lippes shal couer hem.

11. Tourmentȝ shul falle vp hem, and þou shalt cast hem in-to dampnacioun; þe gode ne shul nouȝt dwellen in mesais.

12. þe man michel spekand ne shal nouȝt be dresced in erþe, iuels shul taken þe unriȝtful in-to deþ.

13. Ich knew þat our Lord shal do þe iugement of þe mesais and vengeaunce of þe pouer.

14. þe riȝtful for-soþe shul shriuen to þy name, and þe riȝtful shul wonen wyþ þy semblaunt.

PSALM 140 (141).

1. Lord, ich cried to þe, here me; vnderstonde my voice, whan y crye to þe.

2. Be myn orison dresced to þe as encens in þy [1]syȝt, and so be þe lifting of myn hondes sacrifice of heuen.

3. Lord, sett kepyng to my mouþe, & þe dore of þe vnderstondynge to my lippes.

4. Ne bowe nouȝt myn hert into wordes of malice for to excusen excusaciouns in sinȝes.

5. Wyþ men wirchand wickednes, & y ne shal nouȝt commune wyþ her chosen.

6. þe riȝtful shal vndernimen me in merci and blame me; þe iuel for-soþe of þe sinȝer ne shal nouȝt grese min[2] heued.

7. For ȝete is myn orisoun in her welelikand, her iuges ioint to þe stone ben[3] swolwed.

8. Hij shul heren my wordes, for hij miȝten here hem; mi worde his lopen bifore as[4] fathede of þerþe.

---

[1] fol. 130. [2] MS. *in in.* [3] Followed by *slo*, which is dotted out. [4] MS. *af.*

---

10. cumpas.
11. —*ne.*
12. much: —*ne.*
13. dome to þe misays (*put instead of* pouer, *which is expuncted*) : —þe.
14. F. s. þe r.: chere.

140. 1. vnd.+to.

2. incense: lyftyng+vp: *h.*]euen.
3. of—þe.
4. *Ne bowe*] Low.
5. —*ne.*
6. f. s. þe euyl: —*ne.*
7. *w.l.*] plesynges : þe iuges ionyd(!): swalowed.
8. my speche is broke as fatnes.

9. Our bones ben wasted bisiden helle, for to þe Lord ben our eȝen; Lord, ich hoped in þe, ne do nouȝt owaie þe soule fro me.

10. Kepe þou me fro þe assaut þe which þe wicked stablist to[1] me, & fro þe sclaundres of [2]þe wirchand wickednes.

11. Þe synȝers shul fallen in her assaut; ich am oneliche, þerwhiles þat y passe.

PSALM 141 (142).

1. Y cried to our Lord wyþ my voice, y bysouȝt our Lord wyþ my voice.

2. Ich held myn orysoun in his siȝt, & y shew forþe my tribulacioun bi-fore hym.

3. In failland of me my gost, and þou knu my besties.

4. In[3] þat way þat y ȝede, þe wicked hidden assautes to me.

5. Y loke[d] on þe riȝt half and seȝe, and þer nas non þat knewe me.

6. Fleing perisce[d] fro me, and þer nas non þat soȝt my soule.

7. Lord, y cried to þe; y seid: Þou art my hope, my porcioun in þe erþe of liuand.

8. Vnderstonde to my praier, for ich am michel lowed.

9. De-liuer [me] fro þe pursuand me, for hij ben conforted vp me.

10. [4] Lade my soule out of þe kepyng of wicked to shriue to þi name; þe ryȝtful abiden me, þerwhiles þat þou ȝelde to me.

PSALM 142 (143).

1. Here, Lord, m[i] praier, & take wyþ þin eren my praier, and her me in þy riȝtfulnes, in þi soþenes.

---

[1] Followed by þe whic þe wicked sta, which words are dotted out. [2] fol. 130b. [3] MS. And. [4] fol. 131.

---

*9. by-syde: —ne: fram me my soule.
10. fram asaute þat þai sett to me & fram sclaunder (l added over line) of wyrchyng w.
11. þ. wh.] to þat.
141. 2. bif.] to-for.
3. knew: paþes.
4. And] in.

5. lokyd: h.] syde: & y seȝ: was.
6. perischt: was.
7. y seid] & sayde: hope+&.
8. much mekyd.
9. D.+me: þe] men: confort.
10. of] fram: habideþ—me: rewarde.

142. 1. my: eres: ryȝtf.+&.

* fol. 49b.

2. & ne entre nouȝt into iugement wyþ þyn seruaunt, for ich liuand ne shal nouȝ be riȝted in þy siȝt.

3. For þe enemy pursued my soule, he lowed my lif in erþe.

4. Hij laiden me in derkenes as þe dede of þe world, and my gost is anoied vp me, myn hert is trubled[1] in me.

5. Ich was bi-þenchand of old daies, &[2] þouȝt in alle þin werkes; y þouȝt in þe dedes of þin hondes.

6. Y sprad out myn hondes to þe, my soule is to þe as erþe wyþouten water.

7. Here me, Lord, swiftliche, my gost faileþ.

8. Ne turne [3]nouȝt fro me þi face, and y shal be liche to þe falland in þe diche.

9. Make þy mercy erliche herd to me, for ich oped[4] in þe.

10. Make þe waie knowen to me, in which y shal gon[5]; for y lifted my soule to þe.

11. Lord, defende me fro myn enemys, ich fled to þe; teche me to do þy wille, for þou art my God.

12. Þy gode gost shal lade me in-to þe riȝt londe; þou shalt quicke me, Loue[r]d, in þyn euennesse for þy name.

13. Þou shalt lade my soule out of tribulacioun, and shalt depart myn enemys in þy merci.

14. And þou shalt lesen al þat trublen my soule, for ich am þy seruant.

PSALM 143 (144).

1. Blisced be þe Lord, my God, þat techeþ min hondes to feȝt and my fingers to batail oȝains þe fende.

---

[1] MS. *myn hert is truis anoied vp me myn hert is trubled.*   [2] MS. *in.*   [3] fol. 131*b*.   [4] *oped* begins a fresh line.   [5] MS. *god.*

---

2. —*ne*: dome: —*ich*: —*ne*: noȝt: iustified.
4. He layde: vp me+&.
5. *in þouȝt ... hondes*] & ych þoȝt in all þe warkes of þin hondes & in þe dedes.
7. faylid.

8. —*ne*: into.
9. hopid.
10. *in w.*] þat: *god*] go in: lift.
12. make me qwyk Lorde.
13. &+þou.
14. sturbleþ.

EARLY ENGLISH PSALTER. PSALM 144 (145). 173

2. He his my mercy and myn help, my taker & my deliuerer of iuel.

3. He his my ¹defendour fram iuel, and ich hoped in hym; þou art my God, þat sitteþ my folk¹ vnder me.

4. Lord, what is man, þat tou madest þe knowen to hym? oþer mannes sone,² for þou wetest hym?

5. Man is made lich to vanite, is daies passen as shadue.

6. Bowe, Lord, þyn heuens, and cum a-doun; for-sake þe wicked, and hij shul be³ dampned.

7. Aliȝt shynyng, and þou shalt wasten hem; sende out þi manaces, and þou shalt trublen hem.

8. Send out þy myȝt fro heuen, and defend me; & deliuer me fram mani perils and fro þe pouste of stronge childer;

9. Whaus mouþe spake vanite, her riȝthalf is riȝthalf of wickednes.

10. Whas childer ben as new settynges in her ȝengnes,

11. Her douȝters ben made & aourned about as liknes of þe temple.

12. Her selers ben ful, shewand fro þis in-to þis.

13. Her shepe ⁴ben plentiuous, wexande in her goinges, & her nete ben fatt.

14. Fallyng ne passage nis nouȝt to her walle, ne crie nis nouȝt in her stretes.

15. Hij seiden, þe folke blisced, to whom þes þynges ben; blisced be þe folk⁵ of which þe Lord is her God.

PSALM 144 (145).

1. Ha mi God, y shal heȝe þe, kyng, and blisce þy name in þe world⁶ & in þe world of worldes.

---

¹ fol. 132. ² MS. *manessones* with the last *s* dotted out. ³ MS. *ben*, with the *n* expuncted and struck out. ⁴ fol. 132*b*. ⁵ Originally with a flourish to the *k*, but it is erased. ⁶ MS. *worls*.

143.*3. setteþ.
4. —þe: or man sonne: trowest.
7. sturble.
8. power: straunge.
9. Whas: is+þe.
10. ȝeuþe.
11. anoured.
12. into þat.

13. oxen.
14. F. of her wall no passyng is þer none, no crying is.
15. 1. þe L.] our L.

144. 1. *Ha . . . kyng*] Godd my kyng y sch. anhie þe: *in þe worls*] in world.

* fol. 50.

2. Y shal blisce þe by alle daies, and praisen þy name in þe world and in [1] world of worldes.

3. He is grete Lord and michel to praisen, & of his michelnesses nis non ende.

4. Kynd and kynd shal herien þy werkes, and shewe þy miȝt.

5. Hij shul speken þe hereing of þe worþship of þin holines and tellen þin wondres.

6. And y shul saien þe vertuȝ of þi dredes, and shul [tel]len[2] þy gretnes.

7. Hij shul putten forþ þe minde of þe mildnes of þyn wexing, and hij shul glade of þy riȝtfulnes.

8. Our Lord[3] is rewful and merciable, suffrand and michel merciable.

9. Our Lord is liþe to alle, and his mercies ben vp alle his werkes.

10. Shriue, Lord, al þy werkes to þe, and þyne halwen blisce þe.

11. Hij shul saien þe glorie of þy kyngdome and speken þy miȝt,

12. Þat hij maden þi miȝt knowen to mennes sones, and þe glorie of þe hereing of þyn kyngdome.

13. Þy kyngdom is kyngdom of alle world, and þy lordship is in kynde and kinde.

14. Our Lord is trew in alle his wordes, holi in alle his werkes.

15. Our Lord arereþ alle þo þat fallen, and dresceþ vp alle þe hurteled.

16. Þe eȝen, Lord, of alle hopen in þe, and þou ȝeuest hem mete in couenable time.

17. Þou openes þyn hondes, and fulfilles ich beste wyþ bliscyng.

18. Our Lord is riȝtful in alle his waies and holy in alle his werkes.

19. [4] Our Lord is neȝe to alle þe clepand him, þe clepand hym in riȝtfulnes.

---

[1] þe, which followed here, is dotted out.   [2] MS. shullen.   [3] MS. lord lcrd.
[4] fol. 133b.

2. —and in (þe) world.
3. is+a : much : muchnes : is.
5. h.] gretenes : —þe w. of : & +schal.
6. y] þai : schal+tell.
7. encresyng.
8. r.] pyteful : much.
9. mylde.
10. Lorde all þi warkes schriue.
11. speke : ioie : tell.

12. make : mensonnes : ioie : gretnes.
13. worldes : fram k. to k.
14. w.+&.
15. þe h.] hurte.
16. Lorde þe e. : all+men : troweþ : hem] her : behofull.
17. honde & fillest.
*19. to all clepyng hym, to all clepyng hym in soþnes.

* fol. 50b.

20. He shal do þe wil of þe doutand hym, and here her praier,[1] and make hem sauf.

21. Our Lord kepeþ alle þat louen hym, and he shal desparplis alle synȝers.

22. My mouþe shal speke þe praisyng of our Lord, and ich flesshe blisce to hys holy name in þe world and in þe world of worldes.

PSALM 145 (146).

1. Ha þou my soule, hery our Lord; y[2] shal herien our Lord in my lif, and y shal syngen to my God as longe as ich haue ben.

2. Ne wille ȝe nouȝt affien in princes, in mennes sones, in which non helþe nys.

3. His gost shal go out and turne oȝayn in-to heuen; and in þat daie shul alle her þoȝtes perissen.

4. Blisced[3] be he which þe God Iacob is his helper, and his help is in þe Lord, þat made heuen and erþe, þe see and alle þynge þat ben in hem;

5. [4] Þe which kepeþ soþenes in þe world and doþ iugement to hem þat suffren wronge, and ȝeueþ mete to þe hungerand.

6. Our Lord vnbindeþ þe fettered, our Lord vnb[l]inded þe blynde.

7. Our Lord dresced vp þe hurteled, our Lord loueþ þe riȝtful.

8. Our Lord kepeþ þe straunge, and he shal taken þe moderles[5] and þe widowe, and he shal desparpel þe waies of þe synȝers.

9. Our Lord shal regnen in þe worldes; ha folk of Syon, þy God shal regnen in kynde and kynde.

PSALM 146 (147).

1. Herieþ our Lord, for it is god songe, ioyful and faire; heryinge be to our Lord.

---

[1] MS. praies. [2] MS. in. [3] i on erasure. [4] fol. 134. [5] First e corrected from o.

---

20. of men dredyng : prayer & +he schal.
21. þat l.] louyng : d.] lese.
22. ich] aH : in þ. w. of w.] withoute ende.

145. 1. O : in] & y : haue] schal.
2. —Ne: beleue: pr.+no: mensonnes : in whom is no helþe.

4. whiche þe G.] þat þe Lorde Godd of : help] hope : þinges.
5. þai þat : dome : hungrye.
6. vnbinded] liȝtid.
7. dresseþ : hurtyd.
9. o þou folk : fram k. to k.

146. 1. Hery.

2. Our Lord is edifiand Ierusalem, and he shal ansemble þe sunderynges of Israel;

3. Þe which heliþ þe contrit of hert [1] and bindeþ her contriciouns;

4. Þe whiche noumbreþ þe multitude of sterres, & clepand ichon of hem a name.

5. Our Lord is grete, & is vertu is grete, & [2]þer nys non noumbre of his wisdome.

6. Our Lord is takand þe mild & lowand þe sinȝers vnto þerþe.

7. Singeþ to our Lord in shrifte, singeþ to our Lord in harpe;

8. Þe which couereþ þe heuen wyþ cloudes, and makeþ redy þe raine to þerþe;

9. Þe which bryngeþ for-þe hay [3] in þe mounteyns, & grasse to mannes þraldome;

10. Þe which ȝeueþ to meres her mete & to crowe-briddes clepand hym.

11. He ne schal nouȝt haue wille in strengþe of hors, ne wele-likeing ne shal nouȝt be to hym in mannes legges.

12. Wele likand is our Lord vp þe doutand hym, and in hem þat hopen in hys mercy.

PSALM 147 (147 *continued*).

1. Þou folkꞌ of Ierusalem, heri our Lord; hery God, þou folkꞌ of Syon.

2. For he strengþed þe lokkes of þi ȝate, and he blisced in þe [þy] childer;

3. Þe which sett pes to þi cuntres, and filleþ þe of fatt [4]of þe whete;

4. Þe which sendeþ his worde to þe erþe; hys worde erneþ swiftlich;

---

[1] MS. *h*ter. [2] fol. 134*b*. [3] MS. *ha*þ. [4] fol. 135.

---

2. gadyr to-gyder þe desparpelynges.
3. He þat: hert.
4. He þat: clepeþ name to hem aH.
5. *nys*] is.
6. meke.
7. schrift+&.
8. He þat couerþ—þe: —*redy*.
9. He þat: haþ . . .] hay & erbe in þe mounetaynes to seruyng of men.

10. He þat: bestes.
11. —*ne: ne w. l. ne*] no plesyng.
12. Plesyng is+to: vp men dredyng: *in—hem þat*.

147. 2. made stronge: gates — *and*: bl. þi childer in þe.
3. He þat s. þi c. pees: of þe fatnes.
4. He þat: erþe+&: ȝerneþ whiȝtlych.

5. þe which ȝeueþ snowe as wolle, and streweþ þe cloude as asken.

6. He sendeþ his cristalle as morsels; who shal hold vp to-fore þe face of his colde?

7. He shal sende out his worde and make hem ernand; his gost shal blowe, & waters shul flowen.

8. þe which telleþ his worde to Iacobes sones, his riȝtfulnesses and his iugementȝ to þe folk[1] of Israel.

9. He ne did nouȝt in þis[1] maner to ich nacioun, and he ne made nouȝt his iugementȝ aperte to hem.

PSALM 148.

1. Ȝe soule[s] of heuen, herieþ our Lord, herieþ hym in heȝnes.
2. Ȝe alle his aungels, herieþ hym; ȝe alle his vertuȝ, herieþ hym.
3. Ȝe sone & mone, herieþ hym; ȝe sterres and liȝt, herieþ hym.
4. Ȝe heuen of heuens, herieþ hym; & alle þe waters þat ben vp heuens, herieþ þe name of our Lord.
5. [2]For he seid, and hij ben made; he[3] comaunded, & hij ben formed.
6. He stablist hem wyþ-outen ende and in þe word of worldes; sett comandementȝ,[4] and it ne shal nouȝt ouerpassen.
7. Ha ȝe helles and alle depenes, herieþ our Lord of þerþe.
8. Fur, haile, snowe, yse, & gost of tempestes þat don his wordes, herieþ our Lord.
9. Mounteins & alle hilles, tres berand frut, and alle þe cedres, herieþ our Lord.
10. Bestes & al maner of bestes, serpentes & feþered foules, herieþ our Lord.
11. Ȝe kynges of erþe & alle folkes, princes & alle iuges of erþe, herieþ our Lord.

---

[1] MS. *his*. [2] fol. 135b. [3] MS. *hij*. [4] MS. *to mandementȝ*.

---

5. He þat.
*7. hem ern.] it malte.
8. He þat: domes.
9. —ne: his] þis: —ne: domes.

148. 1. soules: Lorde+&.
2. Aꝉꝉ ȝe aungels heriþ hym, & aꝉꝉ ȝe his vertus heriþ hym.
3. sonne and+þe.
4. heuen] heuens.

5. hij com.] he commaundyd (*put instead of* sent, *which is expuncted*): fourmyd.
6. sett: world of w. he s. commaundement: —ne.
7. Ha] Aꝉꝉ: & depenesses of þe erþe h. our Lorde.
8. —yse: gost] þe gostes.
11. folke: of þe erþe.

* fol. 51.

12. ȝe ȝonge & ȝe v*i*rgines, old wyþ þe ȝonge, herieþ þe name of our Lord, for þe name of hym alon is anheȝed.

13. His [shrift] is vp heuen & erþe, and he anheȝed þe myȝt of his folke.

14. Praiseyng be to alle hys halwen, to þe childer of Israel, to folk' þat draweþ to hym.

[1] PSALM 149.

1. Syngeþ to our Lord a new so*n*ge; hys hereyng hys in þe chirche of holy.

2. Glade þe folk of Isra*e*l in hym, þat hym made, and ioisen þe douȝt*er*s of Syon in her kynge.

3. Herien hij his name in croude, and singen hij to hym in tabor and sautri.

4. For weleplesand it is to our Lord in his folk', and he a*n*heȝed þe milden in-to helþe.

5. Þe holy shul gladen in glorie, and ioien in her couches.

6. Þe ioies of God ben in her þrote, & swerdes sharppe a boþe half in her hondes.

7. To do vengau*n*ces in naciou*n*s and lackei*n*ges in folkes.

8. To bynde her kynges in feteris and her nobles in manicles of iren.

9. Þat hij maken in hem iugement wryten, þys ys þe glorie to alle his halwen.

PSALM 150.

1. Ha ȝe folk, herieþ our Lord [in his halwen], herieþ hym in þe stedfastnes of his uertu.

[2] 2. Herieþ hym in his vertuȝ, herieþ hym efter þe michelnes of his gretnes.

---

[1] fol. 136. [2] fol. 136*b*.

---

12. w*i*th — þe.
13. His+schryft: off.
14. halowes: & to þe folke.

149. 1. herying: holy+me*n*.
2. made hym & ioye.
4. —*wele*: —*it*: meke.

5. *glorie and*] ioie & þay schal.
6. *s. sh. a b. h.*] trenchyng swerdes.
7. vengaunce: blamynges: folke.
8. noble me*n*: ire.
9. dome.

150. 1. —*Hu*: Lorde + among his halowe*n*.

3. Herieþ hym in sowne of trumpe, herieþ hym in sautri and in harpe.
4. Herieþ hym in croude and tabor, herieþ hym in cordes¹ and organ.
5. Herieþ hym in cymbals wele sounand, herieþ hym in cymbals of ioie; ich gost herieþ our Lord.

PSALMUS ISAYE.⁴

(Isaie xii. 1–6.)

1. Y shal shryue to þe, Lord; for þou art wroþ to me; þy vengeaunce is turned, and þou conforted me.
2. Se, God ys my saueour, and y shal do faiþlich, & y ne shal nouȝt douten.
3. For our Lord is my strengþe and my praising; & he is made to me in-to helþe.
4. Ȝe shul haue solas in ioie of þe grace of þe saueour, & ȝe shul saie in þat daie: shriueþ to our Lord and clepeþ his name.
5. Singeþ to our Lord, for he did worþshipfullich; sheweþ þis þyng in alle erþe.
6. Þou² wonynge of³ þy Syon, glade and herie, for þe holy of Israel is grete in-middes of þe.

PSALMUS EZECHIE.⁴

(Isaie xxxviii. 10–20.)

1. Y seid: In þe midel of my daies y shal go to þe ȝates of helle.
2. Y souȝt þe reme-nanȝt of my ȝeres, and y ne shal nouȝt sen our Lord in þe londe of liueand.
3. And y ne shalt nouȝt se man ouer, and wonier of rest.
4. My kinde ys bi-numen and don owaie fram me as wonyng of herdes.

---

¹ d added over the line. ² fol. 137. ³ Followed by an s, which is expuncted.
⁴ No heading in MS.

*5. goste h.] goste hery.

Isaie xii. 2. trewlich: —ne.
5. worschipfullich.
6. —þy.

Isaie xxxviii. 2. remenaunte: —ne.
3. —ne: schal: & þe wonner.
4. fram me before &: hirdmen.

* fol. 51b.

5. My lif is coruen as of þe weuand;[1] [he] by-share me, þer-whiles þat ich werped.

6. Þou shalt ende me fram morwen to euen: ich hoped lyf in þe morwenyng, my bi-ȝeteing, defouled al my bones as a lyon.

7. Þou shalt ende me fram morwen to euen, y shal alway crye mercy as a swolwe-bridde, y shal þenche as coluer, as þe quiked þurȝ þe holi gost.

8. Myn eȝen ben made þinne, lokand vp on heȝe.

9. Lord, answere for me, y suffred [strengþe]; what shal y saie, oþer [2] what shal answere to me, whanne ich my seluen haue don?

10. Y shal þenchen alle myn ȝeres in bitternes of my soule.

11. Lord, ȝif man liueþ in þis maner, and þe lif of my gost ys in swich [3] þynges, þou shalt reproue me and quike me; se my bitterest [4] bitternes is in pees.[5]

12. Þou for-soþe defended my soule, þat it ne shuld nouȝt perissen; & þou cast by-hynde þy rigge alle myn synȝes.

13. For helle ne shal nouȝt shriue to [6] þe; ne þe deþ ne shal nouȝt herien þe; hij þat fallen into pyne, ne shul nouȝt abide þy soþnes.

14. Þe liueand shal shryue to þe leuiand as ich to-daie; þe fader shal make knowen þy soþenes to his childer.

15. Lord, make me sauf; & we shul synge our psalmis al þe daies of our liif in þe hous of our Lord.

PSALMUS ANNE,

In uanitate filij sui Samuelis.

(I. Samuelis ii. 1-10.)

1. Myn hert gladeþ in our Lord, and myn helpe his anheȝed [7] in my God.

---

[1] MS. *woniand*. [2] fol. 137*b*. [3] *c* is added over the line. [4] The latter *e* is corrected from *u*. [5] MS. *pres*. [6] MS. *to to*. [7] fol. 138.

---

5. cutte as of man weuyng he cutte: —þat: warped.
6. morow: morunyng: generacion.
7. morow: *as þe qu*.] inspired.
9. suffre+strengþe.
11. make me qwyk (*followed by* me, *which is dotted out*): lo: pees.
12. F. s. þou: —*ne*.
13. —*ne*: ne þ. d. *ne*] no deþ: payne: —*ne*.
14. —Þe: lyfyng+he: lyfyng.

Samuel, 1. gladid.

2. My mouþe ys made large vp myn enemys, for þy þat y ioied in þyn helþe.

3. Þer nys non holy as our Lord is; and þer nis non oþer wyþ-outen þe, & þer nis non so stronge as tou our God.

4. Ne wil ȝe nouȝt manifold speken heȝe þynges, ioiand;

5. De-part[1] olde þinges out of ȝour mouþes; for God ys Lord of cuninges, & þoutes ben diȝt to hym.

6. Þe assaut of stronge ys ouercumen, and þe syke ben gird wyþ force.

7. Þe fulfild to-fore sett hem for loues, and þe hungry ben fild;

8. Þer-whyles þat þe barain childed many, and she þat hade mani childer, is made sike.

9. Our Lord doþ to deþ, & quikeþ, and ladeþ to helle, & ladeþ oȝayn.

10. Our Lord makeþ man pouer, and makeþ hym riche, & loweþ & arereþ hym,

11. Heȝand þe nedeful out of poudre, & drescand vp þe pouer out of dung,

[2] 12. Þat he sitt wyþ princes, and holde þe sege of glorie;

13. For þe sules of erþe ben our Lordes, & he sett þe world vp hem.

14. He shal kepe þe fete of his holy, and þe wicked shul fallen in derkenes; for man shal be strengþed in his strengþe.

15. Þe enemis shul dreden our Lord, and he shal desparplis vengeaunce vp hem in heuen.

16. Our Lord shal iugen þe cuntres of erþe; he shal ȝeue comaundement [to hys kyng¹, & shal anheȝe þe helpe] of his preste anoynt wyþ creme.

---

[1] Here *or* is dotted out in MS.   [2] fol. 138*b*.

---

2. —þy þat.
3. is none+so: Lord—*is*: is: is.
4. —*Ne*: multyplye+to.
*7. wi*t*h loues sett he*m* : wer.
8. —þat : *childed*] broȝt forþ : *ch*.] sonnes.
9. *d. t. d.*] sleþ.
10. —*makeþ hym*.
11. Araysyng.

12. sete of ioie.
13. *s.*] oules.
14. holy + men :   *strengþed*] stronge.
15. *desp.*] sprenge.
16. deme : of+þe : com.+to his kyng & he schal anhie þe helpe : anoyte.

* fol. 52.

PSALMUS MOYSES ET FILIORUM ISRAEL,

In exitu de Egipto transeundo Mare Rubrum.

(Exod. xv. 1–19.)

1. Synge we to our Lord, for he is gloriousliche[1] heried; Pharaon he adrenct in þe see, and hys Eyipciens.

2. Our Lord ys my strengþe and my praiseinge; & he is made to me in-to helþe.

3. He ys my God, and y shal glorifien hym; he his God of my fader, & y shal anheȝe hym.

4. Our [2] Lord is as man fiȝter, his name is al-myȝtful;[3] he drunkened in þe Reed [4] See Pharaons cartes and hys hoste;

5. His chosen princes ben adreint [5] in þe Reed See; þe depenes [couered hem, hij fellen into depenes] as stone.

6. Lord, þy miȝt is [heried] in þy strengþe; Lord, þi myȝt smote þyn enemy, and in þe multitude of þi glorie hadestow min aduersaries;

7. Þou sent þi wraþe, þat deuoured hem as stuble; waters ben gadered in þe gost of þy vengeaunce;

8. Þe ernand water stode, þe abimes ben gadered to-gidres a-middes þe see.

9. Þe enemy Pharaon seid: Y shal pursuen & take & depart [6] spoiles of þe .xij. kynredens of Iacob; my wille shal be fulfild.

10. Y shal drawe out my swerde; myn honde shal slen [7] hem.

11. Ha God, þi gost bleu, & þe see couered hem; & þe childer of abyme ben adreint as lede in grete waters.

12. Ha Lord, who is liche to þe in stronge þynge, who is liche to þe? þou art worþshipful in holines; þou art dredeful, and to praysen, & doand wondres.

---

[1] Second o corrected from e. [2] fol. 139. [3] MS. as myȝtful. [4] The second e added over line. [5] MS. be nadreint. [6] spolies follows, but it is expuncted. [7] shen, MS.

Exodus xv. 1. *Pharaon* . . .] he cast & drenkyd Pharaon & Egipcians in þe se.
4. *man*] a man: *as myȝtf.*] al-miȝty: drenkyd: —*reed*: oste.
5. beþ adrenkyd: depenes + couerd hem þai fell into depenes: as+a.

6. is+heried: —þy: þou hadd.
8. . . . *abimes*] þe water stode flowyng þe depe waters.
9. kynredes.
10. sle hym (!).
11. O: adrenchyd.
12. O: þynges: worschypful.

13. Þou sprad out þin honde, and þe erthe swolwed hem;
14. Þou was lader in þy mercy to þe folk⁎, which þou rau*n*sou*n*ned.
15. And þou bar hym in þy strengþe to þy holy wonyng.
16. Þe folk⁎ steȝe vp, and ben wraþed; sorowes hadden þe woniers of Philistyn.
17. Þe princes of Edon were þan trubled; quakyng had þe stronge of Moab; alle þe woniand in Chanaan dreden.
18. Falle vp hem doute and drede in þe gret-nes of þy myȝt.
19. Ben hij made faste as þe stone, þer-whiles þat þy folk⁎ passe; þi folk⁎, Lord, þe which þou had in welde.
20. Þou shalt laden hem in, Lord, and sett hem in þe monteyne of þyn heritage, þy fastest woni*n*g, þe which þou wroȝt.
21. Lord, in þy ho¹ly stede² þou art, þe which þin hondes fastened; our Lord shal regnen wyþ-outen ende & euer.
22. Þe kniȝt Pharao is entred in-to þe see wyþ his cartes and kniȝtes, and God brouȝt on hem þe wat*er*s of þe see.
23. Þe childer of Isra*e*l for-soþe ȝede in dryhede a-middes hym.

PSALMUS ABAKUK,

De passione et resurrecione Christi.

(Habakuk iii. 2-19.)

1. Ich herd, Lord, þyn hereing, & y dradde.
2. We ben, Lord, þy werk⁎; quik⁎ þis in-middes of our ȝeres.
3. Þou shal make knowen amiddes our ȝeres: as tov³ hast ben wroþ, þou shal by-þenche mercy.
4. God shal cu*m* fram þe norþe, & þe holi fram þe mou*n*te⁴ Pharaon.⁵

---

¹ fol. 140.   ² First *e* corrected from *o*.   ³ Followed first by *hastov*.   ⁴ After *mounte* a letter is erased.   ⁵ This verse is repeated in MS. with exactly the same spelling.

---

14. *wh.*] þat.
16. wroþe: wonners.
*17. stu*r*bled: wo*n*nyng: drede.
19. þe *w.*] þat.
20. Lord *before* þou: þy . . . *which*] in þe moste faste w. þat.
21. þe *w.*] þat: *f.*] made: *euer*] ouer.

22. kniȝtes] with his kn.
23. Forsoþe *before* þe: drynes.

Habakuk, 1. Lorde y herd.
2. Lorde we beþ: in-myd of.
3. *kn.*] þing know: —*hastov*.
4. souȝþe.

* fol. 52*b*.

5. Hys glorie couered þe heuens, and þe erþe is ful of his hereing.
6. His shinyng shal be as liȝt; þe helpes shul ben in his hondes.
7. Þer his hys strengþe hid; þe ded shal go to-fore his face.
8. Þe fend shal go to-fore his fete; he stode, and [1]mesured þerþe.
9. He loked, & vnbond þe folkes; and þe mounteyns of þe world ben defouled.
10. Þe helles of þe world ben [2] croked, fram þe waies of his euerlastend-hede.
11. Y seȝe þe tentours of Echiop for her wickednes, & þe skynnes of þe londe of Madian shul ben trubled.
12. Ne artou enired, Lord, in flodes? oþer þy uengeaunce is in flodes? oþer þin indignacioun in þe see?
13. Who shal lepen vp þin hors, and þy chares ben sauacioun.
14. Þou heiȝand shal heiȝen þy bowe for þe sweringes, þat þou spak[1] to kindes.
15. Þou shalt kerue þe flodes of þerþe; þe folk of þe mounteines seiȝen it, & sorweden; & swolȝe of waters passed.
16. Depnes ȝaf his voice, þe heȝenes lifted vp his hondes.
17. Þe sunne and þe mone stode in his wonyng, in þe liȝt of þin arwen; hij shul gon liȝtande in þe liȝt of þin launce.
[3]18. Þou shal defoulen þe erþe in gnasting, and þou shalt maken þe folk afferd in wreche.
19. Þou art gon out in-to þe helþe of þy folk[1], to þe helþe wyþ þy prest anoint wyþ creme.
20. Þou smot þe heued of þe wicked in þe hous; þou madest naked his foundement vnto his nek[1].
21. Þou forwardest his septres, þe heuedes of his fiȝters, to þe cumand as whirle-wynde to disparplen me.

---

[1] fol. 140b.   [2] Followed by a b, which is expuncted.   [3] fol. 141.

---

5. ioie: herying.
6. in—his.
7. deþ.
9. folke.
10. hilles: euerlastynghode.
11. Ethyope fo (!): sturbled.
12. Lorde artow noȝt wraþed.
13. saluacion.
14. anhying schalt arere.
15. seȝ: & swolȝe] þe swoloȝ.
16. He ȝaf his v. to depe waters: lift.
18. grentyng—and.
19. anoyte.
20. his n.] þe neke.
21. cursyd.

22. Her ioie is as of hym þat deuoreþ þe pouer in hidels.
23. þou madest me waie in þe see to þyn horses in sharpnesses of many waters.
24. Ich herd, and my wombe is trubled; my lippes trembleden for þy voice.
25. Rotennes entred in my bones and spring¹ vnder me;
26. þat y rest in þe daie of tribulacioun, þat ich wende vp to our¹ folk¹ girt wyþ godenes.
27. For þe figer ne shal nouȝt floris, and burioun ne shal nouȝt be in uines.
28. þe werk¹ of þe olyue shal liȝe, & þe ²feldes ne shul nauȝt bringe mete.
29. þe beste shal be shorne fram þe fold, and no bestaile ne shal be in cracches.
30. And y shal ioien in our Lord, & y shal gladen in Iesum, mi God.
31. God, our Lord, ys my strengþe; and he shal sett my fete as of hertes.
32. And þe ouercummer³ shal lade me vp myn heȝtes, singand in psalmes.

PSALMUS MOYSI,

Quem scripsit quando tradidit legem et assignauit Iosue filium suum populo⁴ Israel.

(Deuteron. xxxii. 1–43.)

1. Ha ȝe heuens, hereþ þe þynges þat⁵ y shal speken; ⁶here þerþe þe wordes of my mouþe.
2. Wex my⁷ teching as rain, melt my worde as dew,
3. As reine vp gras, and dropes vp cornes, for þat ich shal klepe þe name of our Lord.

---

¹ *lord* follows, but is expuncted.   ² fol. 141*b*.   ³ MS. *ouercunner*.   ⁴ MS. *populi*.
⁵ MS. ꝗ.   ⁶ MS. repeats *speken*.   ⁷ *the* follows, but is dotted out.

---

22. priuyte.
23. made—*me*: horse: scharpnes.
*24. sturbled: þy] þe.
25. entre.
26. gyrd.
27. figtre—*ne*: burgon: —*ne*.

28. —*ne*.
29. —*ne*.
32. ouercumer.

Deuter. 1. O: &] þat.
3. rayne: —þat.

* fol. 53.

4. ȝeueþ hereing to our Lord; þe werkes of God ben parfiȝt, and alle his waies ben iugementȝ.

5. God is trewe and wyþ-outen ani wickednes; þe riȝtful & þe riȝt synned to hym, and hys childer ne ben nouȝt in filþes.

[1]6. Ha wicked kinde and iuel, ha þou foled folk⸱ and nouȝt wys, þou ȝeldes þes þynges to our Lord?

7. Nis nouȝt he þy fader, þat had þe in welde, and fourmed þe and made þe?

8. By-þenche þe of old daies, þinche þou ich kinde bi it self.

9. Aske þy fader, and he shal telle þe, and þi gretter, & hij shul saien to þe.

10. Whan þe heȝest departed folkes, whan he departed þe sones of Adam,

11. He sett termes of folkes efter þe noumbre of þe childer of Israel.

12. Þe partye of our Lord forsoþe is his folk⸱; Iacob is þe corde of his eritage.

13. He fonde hym in londe forsaken, in hidous stede, and of waste on-hede.

14. He ladde hym a-boute, and tauȝt hym, & kep hym as þe appel of his eȝen.

15. As þe egle clepand hir briddes to fleȝe, and fleȝand a-bouen hem,

16. He sprad out his wenges, and toke hem, and bare hem vp his shuldres.

[2]17. Our Lord alle one was hys lader, and oþer god nas nouȝt wyþ hym.

18. He stablist hym vp an heȝe londe, þat he shuld ete þe fruite of þe feldes;

19. Þat he shul souke þe huny of þe stone and oile of þe ardest[3] roche,

20. Butter of þe bestes & melk⸱ of þe ȝowes, wyþ þe fattnes of lombes & weþers, of þe childer of Basan;

---

[1] fol. 142.   [2] fol. 142b.   [3] h is added before a by a different hand.

---

4. herȝing: L.] Godd: domes.
5. —ne.
6. foly.
7. Is.
8. þinche] þench.
12. F. s. þe party of o. L.

13. forsaken . . . stede] desert in stede of drede: onh.] wyldernes.
14. kept: eȝe.
17. was.
18. sett: an] on: frutes.
19. schuld.
20. ȝ.] schepe: & of þe weþeres.

21. And kiddes wyþ þe merȝþe of wete,[1] þat hij drunken alder-bitterest licor of þe grape.

22. Þe loued ys fatted, & he fatted & gresed & en-larged, refused God.

23. He for-soke God, hys maker, & departed fram God[2] his helþe.

24. Hij cleped hym forþe in straunge goddes, and stired hym to wraþ in abhominacioun.

25. Hi sacrified to deuelshippes, & nouȝt to God, to goddes which hij ne knew nouȝt.

26. Newe and fresshe goddes commen, þe which her fadres ne honured nouȝt.

27. Ha þou fol[k] of Israel, þou for-s[3]oke God, þat saued þe, & þou for-ȝate my God, þi fourmeour.

28. Our Lord seȝe þes þinges, & he is stired to wraþe; for his sones and his douȝters cleped him in maumettries.

29. And he seied, Y shal hide my face fram hem, and y shal sen her last endinges.

30. Her kinde is wicked, and her childer vntrewe.

31. Hij clepeden me forþe in hym, þat [nas] nouȝt God, and tariden in her uanites.

32. And y shal clepen hem forþ in hym, þat nis nouȝt folkˁ, & y shal tarien hem in foled folkˁ.

33. Fur is aliȝt in my vengeaunce, & it shal brenne vnto þe last endes of helle.

34. And it shal swolwe þerþe wyþ his burron and brennen wiþ his foundementȝ of þe mounteines.[4]

35. Y shal ansemble iuels vp hem, & y shal fulfillen my manaces in hem.

36. Hij shul ben wasted þurȝ hunger, & foules shal deuore hym wyþ bitterest biting.

---

[1] MS. *swete*. [2] MS. repeats *hys maker . . . god*. [3] fol. 143. [4] Last *e* added over line.

---

21. *And*] þe : merȝe of whete : most bitterest.
22. *enl.*] larged.
24. abhominacions.
*25. deuels : *wh.*] þat : —*ne*.
26. come : —*ne*.
27. O þou folk.
31. þat+was.
32. is : —*& y shal tarien h. in f. f.*
34. swalow : burgunnyng (r *added over line*).
35. gader.
36. þurȝ] for.

* fol. 53b.

37. Y shal sende into ¹hem teþ of bestes and of serpentes drawand wyþ wodeship vp þerþe.

38. Swerde shal waste hem wyþ-oute² & drede wyþ-innen,

39. Þe ȝong to-gidres and þe maiden, þe soukand wyþ þe olde man.

40. Y seid, For where ben hij? y shal make her mynde to cesen³ of men.

41. Ac ich for-bare for þe ire of her enemis, þat her enemis perchaunce ne prouded nouȝt,

42. And hij seiden, Our Lord miȝt is heȝe, & alle þes þynges ne made noȝt our Lord.

43. Þys ys folk¹ wy[þ]-outen conseil and wyþ-outen queintise; God, ȝif, þat hij were wys & vnderstonden, & puruaiden þe laste þinges.

44. Hou pursued on þousand, & .ij. chaceden .x. þousand?

45. Nouȝt for þy þat her God solde hem, & her Lord sett hem to-gidres?

46. For our God nis nouȝt as her goddes, and our enemis ben iuges.

47. Her uines is of þe uine of Sode-mens & of þe suburbes of Gomorre.

48. Her grape is grape of galle, & her berye hys bitterest.

⁴49. Þe galle of dragons is her wyne, and venim of aspides, þat ne mai nouȝt be heled.

50. Ben nouȝt þes þynges hidded to me, & merked in my tresories?

51. Þe wreche is myne, and y shal ȝelde to hem in time, þat her fote⁵ slide.

52. Þe daie of lesinge is nere, & þe times hasten to me.

53. Our Lord shal iugent his folk¹, & haue pite of his seruauntes.

54. He shal sen,⁶ þat þe honde is made sike, & þe bishett faileden, & þe remauntȝ ben wasted.

55. And þe gode shal sain, Where ben her goddes, in which hij had affiaunce?

---

¹ fol. 143b.   ² MS. *wyþ outen*, but *n* is expunged.   ³ MS. *ceser*.   ⁴ fol. 144.
⁵ MS. *fore*.   ⁶ MS. *ben*.

---

37. wodenes.
39. mayde.
40. *ben hij*] þai be : cese.
41. Bot : —*ne*.
42. Lorde : —*ne*.
43. *with*-oute consele: wysdome: ȝif] wold : vnderstondyng.
45. —*þy* : *sett*] closed.
46. is.

47. *is*] beþ : Sodomens : subbarbes.
49. venum : —*ne*
50. hid : tresourres.
51. fote aslyde.
52. neȝ : *me*] cum.
53. deme.
54. *ben*] se : *bishett*] closed : remnaunte beþ.
55. —*gode*.

56. Of whas sacrifices[1] hij eten þe fatthede, & drunken wyn of sacrifices,
57. Arise hij, & helpe ȝou, & defende ȝou in nede.
58. Seþ þat ich am al-on,[2] and þat þer be no noþer God bot y.
59. Y shal slen, and make to liuen; y shal smiten, & y shal helen; and þer nis non þat may deliuer fram my honde.
60. [3] Y shal lift my honde to þe heuen, & saie, Y liue wyþ-outen ende.
61. ȝyf ich sharp my swerde oþer my wreche as liȝtinge, & myn hondes han tauken iugement,
62. Y shal ȝelden vengeaunce to myn enemis, [& y shal ȝelden to hem] þat hateden me.
63. Y shal baþe[4] my manaces in confusion, and my vengeaunce shal swolwe flesshes,
64. Of blode of þe slain & wreched-hede of þe naked heued of þe enemis.
65. Ȝe folk wyþ-outen lawe, herieþ[5] his folk; for he shal venge þe blode of his seruauntes.
66. And he shal ȝelde vengeaunce[6] to her enemis, & he shal be propice to þe londe of his folk.

PSALMUS ANANIE, AZARIE, ET MISAEL.
(Danielis iii. 57—88.)

1. Ȝe alle werkes of our Lord, blisceþ our Lord, herieþ & vp-heȝeþ hym in-to þe worldles!
2. Ȝe our Lordes aungels, blisceþ our Lord! ȝe heuens, blisceþ our Lord!
3. Ȝe alle[7] waters þat ben vp heuens, blisceþ our Lord! ȝe alle vertuȝ of our Lord, blisceþ our Lord!
4. [8] Ȝe sonne and mone, blisceþ our Lord! ȝe sterres of heuen, blisceþ our Lord!
5. Ȝe raine & dew, blisceþ our Lord! ich gost of God, blisceþ our Lord!

---

[1] MS. *sacrifiees*.   [2] MS. *as on*.   [3] fol. 144b.   [4] MS. *laþe*.
[5] *h* on erasure.   [6] MS. *vengeuance*.   [7] MS. repeats *alle*.   [8] fol. 145.

---

56. sacrifice: fatnes: sacrifice.
58. allon: *be no no.*] is none oþer.
*59. —*to*: *helen*] make hole: is.
60. to—þe.
61. take.
62. enemys+& y schal ȝelde to hem.
63. *l.*] baþe: manace: swalow.
64. slaw: wrechidhode.
65. ȝe *f.*] þe f.
66. vengance: mercifull.

* fol. 54.

6. ꝫe fur & bruelinɡ, blisceþ our Lord! ꝫe cold & somer, blisceþ our Lord!

7. ꝫe dewes & rime-frost, bliseeþ our Lord! ꝫe frost & colde, blisceþ our Lord!

8. ꝫe yse & snow,[1] blisceþ our Lord! ꝫe miꝫtes & daies, blisceþ our Lord!

9. Þe erthe blisceþ our Lord, and herieþ him, & heꝫe him in þe worldel!

10. ꝫe mounteins & smale hilles, blisceþ our Lord! ꝫe alle þinges burionand in erþe, blisceþ our Lord!

11. ꝫe whalles & alle þinges þat ben stired in þe waters, blisceþ our Lord! ꝫe alle þe foules[2] of heuen, blisceþ our Lord!

12. ꝫe alle bestes, blisceþ our Lord; ꝫe mennes sones, blisceþ our Lord!

13. Blisce þe folk of Israel our Lord! herie hym, & heꝫe hym in þe world!

14. ꝫe prestes of our Lord, blisceþ our Lord! ꝫe seruauntes [3]of our Lord, blisce our Lord!

15. ꝫe gostes & soules of riꝫtful, blisceþ our Lord! ꝫe holy & meke of[4] hert, blisceþ our Lord!

16. ꝫe Anani & Azary & Mysael, blisceþ our Lord! herieþ hym, & heꝫeþ hym in þe world!

17. Blisce we þe fader and þe sone wyþ þe holy gost! hery we, and heꝫe we hym in þe worldel!

18. Lord, þou art blisced in þe firmament of heuen and ful of heryynge & gloriouse and vp-heꝫed in þe worldes!

PSALMUS ZACHARIE.[5]

(Luke i. 68–79.)

1. Blisced be our Lord, God of Israel; for he uisited, and made þe raunson of his folke.

---

[1] MS. *swo*.   [2] MS. *folkes*.   [3] fol. 145*b*.   [4] *hym* follows, but is expuncted.
[5] No heading in MS.

Anan. 6. *br.*] hete.
7. horefroste.
8. snow.
9. blys: hery+it: vphie: worldes.
10. aH maner of þinges buriounyng in þe e.
11. walles: *stired . . . folkes*] mouyd in þe w. ꝫe aH byrdes (r *added over line*).
12. ꝫe sonnes of men.

13. þe f. of I. blyss: hyꝫe—*hym*: into þe worldes.
14. & ꝫe s.
15. & ꝫe souleꝫ of r.+men: & ꝫe meke.
16. enhiꝫe.
17. Blysse—*we*: with—þe: anhiꝫe: worlde.
18. in þi: anhyed.

Luke. 1. *our*] þe: visett.

2. And he dresced þe helpe of his helþe to ous in þe hous of Dauid, his childe.

3. And as he spake þurȝ þe mouþe of holy his prophetes, þat ben in þe world.

4. Helþe of our enemys & of þe honde of alle þat hated us.

5. To do merci wyþ our fader, and forto by-þenchen of hys holy testament.

6. Þe oþe þat he swore ¹to Abraham, our fader, to ȝif hym to us.

7. Þat we, de-liuerd fram þe honde of our enemis, serue to him, wyþ-outen drede.

8. In holynes & riȝtfulnes to-fore hym alle our daies.

9. And þou, childe, shal be cleped prophete of þe heȝest; for þou shal go to-fore þe face of our Lord to diȝt his waies;

10. To ȝif coning of helþe to his folke, in forȝeuenes of her synȝes;

11. Þourȝ ² þe workes of þe mercy of our God, in which he viseted vs born fram heȝt;

12. To liȝten to hem þat sitteþ in derkenes & shadue of deþ, & to drescen our fete in-to way of pees.

TE DEUM.³

1. God, we herieþ þe, we knoweleche [þe].
2. Alle þerþe honureþ þe, fader wyþ-outen ende.
3. To þe crien alle aungels, to þe crien þe heuens and alle miȝtes.
4. To þe crien cherubin and seraphin, and wiþ voice nouȝt cessand.
5. Holy! holy! holy!
6. Lord, God, Sabaoth.
7. Þe heuens ⁴& þe erþe ben ful of þe maieste of þye glorie.

---

¹ fol. 146. ² MS. þe urþe, the latter þ being corrected from ȝ. ³ No heading in MS. ⁴ fol. 146b.

---

2. arered vp þe helpe of helþe.
3. in] of.
*5. faders: of hys] on.
7. þat] & þat.
9. ordeyne.
10. cunnyng: remyssions.
11. þe urþe] By: in+þe: viset.

Te Deum. 1. knowligge+þe Lorde.
2. All erþe worschepeþ þe, euer-lastyng fader.
3. to þe cr. þe h] & heuens.
4. a.—and: with a incessable voyce.
6. S.] of ostes.
7. þe heuens & þe e.] h. & erþe: maieste .. gl.] ioie of þi mageste.

* fol. 54b.

8. þe glorious felaw-es-hip of apostels herieþ þe.
9. þe praiseable numbre of prophetes herieþ þe.
10. þe whit felaweship of martirs herieþ þe.
11. þe holi chirch knowelicheþ þe þurȝ þe world.
12. Fader of gret maieste!
13. And it is to honouren þy soþefast & onelich sone,
14.' And þe holy gost confortour.
15. Þou, Christ, art kynge of glorie.
16. Þou art þe euer-lastand sone of þy fader.
17. Þou [forto] take to deliuer man ne drad nouȝt þe wombe of þe virgine.
18. Þou opened þe kingdomes of heuens to hem þat bileuen in þe carnacioun, þe broche of þe deþ ouer-cumen.
19. Þou sittest at þe riȝthalf of God in þe glorie of þe fader.
20. Þou art leued for to be iuge to comen.
21. For-þy bi-seche we þe, Helpe þy seruauntȝ, which[1] þou raunsouned wyþ þy preciouse blode.
22. Make þy[2] seruauntes to be rewarded wyþ glorie euerlastand.
23. Make sauf, Lord, þy folkꞌ, & blesce þyn heritage.
24. [3]And goueren hem, and heȝe hem to wyþ-outen ende.
25. We blisceþ þe by ich daie.
26. And we herie þy name in þe world & in heuen.
27. Be it þy wille, Lord, þis daie to kepe us wyþouten sinȝe.
28. Haue mercy on vs! Lord, haue mercy on vs!
29. Be, Lord, þy merci made vp vs, as we hoped in þe!
30. Lord, ich hoped in þe; ne be y nouȝt confounded wyþ-outen ende.

---

[1] MS. repeats *which*.   [2] MS. *my*.   [3] fol. 147.

---

8. cumpany of postels.
10. whyte cumpany.
11. þe h. ch. kn.] Holy chirches knowlegeþ.
13. & þi verrey onlych sonne to be worschypt.
15. ioie.
16. þy] þe.
17. þou+forto: —ne.
18. be-leuyd: incarnacioun: br.] pryk.
19. atte r. side.
20. be . . .] cum a domes-man.
21. we besecheþi help: *wh. wh.*] þat.
22. *my*] þi.
24. gouerne: anhie: —*to*.
25. *The English is omitted.*
27. Lorde be it þy w.
28. Lord haue m. on vs.
29. Lord be: trowed.
30. haue hopid: —*ne*.

PSALMUS MARIE.[1]
Luke i. 47–55.

1. My soule herieþ our Lord.
2. And my gost gladeþ in God, myn helþe.
3. For he seʒe þe mekenesse of his honde-maiden; se for-þy, of þat shal alle kindes saie me blisceed.
4. For he þat his miʒtful made to me grete þinges, & his name is holy.
5. And his mercy is fram kinde in-to kindes to þe dredand hym.
6. He made miʒt in hys helpe, he sprad abrode þe proude þurʒ þe þouʒt of his hert.
7. He did doun þe miʒt-ful of her setes, & anheʒed þe meke.
8. He fulfild þe hungry of godes, & left þe ryche empty.
9. He toke Israel, his childe, & he by-þouʒt of hys merci,
10. As he spak to our fadres, Abraham & to his sede in þe worldes.

PSALMUS SIMEONIS.[1]
(Luke ii. 29–32.)

1. Nou late stonde, Lord, þy seruant in pees efter þy worde.
2. For myn eʒen seʒen þyn helþe,
3. Þe which þou diʒted to-fore þe face of alle folkes,
4. Lit to sheweinge of men, & glorie of þy folk of Israel.

ATHANASIAN CREED.[1]

1. Who so wyl be sauf, nede it is to hym to-fore alle þinges, þat he holde þe catholich faiþe;
2. Þe which bot ʒif ichon kepe hole & nouʒt de-fouled, wyþ-outen drede he shal peris wyþ-outen ende.

---

[1] No heading in MS.   [2] fol. 147b.

Luke i. 1. hyried.
2. gladyd.
3. honde-mayde lo: all k. schall.
5. into] to.
*6. spr. ab. þe] disparpled: þurʒ þe] in: his] her.
7. put: —þe: miʒty: setes] sett.
8. empty] in vayne.

* fol. 55.

Luke ii. 1. Lord now þou letest —stonde.
2. haþ sey.
3. þat þou hast ordeynyd: folke.
4. Liʒt.

Creed, 1. catholy.
2. n.d.] vndefoylid: doute.

3. Þe faiþe for-soþe of holy chirche is þis, þat we honuren o God in trinite & þe trinite in on-hede,

4. Noiþer confoundand persons, ne departand þe substaunce.

5. On for-soþe is persoun of þe fader, anoþer of þe sone, anoþer of þe holy gost.

6. ¹Bot of þe fader and of þe sone & of þe holy gost is o god-hede, euen glorie & maieste to-gidres euer-lastand.

7. Swich as þe fader is, swich is þe sone, swich is þe holi gost.

8. Vnfourmed is þe fader, vnfourmed is þe sone, vnformed is þe holi gost.

9. Mychel his þe fader, mychel his þe sone, michel his þe holy gost.

10. Þe fader hys euer-lastend, þe sone is euerlastend, þe holy gost is euerlastend.

11. And neuer þe lesse þer ne be nouȝt þre euerlastend, ac þer is on euerlastend.

12. As hij ne ben nouȝt þre vnfourmed, ne þre grete, ac on vnfourmed, & on grete:

13. Also his þe fader almiȝti, þe sone almiȝti, þe holi gost almiȝti.

14. And neuer þe les þer ne ben non þre almiȝti, bot on is almiȝti.

15. So is God fader, God² is sone, God ys þe holy gost.

16. And na-for-þan þer ne ben nouȝt þre goddes, bot þer is o God,

17. So is þe fader Lord, þe sone Lord, þe holy gost Lord.

18. And na-for-þan þer ne ben nouȝt ³þre lordes, ac on is Lord.

19. For as we ben constreint þurȝ cristen soþenes to knowelich on-lich God and Lord ich a persone, so we be defended þurh catholik religion to sai, þre goddes & þre lordes.

---

¹ fol. 148.   ² Twice *god* in MS.   ³ fol. 148*b*.

---

3. *o*] one: onhode.
4. *ne*] no.
6. *of þe sone & of*] þe sonne &: on goddhode.
9. Grete: grete: grete.
10. Euerlastyng is þe f., euerlastyng is þe sun, e.l. is þe h. goste.
11. neþþeles: —*ne*: bot one euerlastyng.
12. *hij ne*] þer: no: bot.

13. Also almiȝty is þe f., almiȝty is þe sun, alm. is þe h. goste.
14. *ne ben non*] be noȝt: —*is*.
15. So Godd is f., Godd is sun, Godd is h. goste.
16. *na . . . ne*] neuer þe les þer: þer is *o*] one.
18. *And . . . ne*] Ac nepeles þer: ac on is] bot one.
19. constreynyd: knowlege: *ich a*] ech.

20. Þe fader nis made of no wiʒt, ne fourmed, ne biʒeten.
21. Þe sone is oneliche of þe fader, nouʒt made, noʒt formed, ac biʒeten.
22. Þe holy gost is of þe fader and of þe sone, nouʒt made, nouʒt fourmed, noʒt biʒeten, bot forþgoand.
23. For-þi o fader is, & nouʒt þre fadres [1]; o sone, and nouʒt þre sones; on holy gost, & nouʒt þre holy gost.
24. Bot in þis trinite noʒt is to-fore, ne nouʒt by-hinde, nouʒt more ne lasse, ac alle þre persons ben to-gadres euerlastand & euen.
25. So þat by alle þinges, as it is sone said aboue, & on-hede in þre-hede & þre-hede in on-hede be to honour.
26. For-þy he þat wil be saued, fele he so of þe þrehede.
[2]27. Bot nedeful þinge is to þe euerlastand helþe, þat he trowe-lich bi-leue þe in-carnacioun of our Lord Iesu Crist.
28. For-þy þe riʒt bileue is þat we bi-leue & knowelich, þat our Lord Iesu Crist, Goddes sone, is God & man.
29. He his God, of þe substaunce of þe fader biʒeten to-fore þe worldes; & man, of þe substaunce of þe moder born in þe world.
30. He is parfit God, parfit man, beand of resonable soule & of mannes flesshe.
31. He is euen to þe fader efter þe godehede, lasse þan þe fader efter þe manhede;
32. Þe which, þeʒ he bi God & man, na-for-þan hij ben nouʒt two, bot o Crist.
33. He is for-soþe on, noʒt þurʒt [confusioun of god-hede in flesh, bot þurʒ] takeing of manhode in-to God.
34. He is on in alle, nouʒt þurʒ confusion of substaunce, bot þurʒ onhede of persone.
35. For as resonable soule & flesshe is o man, so is God & man o Crist;

---

[1] Instead of the *e*, the MS. has a loop to the *r*.   [2] fol. 149.

20. is : no þing no : no.
21. of þe onlych f. : bot.
22. *nouʒt fourmed*] no *f.* : —*n. biʒ*.
23. one : one : one : gostes.
24. *ne nouʒt*] no noʒt: *nouʒt m. ne l.*] no lesse bot : togyders.
*25. *sone*] now: & *o.*] as onehode: þrehode: þrehode: onehode is to be honouryd.
26. *s.f.*] safe frede : trinite.
27. trewlych.
28. riʒtful : knowlege.
31. goddehede+& : manhode.
32. *bi*] be : neþe les.
33. noʒt one þurʒgh+confusion of godd-hode in flesch bot þurʒgh.
34. ac : onhode.
35. one : one.

* fol. 55*b*.

36. Þe which suffred for our [1]helÞe, went to helle, & aros Þe Þridde daie fram deÞ to lyf.

37. He steȝe vp to[2] Þe heuens, sitteÞ at Þe riȝt half of God, fader al-miȝti, fram Þennes he is to cum to iugen Þe quike and Þe. ded.

38. Tho whos cumyng al men han to rise wyÞ her bodis, & ben to ȝelden rekening of her propre dedes.

39. And hij Þat deden wele, shul gon to Þe lif euerlastand; & hij Þat han don iuel, shul gon into fur euer-lastend.

40. Þis ys Þe bileue catholik, Þe which bot if ich man haue bileued trewlich & fastelich, he ne may nouȝt be sauf.

---

[1] fol. 149b. [2] he follows here, but is expuncted.

---

37. Þe heuens] h.: sittyÞ (but instead of the Þ the MS. has only a long downward flourish): r. side: deme: & —Þe.
38. Tho] To: —ben.

40. cath.] of holy chyrche: —ne.

Explicit psalterium translatum in anglicum John Hyde constat.

END OF THE TEXT
AND OF PART I.